NO STRAIGHT PATH

NO STRAIGHT PATH
BECOMING WOMEN HISTORIANS

EDITED BY
ELIZABETH JACOWAY

WITH A FOREWORD BY
GLENDA ELIZABETH GILMORE

Louisiana State University Press
Baton Rouge

Published by Louisiana State University Press

Manufactured in the United States of America
First printing

Designer: Barbara Neely Bourgoyne
Typeface: Whitman
Printer and binder: Sheridan Books

Cataloging-in-Publication Data are available at the Library of Congress.

ISBN 978-0-8071-7043-4 (cloth: alk. paper) — ISBN 978-0-8071-7211-7 (pdf) —
ISBN 978-0-8071-7212-4 (epub)

The paper in this book meets the guidelines for permanence and durability of the Committee on Production Guidelines for Book Longevity of the Council on Library Resources. ♾

CONTENTS

FOREWORD

Personal Histories, Professional Historians, and Truth in the Academy

GLENDA GILMORE

Anthropologist Bianca R. Williams uses "radical honesty" as a practice to change the classroom and the academy at large. As a black woman professor, she vividly portrays the "shame" and "hauntings" of academic spaces and how her presence "disrupts" those spaces. She writes about how professors, particularly black women, face down imposter syndrome, the pervasive feeling of not belonging. Williams's teaching practices include "truth-telling," "valuing narrative and personal experience," and "acting" with radical honesty.[1] Taking up imposter syndrome, Amy Olberding, a philosopher, writes about the ways in which her rural farming background and accent limited her as a white southern woman in academia. But at the end of the day, "as a philosopher, I can't conceal my class." Moreover, she avers, "I would experience belonging as a loss. . . . [B]eing ill-adapted has a value I would not forfeit."[2] As academics, Williams and Olberding embrace their life experiences to ask new questions of their disciplines and to reach their students. Following their practices, the essays in *No Straight Path: Becoming Women Historians* prove the value of hard truth-telling about personal experiences as a practical and inspirational guide for women inside and outside of the academy.

The ten essays that comprise *No Straight Path* are radically honest. Written by women who were among the first sizeable cohort of women teaching at the university level in the South—and by one who benefited from their trail blazing—they tell us about love and struggle, race and class, persistence and resilience, improbability and destiny. The writers are white, black, LGBT, single, married, widowed, middle-class and working-class. Most were in their thirties or forties when they earned the PhD. As a white woman and southern historian in the generation that followed them who became a professor in my forties, I knew them. But I now know that I knew nothing about them. Perhaps I knew even less about the fraught history of the academic profession that I so breezily entered in the 1990s.

No Straight Path sprang from a 2016 conversation among the Delta Women Writers (DWW) group on a day when they "shared our personal stories for the first time." Women historians tend to submerge their personal biographies under their identity as historians. We become our work, and the personal perspectives that caused us to take up that work often become invisible. Yet, family history, gender, race, and class continue to inform the questions we ask, the ways that we interpret evidence, our identification with our institutions, and our teaching. By 2016, this group of ten essayists had already been meeting with ten other DWW members for eight years to talk about their work. Finally, they talked about themselves.

The result is a powerful antidote for imposter syndrome. Elizabeth Payne recounts trying to put off her comprehensive exams to study more when her adviser, historian Joan Scott, who became a leading theoretician at Princeton's Institute for Advanced Study, confronts her. Scott puts "her hands on her hips" and says, "Elizabeth Payne, don't you realize that every morning when I am brushing my teeth, I say to myself, 'Joan Scott, today is the day somebody will find out that you are a fraud!' Now take the exams." Moreover, these narratives serve as models for other women academics and those who aspire to join their ranks. Janann Sherman's searing story of abject poverty and misfortune is a powerful lesson in persistence for working men and women anywhere who hope for fulfilled vocations. Elizabeth Jacoway, Gail Murray, and Pamela Tyler tell us about what they did and didn't do for the love of family and the impact of those choices on their lives and careers.

Many essayists highlight "happenstance": the times when a professor's note—"Miss Payne, you should go to graduate school," a temporary job, or sheer desperation finally cracked open the profession's gate. But along with happenstance, single-mindedness is a recurring theme, from Martha Swain's conviction from the eighth grade onward that she would teach history, to others who realized they would follow their research wherever it led them with little hope of academic reward. They speak of history as love. Sheila Skemp realized, "There was no right or wrong answer. History was open-ended. I was hooked." Emily Clark bonded with her subjects: "Historians don't take final vows like nuns, but I knew now that my commitment to my vocation was forever." Beverly Bond understood her family of strong women as historians themselves. In the "beehive" of queen bees in which she grew up, lost histories in slavery, passed down through generational knowledge, grounded her. Likewise, Sylvia Frey, of French Acadian and German ancestry, calls upon her childhood speaking French and German in Eunice, Louisiana, to underscore the Global South and her interest in "diasporic studies."

Confronted with a white male academy—many of the essayists never had a woman professor or professor of color—their personal histories bore little resemblance to those of their teachers or, later, of most of their colleagues. The parlance of academia might as well have been a foreign language. The essayists are blunt, poignant, and often funny about what they didn't know. Sherman recalls that a professor "encouraged me to consider graduate school. I didn't know what that was." Tyler was surprised that her dissertation might be published. Many were astonished—as was I in 1985—at the existence of graduate school fellowships and even more astonished when they were offered one. Gail Murray enrolled in graduate school, as did I, as a "special student," taking a limited number of courses and then the GRE, hoping to earn a place as a real graduate student.

They persevered against adversity because they expected adversity. The essayists had always faced sexism as a fact of life; for example, her public high school initially barred Payne from taking geometry (just as mine excluded girls from Latin). Taking years off to teach high school or work in menial jobs slowed their dissertation writing, but the thrill of writing made up for it. Most gratefully accepted positions on the margins of the academy: one-year visiting slots, administrative jobs, summer school courses. The academic job market features as a black hole for which no one prepared them, save Linda Kerber, who gave Sheila Skemp pointers. Only one woman, Martha Swain, secured a teaching slot through the old-boy network of the 1950s when Vanderbilt professor Dewey Grantham recommended her for a job at Texas Woman's University, which hired her on his say-so and without an interview.

Their portrayal of the sexism rampant in the field of southern history takes my breath away, even though I followed them into the field by only a few years. I realize now that, but for them, their experience would have been mine as well. Sometimes it borders on subtle: as a new hire, the lone woman in the department is assigned to take departmental meeting minutes. Other times, it is structural, as women toil as adjunct or non–tenure track professors until long-neglected sex discrimination laws finally impact the academy. Gail Murray recalls, "So in the fall of 2000, I became a tenured associate professor after having been fired in the spring of 1998!" Occasionally, the sexism is vulgar. All dressed up for her first conference reception, Elizabeth Jacoway spots a professor she does not know and gushes that she loved his book. He responds "in the most casual way possible" by asking in the vernacular if she wants to have sexual intercourse.

But the essays also repeatedly introduce whole-souled male professors who stood above the sexist cesspool that trickled through the field of southern history. Women's entrance into their profession must have made it a better place for them as well. These men delighted in mentoring these women and took into account their familial, economic, and logistical constraints by helping them find a way out of no way. The essayists learned from them how to mentor and never to write off their own nontraditional students. In a historical moment when the humanities are under siege in the academy and history as a discipline is shamelessly devalued in the world at large, this book demonstrates that the academic career path is not always linear; it is often circuitous.

Most importantly, *No Straight Path* teaches us powerful lessons about how to reshape the academy to make it better suited to the world we now face. In part as a response to market conditions, in part because of ethical commitments, universities now seek first-generation college students, people of color, students of nontraditional ages. Once admitted, those students are expected to conform to an educational structure and culture that has changed little since the essayists experienced it when it served middle- and upper-class white men. When that structure ill serves those students, most universities do little to accommodate their needs. Indeed, universities fail even to fathom those needs. For example, students of limited means find themselves on an academic calendar that requires them to leave campus for holidays, use summers to study abroad, or follow a strict credit-hour formula to stay enrolled and defer student loans. The women of *No Straight Path* contradict that model of academic success with practical strategies that they cobbled together by hook or crook, often at great career cost. When they became successful, they tried to change the rules. For example, when Janann Sherman, who camped in an RV parked at the archives, got the opportunity as departmental chair to adopt online courses, she understood the flexibility that they could afford working students.

As students who were "different," these writers' wisdom suggests powerful ways to deal with differences that go past complaining about "college students these days." Beverly Bond, among the first black students to desegregate Memphis State, shrank in her seat amid a "sea of white students" when history professor Marcus Orr went around the class asking students to state their ethnic origins. Hoping to be overlooked in the ethnicity rounds, she shrank when he called on her. "I realized that his question had actually forced me to claim my right to a place on this campus," Bond recalled. She learned from Orr, who became her favorite professor, how to practice radical honesty by exploring and acclaiming difference. Since most of the essayists never had a woman professor, they understand how gender differences impact the classroom experience. These are real, not theoretical, considerations in today's universities. A few years ago at Yale, an African American first-year man from Jackson, Mississippi, confided in me that I was the first white woman teacher he had ever had.

The essays in *No Straight Path* not only sensitize us to difference in the academy, but they also suggest how we might construct different academies. They reveal in large and small ways the embedded discrimination that deters women, people of color, and nontraditional students who become academics and offer real suggestions for making the academy a place that responds to diversity. They provide a history of the academic practices that routinely disadvantage women. For example, universities customarily move "the goalposts" for tenure and promotion, cutting years to tenure while increasing publication requirements. This turns out to be a game with a long history, one that confounds the promotion of women with families.

Many universities now attempt to retain women and faculty of color through mentoring committees or random assignment of mentors. *No Straight*

Path offers vivid testimony to the kind of mentorship that works. Every essayist writes of mentorship so direct, so committed, and so acute that it literally saved their careers, most of it practiced by male professors. As long as universities treat mentoring as simply one more service contribution to be ticked off, they will never enable the kind of radical academic leadership that renowned professors such as David Oshinsky, John Boles, or Clarence Mohr offered these scholars. Moreover, to retain and nourish faculty, universities would do well to provide their faculty with sponsorship to summer institutes, such as the one that Sylvia Frey attended at Princeton, where she found the women historians who changed her work.

Knowing the value of mentoring, these contributors built mentoring structures in their universities and the profession at large. They built an organization dedicated to mentoring women, the Southern Association for Women Historians (SAWH), and four have been its president. I met many of them for the first time at an SAWH conference where I gave my first professional paper. The SAWH has been the wellspring of southern women's history and the collective mentor of us all.

Taken together, the essays also portray a sea change in the way we write history, particularly southern history. In the essayists' lifetimes and in part because of their work, history became more inclusive to include social history and new historical actors. Many of the essayists actively sought out collaboration with groups of historians, for example, Martha Swain and Elizabeth Payne for the project that resulted in *Mississippi Women: Their Histories, Their Lives*. Other cowrote works. Frey notes: "History is, for the most part a solitary profession. But it also is or can be a collective experience." The act of banding together in the Delta Women Writers group is itself collaboration.

When contributor Elizabeth Payne mentioned Eudora Welty's *One Writer's Beginnings*, that lyrical account of a southern childhood spent listening, I realized that this volume evoked Welty's book for me. As Janann Sherman writes here, "Nothing you learn is ever wasted." Perhaps that is the most important lesson that the reader takes away from *No Straight Path*. There are many different kinds of knowledge; there are many paths toward a life of the mind. The essayists in *No Straight Path* are women on whom nothing was lost. And, like Welty, they tell their stories with gratitude and grace.

NOTES

1. Bianca R. Williams, "Radical Honesty: Truth-Telling as Pedagogy for Working through Shame in Academic Spaces," in *Race, Equity, and the Learning Environment: The Global Relevance of Critical and Inclusive Pedagogy*, ed. Frank Tuitt, Chayla Haynes, and Saran Stewart (Sterling, VA: Stylus, 2016), Kindle.

2. Amy Olberding, "The Outsider," https://aeon.co/essays/how-useful-is-impostor-syndrome-in-academia.

NO STRAIGHT PATH

INTRODUCTION

ELIZABETH JACOWAY

At the 2016 annual meeting of the Organization of American Historians in Providence, Rhode Island, four members of the Delta Women Writers shared our personal stories with each other for the first time. We were stunned by the divergence of our experiences, even though we had all followed paths into the historical profession, into the Delta Women Writers, and into an exceptional meal together. We came away feeling inspired to share our stories, and *No Straight Path: Becoming Women Historians* is the product of that inspiration. It traces themes and experiences that many women of the post–World War II generation shared if they chose to enter the professional world.

Twenty female historians who live in or near the Mississippi Delta from Memphis to New Orleans, the Delta Women Writers meet twice a year in Jackson, Mississippi, to read and critique each other's work. What began as strictly an academic exercise grew very quickly into a tight-knit, fully bonded support group of dear friends who range in age from their late twenties to late seventies. On the chosen Friday afternoons in October and April, the group gathers at our favorite hotel for Happy Hour popcorn and wine, followed by a raucous supper at a nearby Cajun restaurant. Saturday morning the tone changes completely as twenty hard-nosed academic women gather at Millsaps College to spend the day dissecting, questioning, and improving four papers that have been circulated in advance. Saturday night the friendly tone returns over an elegant meal at one of Jackson's finest restaurants, and Sunday morning the group disperses amid hugs and promises to remain connected through email.

The four of us who gathered in Providence included a full professor at Tulane—a native of New Orleans and daughter of a professional mother—who pursued careers as an archaeologist, then a social worker, then a university administrator, and finally a historian; a first-generation college graduate who grew up in Minnesota, then attended college in Arkansas before landing a full scholarship at Rutgers, and then becoming the first woman chair of her department at the University of Memphis; an African American high school teacher in Memphis who went to graduate school past the age of forty; and a privileged southern daughter who pursued graduate study straight out of college only because her father instructed her to do so. All four of us became recognized, published scholars with extensive research interests and wide networks of professional friends and colleagues. As we told our stories that night in Providence, we all marveled that we had landed at the same table even though we had followed paths that were so very different. As we queried other members of our writing group, we were amazed to discover an even wider diversity, and yet we also recognized the undeniable similarities in our stories.

With a shared trepidation, we each tackled the assignment of writing about our own trajectories into and through the profession, and each one of us felt that we were descending into the rankest form of self-absorption and narcissism. For each of us it was a surprisingly painful exercise. Surveying the landscapes of our own histories, we confronted head-on the mistakes and failures that busy lives keep buried under the surface. We also laid bare the connective tissue that had kept our lives integrated and coherent, and sometimes these discoveries were unsettling. Finally, we were accustomed to writing about other people and their fascinating lives, and our own stories often seemed bland and insignificant by comparison. But as we began to read each other's work, several themes emerged that surprised us in their consistency and gave our individual stories a larger importance. First, as children raised by Depression-era parents, most of us were born into a world of expectation that we would achieve and succeed where our parents had not had those opportunities. As little girls we expected to grow up and become teachers, nurses, secretaries, or society ladies, the only respectable choices available to the women we knew at that time. Even then, those of us who thought in terms of a career expected our work life to be little more than a "fallback position" if Prince Charming failed to come along, or if he died before our children were educated and independent. Few of us took a straight path into the profession, opting instead to attempt the more conventional pursuits of public school teaching, marriage, and motherhood. As we made the unusual decision (for our time) to go to graduate school and move beyond high school teaching (which many of us had tried and found abhorrent), almost all of us failed to grasp that we would be entering a man's world, and that most likely we would not be welcome there—or that we would be perceived by many as sex objects. At the same time, most of us had the good fortune to find men who recognized our potential and who encouraged us in our quest to pursue this "unusual" path. For all of us, the work-life balance has been an issue throughout our careers, as we have struggled to combine the needs and demands of our families with the expectations of our profession. We had no roadmaps to follow, and very few role models. The giants who preceded us—Gerda Lerner, Anne Scott, Linda Kerber, Joan Scott, A. Elizabeth Taylor, and others—had battered down the gates, but they had to be superstars to do it. Very few of us expected to undertake such heroics or to rise to that level of accomplishment. All of us had the experience that someone kept moving the goalposts. Just about the time we would approach a milestone in our careers, the rules or the expectations would become more rigorous. In part a result of our own presence there, this rigor was also a part of the transformation of the profession that has taken place in our lifetimes from the gentlemanly preserve of largely upper-middle-class practitioners to one that is much more diverse and meritocratic. In the long run we have all benefited from these changes.

All of us found support and solace in our relationships with other female scholars, and all of us benefited from the work and networking of the Southern Association for Women Historians, of which four of us have served as president. All of us discovered in the Delta Women Writers a group of congenial and supportive women who made us feel truly at home as scholars and as historians.

For all of us, the key words have been persistence and tenacity. Some of us may have backed into our careers, but all of us have taken the opportunities that have presented themselves and walked through those open doors. We may have had low expectations, we may have been willing to settle for less than was our due, but we kept climbing, and by the end of our careers we had all achieved a level of success within the profession that we have found deeply gratifying. It is our hope that by sharing our stories, we will encourage younger scholars to believe that with similar persistence and tenacity—and with the added benefits of the opportunities for women that were not available to us—they may be able to transcend our achievements and soar to new heights within the historical profession.

MY IMPROBABLE JOURNEY

JANANN SHERMAN

I do not remember much of my childhood, and what I do remember, I often wish I didn't. The basics are pretty simple. I grew up in 1950s Minnesota in a family with too many children and too little income. I had four siblings: an older brother and three younger sisters. My mother suffered from headaches and a variety of unnamed maladies. Frequently taking to her bed, she seemed perpetually burdened by her lot in life as the mother of five ungrateful children. As for me, my mother made sure I understood that I wasn't going to amount to anything. First of all, I was fat. That sealed my fate right there. All I was good for was taking care of the house, cooking, and looking after my siblings. What I remember most about my father is that he was always angry. He didn't drink, but he always seemed to be seething, and the anger was clearly our fault. His daily homecoming was fraught with suspense and fear. We all became very good at sensing his mood and steering clear of him as much as possible, trying to make ourselves invisible.

I felt smothered by my family. Until the day I married, I shared a bedroom with my three sisters. My brother usually had a cot in the living room. All seven of us shared one bathroom. Our homes were often tiny and mostly dilapidated. Until I was an adolescent, we lived in a series of rural communities in Minnesota and northern Iowa, too many for me to count or remember. I realize now that was probably because we were trying to stay one step ahead of bill collectors.

When we moved to the city, I went to junior high in Minneapolis. At the time, Lincoln Junior High was designated, by *Life* magazine no less, as the most dangerous junior high in the nation. The school straddled the black community and the Jewish community. We lived pretty much on the line. Clashes on the playground were common and frequently escalated into knife fights. One afternoon at the playground, I watched two of my classmates, one black and one white, both girls, engage in a knife fight. The white girl died. Our neighborhood, not just the school, was a place of danger, but to me it was just the way things were.

The year I turned thirteen, doctors told my parents that my asthmatic sister could not survive another winter. Dad got an old truck, built up the sides, piled our belongings in and on the truck, and headed west. Leaving was also auspicious for me. In my neighborhood, gangs were putting pressure on girls my age to choose allegiance and to "prove it" by "putting out."

We landed in Phoenix, where Dad searched fruitlessly for a job as a machinist. He eventually opened his own shop repairing large appliances, which he apparently learned while doing. My family had arrived just in time for me to begin my freshman year in high school, albeit a couple months late. I had only two outfits to wear, and I felt shabby and embarrassed. High school was very difficult for me. I always felt like an outsider. I was awkward, poor in relation to my peers, and tried my best never to draw attention. My only social group in high school was made up of the students in my journalism class with whom I worked on the school newspaper. Writing seemed to come relatively easy. Best of all, it didn't involve much interaction, which I was sure I'd make a mess of. My senior year, we all took a bus to Tucson for the state competition for best high school newspaper. We won. I'll never forget the joy and the pride of that journey home. For that brief time, I was part of the in-crowd.

I graduated from high school in 1961, when I was seventeen, and graduated into a full-time, unpaid job in Dad's laundromat in Phoenix. A dreadful place. Hot, no point in air-conditioning. Washing, folding, and ironing clothes. I was already a skilled worker in that regard. Besides doing the cooking and taking care of the household while in high school, I washed, starched, and ironed men's white shirts at home to make spending money. A number of fellows would stop by the house in the mornings on their way to work, pick up a clean shirt and drop a dirty one. Ten cents for a short-sleeved starched shirt, fifteen cents for long sleeves. At a time when my allowance was twenty-five cents a week, that was real money. I split it with my mother. I had no plans for the future. Given my abilities and my family's circumstances, college was unthinkable. People like me did not go to college. Interesting work, perhaps one day for pay, was my aspiration.

At the laundromat I made friends with a young woman, Rose, recently married to an auto mechanic. She and her husband, Denny, rented a small home nearby and, to make extra money, had sublet a tiny bedroom to a man who had recently gotten a job at the same service station. (Remember when gas stations had service bays and hired mechanics?)

Charlie had just left the U.S. Air Force on a temporary disability for arthritis and moved to Phoenix for the hot, dry air. When I met him, he was twenty-nine; I was seventeen. Though we spent time together with Rose and Denny, sharing meals, playing cards, I entertained no romantic notions about him. Mostly we just listened to music and talked. We found it remarkable that we immediately felt at home with one another, like picking up a conversation begun years earlier. Yet we could hardly have been more different. When he enlisted at the beginning of the Korean War, I was in first grade. He had traveled the world for ten years in the service, and I had scarcely left my neighborhood. I was soon enamored of this quiet man with the bright hazel eyes and strong hands who treated me with regard and great tenderness. I don't know what he saw in me, but we both knew we were fated to be together.

Our courtship was short. We met in late October; he asked me to marry him in early December. We married in May 1962, after I turned eighteen. My parents denied their consent. My mother harped continuously that I was marrying an old man with no future, that the marriage would not last six months. She chose not to attend.

She was right about the "no future" part. He had crippling arthritis, a one-hundred-dollar-a-month disability pension, and minimal security as an auto mechanic. But I was okay with that. I was used to no future. We'd figure it out together. We bought a small trailer, 8' x 28', in a park next to the airport. He worked mostly nights at the station in order to minimize time on his feet. I worked in a discount drugstore. We ferried cars to Las Vegas on weekends to make some extra money, until the police arrested our boss for trafficking in stolen vehicles.

I decided to make it my mission to get hired by the largest employer in town, Motorola, Inc. I took every opportunity to travel to the personnel office and fill out yet another application. One day, I noticed a stack of applications sitting on a counter. I gathered a handful and took them home. I mailed a completed application every two days until they finally called me in for an interview. I was hired for the graveyard shift. I sat on an assembly line with needle-nose pliers in one hand, grasping a transistor in the other, straightening the lead wires, and threading the unit into a carrier to take it through a testing machine. I earned good money and even had benefits. When I learned that the company encouraged family members to work there, Charlie applied. He had to pause to earn his GED before he was eligible. He had never completed high school. After a series of altercations with his father, he left home at age fourteen and took a job topping trees in the lumber camps. Able to support himself, he saw no need to continue his education. He later regretted that decision, but for the moment taking the GED solved his problem and got him the job at Motorola. We worked the same shift and often in the same areas of the plant. About this time, military doctors gave Charlie an experimental drug that appeared to almost completely "cure" his arthritis. He was pain-free for the first time in years. Eventually, we were able to buy a small home. Life was good.

I was not content to straighten leads for eight-hour shifts for the rest of my life, so I took all available training opportunities at the plant to increase my skills and responsibilities. Still, I found the work intellectually deadening. One evening on our way to work, I spotted a sky-writer high overhead, spelling out the word "Pepsi." I told Charlie, "I'd like to try that. I think I'd like to learn to fly." "OK," he replied. I showed up at the airport the following Saturday and began lessons. Charlie loved flying in the air force, though he was trained as an aircraft mechanic, not a pilot. Soon he decided he'd like to take lessons, too. When he took the physical and vision exam, we got the first inkling that all was not well in paradise. He found out that he was color-blind, a new development. But Charlie just noted that "one pilot in the family is enough," and no more was said.

Once I got my pilot's license, we bought an old two-seater airplane from an old man who lived out in the desert. Clad in tarnished aluminum with torn upholstery, it looked pretty bad, but it flew and it was cheap. We parked it at the airstrip and spent countless hours polishing the aluminum with steel wool. I sewed new upholstery and lined the cockpit with matching fabric. We took it up on weekends, sometimes flying to Las Vegas for brunch on Sundays at a restaurant north of town with an airstrip. Sometimes to San Diego for the weekend. It was a delightful toy.

A few months later, as we approached the car to drive to work, he said, "You'd better drive." I *never* drove when we were together, and we were always together. He went on to explain that he'd had a near miss earlier in the day because he no longer had any peripheral vision. I was stunned. What did this mean? He hadn't told me sooner, he said, because he "didn't want to worry me." So he had saved the bad news until it was no longer deniable. It took many weeks and multiple doctor visits to find out what was going on. It seems that the medicine that "cured" his arthritis, and that he had stopped taking almost a year before, had burned his retina and damaged his optic nerve. The Veterans Administration declared Charlie "legally blind" in 1968, based on his diminished visual acuity and his narrowed field of vision. His field of vision chart resembled a screen door splashed with paint. He could see clearly only through two small openings in the lower quadrant of both eyes. Ophthalmologists told us that the damage was continuing, and there was nothing they could do to stop it. I would not accept that prognosis. Over the next few months, we used our little plane to fly to see specialists in California, Texas, Washington, Colorado, trying to find someone who could give us hope. But their conclusions were unanimous.

The progress of the deterioration of his sight was very gradual. We managed to work for several more years, largely because, by this time, I was an electronics technician and he was an electronics mechanic. We worked from a central lab. I was often able to accompany him when he was called to work on machines in the plant because they would frequently require reprogramming from me after his repair was completed. We worked out a system so that I could be there to be his eyes, alert him of people approaching in the hallways, and, most importantly, sign both of us in and out of the plant at the guard station. We knew the end was approaching, but we were desperate to pay the accumulated medical bills from visits to those specialists that we dared not turn in on the factory-provided insurance. The stress increased in severity, taking a physical toll on us both, as his sight continued to worsen. In 1973, during the first energy crisis, the plant extinguished every third light to save energy. We were done. We could no longer keep up the charade. We asked a friend to anonymously reveal Charlie's disability, and they let him go.

I went, too. Our dream of a houseful of children had never materialized. We abandoned adoption proceedings when we got his diagnosis. We had the freedom to just quit it all and start over somewhere else. By the time we sold the house and the plane and paid the outstanding medical bills, we were left with five thousand dollars and a pickup truck. We headed for the Ozarks, where my research told me Charlie's VA pension would stretch the farthest. We had been married twelve years. Charlie was forty-two, I was thirty, and we were "retired." We bought a small lot in a failed development on a lake in northern Arkansas, bought an 8' x 28' trailer to put on it, and settled in.

The next few years were tough. Charlie felt like his life was over, and I didn't know how to help him. I took small part-time jobs in the community to help keep our finances and my own sanity afloat. But every time I had to leave him alone, I was afraid he might take his life while I was gone. I did my best to enrich his life as much as I could and made every effort to communicate how much I loved him and that life for us was not done yet.

We lived twenty-eight miles from the nearest town with basic services. On our bimonthly trip for groceries, we stopped at a van in the parking lot, labeled Disabled Veterans of America. "Come in and see about your veteran's benefits," a sign beckoned. Well, we figured we had all the VA was going to offer, but we went inside anyway. The representative asked Charlie if he had used his GI Bill for education. No. "Since you are a 100 percent, service-connected, disabled veteran," he told us, "your wife or your children can use it." We took the literature home, and, after some discussion, we decided I should try to take advantage of that program. We could certainly use the money, and this would be a chance for me to go to college. So at the age of thirty-five, I showed up at the registration office of the North Arkansas Community College (NACC). I seriously didn't think they'd let me in. I'd barely graduated from high school; I was more concerned about my home situation than my studies in those days. When they asked for my high school transcript, I demurred, saying I thought it probably no longer existed. When that didn't work, I said that I'd been out of high school for eighteen years. Couldn't I just take a test? They gave me the ACT that afternoon, and while I merely filled in ovals at random on the math section, I scored high enough that they congratulated me and said they'd waive my tuition for the first year. Welcome to NACC.

Maybe I could do this after all, but I was terrified to build a life for myself that didn't include Charlie. We had always been inseparable. What would happen now? I ended up doing the only thing I knew to do. I brought my learning home to him. When I came home from class, I recapped my lectures to him, read all my assigned readings aloud, shared multiple drafts of my papers as I wrote them. That turned out to be the very best way to study. I got straight As that first semester and fought fiercely to keep that 4.0 all the way through the community college. I had to attend full-time to keep my funding, but managed, at least at first, to keep my time at college to just two days a week. On the days I was gone, Charlie managed to make his own lunch, work a bit in the yard, become just a bit more independent. His eyesight seemed to stabilize, leaving him a small window in his right eye to navigate his restricted world.

I discovered a world I did not know existed: a life of the mind, a life built around reading and thinking and grand ideas. I fell in love with that world, and to this day I frequently stop to think about how fortunate I was to find this life, and to live it. I began with a major in journalism but changed after I learned I'd be required to work on the student newspaper, which would necessitate extensive extra time on campus. I switched to history and then added psychology, stretching the two-year curriculum to three by picking up that second major. I had five years of funding so I tried to keep it as long as possible. After I graduated with an associate's degree, Charlie encouraged me to find a way to continue. With two years of funding left, I enrolled at the School of the Ozarks, a private Presbyterian college about forty-five miles away. The School of the Ozarks (now the College of the Ozarks) is a unique self-contained institution in that all functions of the college, except teaching and administration, are done by students. They work in the cafeteria, keep up the grounds, perform secretarial duties, build the dorms, manage the farm, and so forth, in return for the cost of their education. Generally, the School of the Ozarks did not accept tuition students, but they made an exception for me, and I tried to manage my schedule to keep my commute to three days a week.

By the time my GI funding ran out, I found work on campus to support the rest of my time there. This required me to be away from home for four days a week. I camped in a small travel trailer on a corner of campus from Sunday evening until Thursday. I had a telephone installed so Charlie and I could continue sharing my experiences. We talked for hours every night, and because the school was in Missouri and Charlie in Arkansas, the phone bill was our largest expense. Charlie gradually became more independent, taking on more responsibilities and finding friends to spend those days with. At some point he came to the conclusion, as he told me later, that "I have no control over what happened to me. All I can control is how I respond to it." This became his guiding philosophy throughout the rest of his life.

I held onto my straight As, and from my double major I acquired two great mentors. I loved psychology best. Dr. Lange hired me to use my newly acquired skills to work in the Student Services department. My job was to help students with study skills and time management. But I soon heard about more serious problems: young women came to me with eating disorders. As we talked, many of them related stories of sexual abuse from their fathers and brothers. Of course, I referred them to the professionals, but I was so disturbed by these revelations, and the large number of them at this tiny religious college, that I knew I could not spend my life in this profession. There was simply no way I could distance myself from the rage I was feeling.

I decided my destiny was to teach high school, so I earned a Secondary Social Studies Teaching Certificate. Things, as they often do, ultimately pushed me into a different track than I had anticipated. First was my experience doing student teaching in a rural country school, where I found all my energy was required to keep a lid on a chronically unruly classroom. No, thanks.

My history mentor, Dr. Kneeshaw, had encouraged me to consider graduate school. I didn't know what that was. Besides, my funding was all gone. He told me that funding was available out there for outstanding students like me. I had shrugged it off, not eager to relocate, until my experience at the secondary school. I was more receptive to the idea after that.

I became his intern that semester. At the same time, I participated in his senior seminar. He hired a van and took eight of us to the LBJ Library in Austin, Texas, to spend a week doing primary research there. I decided to write about Lady Bird and her role in the Johnson administration. Doing primary research was a revelation to me. I would later tell my own students that I became a historian because I like to read other people's mail. That was only partially in jest.

It was an internship in name only. The only work Dr. Kneeshaw required was for me to produce essays and applications to graduate schools. I applied to a dozen schools and was accepted at all of them. Some even offered me a bit of funding. Dr. Kneeshaw also put me up for a Mellon Fellowship (eight thousand dollars a year at that time) that I could take with me anywhere I chose. I told him that I thought I wanted to go to Sarah Lawrence and study women's history. He reacted quite negatively, telling me that women's history was "one of those fad histories, like black history" and would be a dead-end career move. I made the finals on the Mellon. They flew me to Dallas to meet with the committee for the final decision. It was grueling and combative. The committee, seeing my double major in history and psychology, fixated on making me explain, and defend, psychohistory. I didn't make the cut. I decided I'd probably go to the University of Texas, Austin, since they offered me an assistantship, albeit one that required me to begin teaching large lecture sections of their American history survey immediately.

Then came the letter that changed my life. It was from the chair of the History Department at Rutgers University, David Oshinsky. He wrote that he was aware that I had made the finals for the Mellon but had not won. The Mellon was housed at Princeton, and I assumed they shared the list of losers with their sister school, Rutgers. Oshinsky encouraged me to apply to their program, saying Rutgers had funding available at least as good as that from Mellon. This caused a good deal of discussion at home. Charlie was eager for the process to be completed. He said he didn't care where I decided to go; he just wanted the decision made. He did care, though. He had asked me to limit my applications to "warm places," steering me away from Minnesota, Wisconsin, Iowa. Still, he thought I should go ahead and try Rutgers, since this was a real solicitation. I reminded him that they were in New Jersey. It gets cold up there, I said. He responded with a story of being stationed near New Brunswick, where Rutgers is, on his way to Korea, and that the winters were relatively mild. So I decided to go for it and held off making a final decision.

It seemed like such a long shot, and I had already worn out my recommenders. I hesitated to ask for yet another letter. As it happened, being a very "nontraditional" student had gotten me noticed by the president and the dean of faculty (both about my age), who had once offered to write for me. I took up their offer, sent in my materials, including a copy of my senior thesis on Lady Bird, and pretty much forgot about it in the closing weeks of the semester. Then one Thursday, when I came home for the weekend, Charlie told me I'd had a phone call from a professor at Rutgers. He said they were offering me funding of ten thousand dollars a year for five years to complete my master's and PhD and they would cover all my tuition and fees. "No," I told Charlie. "You must have misunderstood." "I thought that's what you'd say," he replied. "He said he'd call back tonight." When Dr. David Oshinsky called, he reiterated the offer. I was stunned, so much so that a long silence ensued. Oshinsky moved to fill it, saying that if I were hesitant about coming to New Jersey, they would be pleased to send plane tickets for my husband and me to visit the campus. More silence. I couldn't believe what I was hearing. Oshinsky added that he could arrange for us to live in student housing to defray the high cost of living in the area. I finally choked out that I would call him back. I hung up and asked Charlie if he thought we should accept the tickets and go have a look. He replied: "How bad could it be? If worse comes to worst, you can just go for a couple years, get your master's, and come home. I think we should go for it; they're paying you. It could be a great adventure." I called David Oshinsky back and accepted.

We loaded up and headed to New Jersey in July. As we came into New Brunswick, Charlie said that some things seemed familiar. Turning down a side road, he pointed out a theater where he had seen the premiere of *Singing in the Rain* when he was stationed near there on his way to Korea. Everything was new to me, and I was thrilled to find a campus that looked like all the campuses in the movies. Founded as Queens College in 1766. A truly colonial college. Red brick, ivy-covered, sprawling lawns. As we crossed the river to find our new apartment on an adjacent campus, Charlie again remarked about how familiar things appeared. It turned out that the complex of student apartments was adjacent to a handful of repurposed barracks and a coal-fired generating plant. Charlie had worked in the plant when he was stationed there. We, or rather he, had come full circle.

On our first day, all of us new graduate students gathered with Professor Oshinsky, arrayed around a large table. There were about thirty of us, but only some had full funding like I did. We were to introduce ourselves, where we had completed our undergraduate studies, and what our major interest area was. They were all young, of course, in their twenties. I was forty-one. They were from Yale, Cornell, Brown, Toronto, William and Mary. I was from the School of the Ozarks. I tried to spin it a bit, describing it as a small private college in Missouri. My interest was women and politics.

I strongly suspected that I had been admitted because of the novelty of my background. I was over forty and had graduated from, of all places, the School of the Ozarks. Still, my GRE was strong (734 verbal), my grades were stellar, I had recommendations from people in the highest levels at my college, and I'd written a pretty good senior honor's thesis about Lady Bird Johnson. For those reasons, I figured, they decided to take a chance and get a look at me.

The reading load was grueling. We were assigned five to eight books a week, often with a handful of scholarly articles. It became evident to me that many of my fellow students were already familiar with at least some of the books, classics in their subfields. But the books were all new to me. All I had ever read for history was textbooks. Some students even knew what "schools" the authors represented. And they were far more comfortable debating the merits of each book in the discussion sections. I mostly sat quietly and tried to soak up as much as I could. I was reading from 6:00 a.m. until nearly midnight every day. Charlie spent his days cooking for me, telling me when to take a break, when to stop for the night. I was constantly aware of the sacrifices he was making for me—though he never pointed that out to me—subordinating his relatively autonomous life back home to live in this tiny apartment, waiting for me.

I soon realized that I wasn't the only student feeling overwhelmed. A group of women students began gathering in the hallway after class to commiserate. Several of them indicated their intention to drop out. I suggested maybe it would help if we met regularly and tried to help one another survive. At Sunday-evening sessions in our apartment, we shared our fears about our inadequacies and developed strategies for sharing the enormous workload we faced. We met from 5:00 to 7:00 p.m., and then our significant others arrived to share a pot-luck meal. This social time became at least as important as the academics, and it was one more way to involve Charlie more directly in my journey. What's more, I learned how valuable the support of a group of women in similar circumstances could be. It was a lesson I took forward throughout my career.

With some research, I discovered a VA program designed to help the blind and near-blind realize their potential. It was a residential program in West Haven, Connecticut, that lasted sixteen weeks. We had never been separated for longer than a week. But it was clearly a great opportunity and just what I was hoping to find when we moved to the progressive Northeast. Charlie retained about 3 percent of his sight, according to the VA, but we were both aware that this might disappear at any point. At the Blind Center, Charlie learned a host of life skills, including how to cross busy streets and navigate through a city, how to cook safely, care for a home and himself. It was truly life-changing; he came home feeling empowered to face whatever the future might hold.

Charlie told me he felt left out during our discussions of history and wished to learn more. He wanted to take advantage of a university program for retired and handicapped persons to audit classes on campus for free. I contacted Princeton to order the required textbooks on tape. I attended with him for a few sessions until he mastered the bus system and the location of the classes, across two busy streets from the bus stop. Then I had to let him go on his own. The most difficult task I had throughout my life with Charlie was to bite my tongue and let him do what he wanted to do.

By the end of that first semester, a bunch of my cohort had dropped out. Almost half of the original thirty students were gone by Christmas. These were bright kids who had sailed through their undergraduate studies. All this reading and studying, plus the far higher standards of graduate study, were just too hard. It *was* hard, the hardest thing I'd ever undertaken. Yet I was keenly aware that someone was paying me to go to school. I was not about to abandon that without a fight.

I came to graduate school knowing I wanted to do something with women and politics. While still an undergraduate, I entertained the idea of a biography of Lady Bird Johnson. When I interviewed her in Texas, I shared that desire with her. "Not in your lifetime, honey," she replied. Her papers would be closed until fifty years after her death. So I had come to New Jersey in search of a topic, and, having survived my first year, I began looking around.

As my second year got under way, David Oshinsky called me into his office and asked me what I knew about Margaret Chase Smith. Not much. I thought I remembered her being nominated for president at the 1964 GOP convention, the one that crowned my then home-state senator Barry Goldwater. She had come to Rutgers for an honorary degree that spring. With me in mind, he said, he'd asked her if her papers were available and if anyone was writing her biography. Yes to the first; no to the second. Was I interested? Absolutely. He offered to write me an introductory letter. I should go up there, he said, and "sew it up." I thought of that charge many times as my relationship to the project and to Senator Smith evolved, from wariness about my motives, through a lengthy "courtship" that involved demonstrating my work ethic, my skills as a historian, and my fairness, to an active working relationship based on mutual respect and trust.

When I met her, she was eighty-eight years old, living in her hometown of Skowhegan in central Maine. Her home had been modified to house also her papers and a museum, filled with the artifacts of her public life. Out of the political mainstream since her defeat in 1972, Smith remained very active in her role as an elder stateswoman. Her opinions were frequently sought by Maine's print and broadcast media, and she made herself available to nearly everyone who came to see her. I was a graduate student of history, I told her, interested in women and American politics. "You must understand," she told me that first afternoon, "that I never was a woman. I never was a woman politician. I never was a woman senator. And I'm not a feminist, either." Oh. Smith dutifully answered my questions about major events in her career, as I avoided asking too much about being a woman.

I began the project with a women's history seminar paper. That's when I learned that there are trends in history; the then-current trend was to focus on working-class inarticulate populations. My project to write a biography of an elite political woman—a Republican!—was well beyond the pale. Yet, here again I found the support and engagement of women in similar circumstances, here grappling with their first attempts at writing history, though somewhat hostile to my project, was immensely helpful in formulating questions, designating strategies, interpreting findings. I found a similar situation when I teamed with a group of women in political science to work on a grant-supported project to measure the "impact of women on American politics."

Funded by the Center for the American Woman and Politics, this project and this group of women, whose focus was the same but methodology so different from mine, challenged me to consider Senator Smith and my own notions of scholarship in new ways. The grant paid for my first laptop and several months' rent in Skowhegan.

Charlie and I traveled to Skowhegan as often as we could while I was still taking classes. Once I finished my comprehensive exams, we found an apartment and settled in for the summer. This was a project of massive proportions. It was a good thing I didn't grasp the enormity of it at the outset, or I might have abandoned it early on. Instead, I was enchanted by the scope and the comprehensiveness of the sources. Smith had held national office for thirty-three years. Her archive contained more than eighty-eight file drawers filled with three hundred thousand primary-source documents, forty bound volumes of statements and speeches, five hundred scrapbooks that she had been keeping since she was a girl, swelled during her career by clipping services, thousands of photographs, hundreds of video and audiotapes. Still, there were significant gaps in the record. Much important legislative work is done face-to-face. Political maneuvers, personal relationships, personality quirks, understandings and agreements, cloakroom conversations and private phone calls are seldom recorded. Office correspondence is routine and purposefully impersonal; speeches and statements are couched in general terms to minimize political consequences. While traditional sources could usually reveal what happened, only Smith could tell me how, and what it meant to her. I gathered more than one hundred hours of interviews to add to the mix. "Sewing it up" ultimately took over six years.

Charlie and I moved back and forth between Arkansas and Maine during those years. Staying as long as we could in Maine, then coming home to raise funds, write grants, work a bit over the winter, then back north in the spring. Charlie and Senator Smith had a great affinity. She liked him very much, and that certainly helped move our relationship into a more personal realm. Smith was just more comfortable with men in general. Charlie didn't ask endless questions, and, nearly blind herself with macular degeneration, she found a sympathetic kindred soul and a role model for coping in him.

When I set up my dissertation committee, there was no question but that my mentor, David Oshinsky, would be the chair. Then I added three women scholars: historians Suzanne Lebsock and Virginia Yans, and Ruth Mandel, director of the Center for the American Woman and Politics. My chapter drafts would come back with Oshinsky remarking that I used the word "woman" too much. The women historians requested I employ more feminist theory, and Ruth Mandel urged sharpening my focus on politics. I ultimately landed somewhere in the intersections of their advice. None of them, though, was willing to stay with me to see the biography all the way through. We agreed upon a logical stopping point for the conclusion of the dissertation (her election to the Senate, the first woman to earn such an election on her own, in 1948), with the understanding that I could finish the full biography on my own once I got a job.

I seriously did not think I would be able to land a tenure-track job. I was forty-nine years old when I completed my dissertation. Jobs were scarce. Moreover, my topic was seriously outside the current trends in historiography. I applied for many positions, traveled to multiple interviews, trying not to lose hope, just like everyone I knew was doing. My first year on the market, I got a job at the University of Wisconsin–Eau Claire. I had it for two weeks, then a letter from the chair regretfully informed me that funding for the position had been rescinded. I made a campus visit to the University of Memphis (at that time, Memphis State) in the spring of 1994. I found a history department composed of white men, most of them over fifty, several a good deal older, and one woman. It wasn't until after I got the job that I learned that I was apparently an affirmative-action hire. The department had been under strong pressure by the university to hire a woman. The other candidates brought to campus had been young feminist scholars who "scared the pants off the men." I was older, perhaps calmer, probably less challenging. I wrote about a conservative woman. I was someone they could live with, I overheard the chair say to a colleague.

The department hired a male scholar at the same time, but since I was both a new hire and female, Dr. Jack Hurley, the chair, told me to take minutes at the faculty meetings. And I did, for a year. After that, the departmental secretary took the minutes. Soon, the next few hires were women and African Americans, and in at least one instance, both. I cannot say I was consciously eager to change the system, but the system was changing, and I was glad to be along for the ride.

My second year on the faculty I was named to a search committee for a position in nineteenth-century African American history. Among our top applicants, one of them was known to everyone on the search committee except me. Each of us took one candidate to examine closely; I was given the assignment of examining Beverly Bond's credentials and deciding whether or not to recommend she be hired. She was a graduate of the program and as such would typically be considered ineligible. I was impressed with her application and presented her to the rest of the committee and the full faculty as the best choice for the position. Everyone agreed, and she got the job. Her office was across the hall from mine, and we began talking. I told her that while I had attended one of the top women's history programs in the country (ironically, after my mentor's warning about Sarah Lawrence), I knew almost nothing about black women's history. She said she knew little about white women in the twentieth century. As we began sharing sources, we decided to design a course and take some graduate students along on our mutual exploration. That became "Black and White Women in American History," structured around those historical moments when black and white women worked together for a specific goal, and a close examination of why and how those alliances did not hold.

Beverly and I became coauthors of a couple books on Memphis history and together produced a coffee-table book for the one-hundredth anniversary of the University of Memphis.[1] During our partnership we learned how to teach together, to trust one another's judgment and strategies; we learned to write together, separately writing portions of the narrative and then collaborating on making the prose "match" in style as much as possible. We learned to scan and prepare images for publication—the hard way, by doing them over and over until we got it right. We learned a great deal about Memphis history, about the university, and about ourselves.

We became friends and, ultimately, sisters. Here's how that happened. As Charlie's health declined, he made many trips to the hospital, and I often called Beverly to tell her. She was always there for me, listening, caring. One night when I knew we were at the hospital for the last time, I called Beverly about 2:00 a.m. She said she would come to be with me. I told her she couldn't, that he was in cardiac ICU, and only family members were allowed. She said, "I'll tell them I'm your sister." Apparently she did, and no one challenged her. She held my hand through the memorial arrangements as I dissolved in grief, and she helped me in myriad ways when I returned to work. She's the very best kind of sister because she chose to be.

But I'm getting ahead of my story.

While I was still in Arkansas, recovering from double knee replacements, I got a book contract, based on my dissertation, from the Free Press, plus something few historians see, an advance. But it came with a strict deadline to revise the dissertation and to write what was essentially another dissertation covering 1948 to the end of Smith's life. I'd taken copious notes and photocopied key documents before I left Skowhegan, so I was certain I could meet their demands, even while teaching as a new assistant professor. But I hadn't reckoned on the decline in the health of the love of my life.

Charlie's health began to deteriorate almost as soon as we settled in Memphis. While still in Skowhegan a few years before, he had contracted a particularly awful strain of the flu. It settled in his heart and left him with a large scar that looked on an X-ray like he'd had a severe heart attack. He appeared to recover well. He took up running while we lived in Maine and even tried downhill skiing! But his apparent recovery was deceptive.

At the beginning of my second year on the faculty, in 1995, Charlie got pneumonia, an apparently stubborn drug-resistant strain. He spent nearly four months in the hospital. I taught during the day and spent the nights on a cot in his hospital room, listening for him to stop breathing. When he left the hospital, he spent several more weeks on a hospital bed in our living room on full oxygen. I overheard his home-health nurse whisper to her replacement one evening that he was not anticipated to survive. I was stunned and very frightened. His cardiologist informed us that, as a result of the pneumonia, the weak spot on his heart had gotten much weaker. He now had stage C (the third of four stages) congestive heart failure and could anticipate to live at best two years more. This was February 1996.

My chair asked me every day how my book was coming along. It wasn't. My mind was full of whirling chaos. My husband was dying. I couldn't imagine my life without him. How could I concentrate on writing? Every spare moment was consumed with keeping Charlie's health records, a spreadsheet recording everything any of his multiple doctors had told him, medicines they had prescribed, any side effects, his daily weight and blood pressure.

For many weeks, he got daily blood tests at a lab across town. He made many ambulance trips to the hospital, usually at night, most of them because some medication or electrolyte got out of whack. And every day, my chair asked me how my book was coming.

The tenure clock was ticking; I had only a year and a half left. Then the Free Press was bought by Simon and Schuster. They canceled my contract because I was a few months late, and they demanded their advance back. It was all the money I had in the bank. I began reading the want-ads for retail and office jobs. Just in time, a new chair, Kenneth Goings, took over. I'll never forget the day he called me in his office. I went in thinking, "This is it. It's all over." Trembling, I lowered myself into the chair across from his desk. He said, "I've been trying to think of a way to help you." I dissolved in tears. After I calmed a bit, he took me upstairs to talk to the dean, Ralph Faudree. Together they came up with a plan that saved my career: a pause on the tenure clock, a double teaching load for the coming semester, then a semester's leave so I could write.

I called David Oshinsky, who sat on the board of Rutgers University Press. The press had earlier expressed an interest in my book, but I had chosen the trade press. The director called me back and said, okay, she'd take it, if I could deliver it in one year. No extensions. No excuses.

No Place for a Woman: A Life of Senator Margaret Chase Smith was published in 2000.[2] *The New York Times Book Review* praised my research and writing, calling my book "thoughtful and satisfying, as straightforward and straight-arrow as its subject." I had done it, and Charlie was still there to share it with me.

His health stabilized a bit, or maybe we just got more used to the routine. He began a garden and some small projects around the house. I hired graduate students to "be his eyes" for ten dollars an hour. After several male graduate students proved unreliable, I asked one of my advisees, Kim Nichols, for a recommendation. "Does it have to be a male?" she asked. No, it didn't. She started working with Charlie and ultimately became something of a quasi-daughter to the both of us.

Meanwhile I turned to finding a topic for my next book. One of my colleagues, who had noticed I'd listed I was a pilot on my resume, noted that the control tower at Memphis International Airport was named for a woman. This intrigued me. Unlike the extremely long odyssey I'd completed with

Margaret, I figured this would be a nice, and fun, local story that I could complete quickly. An examination of the clippings file on Phoebe Fairgrave Omlie in the public library disabused me of that notion. There was little information about her, but what there was told me that this was not a local story but a national one. The handful of clippings revealed her early career in the 1920s as a barnstormer, wing-walker, and air racer; her and her husband's involvement in the foundation and management of the Memphis airport; her appointment to an aviation policy post in the federal government in 1934; her obituary noting she died broke and alone in Indianapolis in 1973.

The paucity of sources offered a stark contrast to the massive documentation on Senator Smith. At every break, Charlie and I traveled to archives and aviation museums trying to find enough information to write a book. As long as Phoebe was in the public eye, I had newspaper sources and a handful of documents from her government service. But once she left public office in 1952, she disappeared for the last twenty years of her life. Multiple times, failing to find sufficient sources, I abandoned the project to take up something else. But Phoebe refused to be forgotten.

Charlie outlived his "expiration date" by six years. His cardiologist had predicted 1998; he died in March 2004. Mostly he did it through pure stubbornness. There was simply too much going on that he had no intention of missing. No matter what his doctors reported about his failing heart, he kept repeating to me, "I'm not ready to leave you yet."

I remember the night when he was finally ready. I had gone to a reception at the university where I dined with Ralph Faudree, now the provost. I beseeched him to tell me if my promotion to full professor had left his desk. "Of course," he said, "and I want you to think about being chair of the History Department. Jack is leaving." I went home to tell Charlie what he'd said. Now very thin and frail, breathing with difficulty, my dear husband sat on the side of his bed, and as I related the news, he took a deep breath and sighed. He knew I'd be able to take care of myself now. Within a couple of months, Charlie let go and died.

Despite significant reservations, I did pursue the chair position, largely because I had apparent support from my colleagues who feared—as I did—that the only other interested candidate would get it. Charlie died in March; I became chair in August, the first female chair the department ever had.

I am completely convinced that being chair saved my life. I threw all my heart and soul into being the best chair I could be; the distraction of the work and the off-hours planning and thinking about it helped me survive the worst time of my life. But I felt woefully unprepared to assume leadership. I was uncomfortable with the male models I knew; they just didn't fit me. I asked Ralph Faudree if there was "a chair school." He sponsored me to attend a leadership-training institute in Nashville, where I was very surprised to learn that the leadership style I was most comfortable with—team decision-making, consensus building, facilitating instead of directing—were the very skills the leadership institute was teaching to the mostly male attendees. I found this validating and empowering, and I never looked back.

I spent nine years as chair of the History Department. The best thing about being chair is that when you have an idea, your colleagues have to listen to you. I had lots of ideas, most of them having to do with the culture of the department. My vision was for a more collegial department and one that was open and accessible to all our students. I hired sixteen new faculty during my tenure, and my primary criterion for a new hire was that they be "nice." This may sound facile, but I had no intention of introducing a prima donna into the faculty, no matter how accomplished. Also during my tenure, we completely transformed our graduate program, from one that assumed graduate students should sink or swim on their own, assuming total responsibility for their own learning, to one that assisted them in a process of systematically building knowledge and skills while supporting their development.

One initiative I'm proudest of, and that had the greatest impact on the entire department, is our online program. The department was urged to develop such a program as an important money-generating initiative for the university, yet they remained reluctant to provide the resources I felt were needed to implement it. I resisted for several years until the dean finally acquiesced. In the final negotiations, I asked for one more thing: I told them I knew the university stood to earn a lot of money from an online history program that processed so many students. I wanted, I told the dean, a "piece of the action." Apparently under pressure to get this done, the dean made me a very generous offer of a percentage of the income. We built a program committed to the highest standards; our online courses are identical to those taught in the classroom; only the delivery system is different. And we realized a funding stream that changed everything in the department. From an annual budget of less than thirty thousand dollars for the entire department, one that required faculty to pay for their own copies and printer ribbons, to being able to fund student and faculty research travel, buy new equipment like computers, software and the like, increase graduate stipends to full support as they completed their dissertations, and a host of other benefits.

Nothing you learn is ever wasted. So much of my training in counseling psychology was a big help in dealing with faculty and students. My door was always open, I listened compassionately, I mentored anyone who would let me, including women chairs in other departments (and in two cases, male chairs). I served on many committees and tried to make myself indispensable to deans, mine and others. I was most fortunate to serve during the tenure of the university's first and only female president, Dr. Shirley Raines. We met when she was a candidate for the job, and we found many opportunities to privately discuss sensitive matters privately. At the reception for my retirement in 2013, she announced that she could not imagine serving at the University of Memphis without me and so would retire the next year. I'm sure she had likely been planning her retirement for some time, but her kindness in making that public announcement is indicative of what a kind and supportive leader she had been for me.

Once I had settled into being chair after a few years, having abandoned Phoebe multiple times for other projects, I remained obsessed with her story. I felt that I had reached the pinnacle of my career. I needed no more books for my resume. Still, I could not bear to abandon Phoebe. I needed help. And once again, I turned to women in similar circumstances, having learned over and over again that talking things through with simpatico listeners, with whom I felt free to share anything and everything, my failings and my insecurities, helped me reach the right solution.

I joined a group that came to be known as the Delta Women Writers, composed of women historians from the mid-South area who valued the company and expertise of other professional women for sustenance and encouragement, professionally and personally. We met twice a year to share and critique one another's work in a spirit of collegial nurturance. In November 2008, I brought my incomplete story of Phoebe to the group and asked for guidance. Following that session, convinced that the story, however incomplete, needed to be told, I set out to write it as a journey of discovery, calling it *Finding Phoebe.* Yet, I was still loath to leave her story unfinished. I took my last sabbatical that fall, determined to retrace all my research, still hunting for the key to her last twenty years. I followed obscure threads through the careers of other women aviators, searched the archives of deceased journalists and aviation magazine writers. I found a bit of information in one of them that indicated Phoebe had maintained contact with a sister air-racer, Louise Thaden. Through the miracle of the internet, I found Thaden's daughter, Pat Thaden Webb, who retained correspondence between her mother and Phoebe. She recalled that when Phoebe died, someone had tried to sell the papers she left behind to the Ninety-Nines Aviation Museum in Oklahoma City. Pat called the museum's former director, who called me and gave me a phone number. That's how I found Della Mae Frazier, the woman who had been with Phoebe when she died, and who had kept all of Phoebe's final effects in her basement, waiting for me to find her. It was a rich treasure trove of personal recollections, scrapbooks, correspondence, and photographs. I finally learned what had happened to Phoebe during those last twenty years of her life.

Eighteen months after my first Delta Women Writers presentation, I returned with a more complete story. Their comments helped me polish the final version, and *Walking on Air: The Aerial Adventures of Phoebe Omlie* was published in 2011, sixteen years after I began my search for Phoebe.[3] I dedicated the book to Charlie, "who taught me how to live."

None of this improbable journey would have been possible without the great love of my life. He saw things in me that no one else had and encouraged me to seize upon the great adventures of life. He taught me how to stand up and deal with great adversity with grace and optimism. Without him, I planned to keep working until I couldn't anymore. After nine years, I felt I'd done all I could as chair. I decided to step down and just go back to being a professor again. From that vantage point, it sounded like a vacation. Yet, one more adventure awaited.

When Charlie and I had been in Maine, we discovered a beautiful island fifteen miles off the coast in Penobscot Bay. The seventy-five-minute ferry ride threading through forested granite islands was, as Charlie put it, "a poor man's cruise." Vinalhaven is roughly the size of Manhattan Island and has

1,200 year-round residents. The island is breathtakingly beautiful. We visited often during those years, made friends there, and promised ourselves we would retire to Vinalhaven. But, as you now know, we relocated to Memphis, Charlie got sick, and we abandoned our plans for the island. In 2010, an old grad school friend, both of us in the Northeast on separate pursuits, talked me into returning to the island for a couple days. She'd never visited and recalled how much I had loved it there. I tried to say no; I thought it would just be too painful. Nonetheless, she was most persuasive, and I gave in. The moment the ferry turned the corner and pulled into the harbor, I knew that this was where I belonged, that this was home. I spent the next couple of summers in a rented cottage in the village, returned for a winter stay, then bought a home. In May 2013, I retired and moved permanently to Vinalhaven, Maine. Every morning I awake into beauty and serenity, and resume the task of constructing my happily-ever-after.

NOTES

1. Janann Sherman and Beverly G. Bond, *Memphis in Black and White* (Charleston, SC: Arcadia, 2003); Janann Sherman and Beverly Bond, *Beale Street* (Charleston, SC: Arcadia, 2006); Janann Sherman and Beverly Bond, *Dreamers, Thinkers, Doers: A Centennial History of the University of Memphis* (Virginia Beach, VA: Donning, 2011).

2. Janann Sherman, *No Place for a Woman: A Life of Senator Margaret Chase Smith* (New Brunswick, NJ: Rutgers University Press, 2000).

3. Janann Sherman, *Walking on Air: The Aerial Adventures of Phoebe Omlie* (Jackson: University Press of Mississippi, 2011).

CLUELESS

SHEILA SKEMP

As much as it embarrasses, even pains me, to admit it, my academic career has been more the product of happenstance and a good measure of luck than anything else. Born in 1945 (old enough so that I am technically too old to be a baby boomer), I was fortunate to have parents who cared about education, and who made many sacrifices along the way so that their children would have access to a college degree. My parents met on a blind date in Seattle during World War II. My dad was on leave from the army; my mother worked at Boeing. Mom had already graduated from the University of Montana—the first person in her family to attend college. My father was also a first-generation college student. Originally from the Chicago area, at war's end he took advantage of the GI Bill, moving all of us to Missoula, where he attended Mom's alma mater, graduating in 1950. He taught school in various tiny Montana towns before returning us to the Chicago suburbs in 1954. There, we continued to move around a lot, going from one rented house to another. By the time I entered college I had attended six grade schools and two high schools. But despite having to endure a peripatetic existence, I never doubted that my basic needs would be taken care of. Nor was I ever allowed to think that getting an education didn't matter.

Although they surely didn't realize it, my folks were also instrumental in giving me a love of history. Each summer we took a vacation, driving across the country in whatever used car we could afford at the time, pulling a pop-up trailer so that we wouldn't have to pay for a motel. We visited friends and relatives, but we also went to any and all historical sites we encountered along the way. My younger brothers and I visited countless Civil War and American Revolution battlefields, walked Boston's Freedom Trail, and gawked at the homes of many of America's great men. (And of course I do mean "men"—not people!) My romantic imagination was in top form on those visits, and they surely made history come alive for me in ways that even the best textbook could not. We also made great use of our library cards. I especially loved historical fiction and the little biographies that introduced me to the stories of famous people—mostly men but a few women—in America's past. And I was fortunate enough to have excellent grade school teachers who nurtured my love of history. Yes, I took advantage of the opportunities that came my way. But I was lucky to have those opportunities.

Raised in the 1950s and early 1960s, I was, like so many white middle-class women of that era, not especially focused on a career of any sort. "Smart" girls in those days thought in terms of becoming nurses or grade-school teachers. Maybe high school teachers if they were truly ambitious. If they didn't follow one of those trajectories, they took shorthand and typing courses and planned to become secretaries. Of course, the real goal of the vast majority of my cohort was to marry someone who would earn enough money to support us and our many children in comfortable middle-class fashion. Men, in other words, needed to think seriously about, to worry about, their career options and to plan accordingly. Women needed something to "fall back on," and little more.

In some ways, this was liberating. I could take courses that interested me, with no thought about their practical ramifications. For me, this meant that once I entered high school, I enrolled in classes in creative and journalistic writing, sociology, psychology, and, above all, history. After taking a Western civilization course my senior year in high school that was taught by an aspiring and inspiring PhD candidate from Northwestern, I was more certain of my love of history than ever. History became my passion, but my father warned me not to make it my college major. He had been a history major in college and had finally gotten a job teaching junior high math. If I rejected his sage advice, my father insisted, I would never get a job. Only coaches obtained positions teaching history. Better, by far, to major in elementary education. Why set myself up for disappointment?

Solid advice, which I had every intention of following. But luck—fortunately

—intervened. Following in my parents' footsteps, I enrolled at the University of Montana in 1963. I was familiar with Montana—we spent parts of many summers there on my grandfather's farm. Moreover, the University of Illinois—which was huge and impersonal—scared me. I was sure I would be a social outcast at so formidable a place, and social life mattered to me back then. Almost as soon as I set foot on campus, I discovered that elementary education majors at the university were required to take three quarters of some sort of mathematics. History majors, on the other hand, could take *either* three quarters of science *or* three quarters of mathematics. That settled it. I had nearly failed high school algebra and had struggled through geometry. I had vowed never to enroll in another math class. That night, I wrote a letter home (no cell phones back in the day!) announcing my decision to major in history. I never looked back.

Indeed, in virtually every way my university experience was life-changing. I had been an indifferent high school student until my senior year. I had also been painfully shy, never dating, hanging out with a few close girlfriends who were as socially awkward as I was. For whatever reason, that changed almost as soon as I began my college career. I loved dorm life, made lots of friends, and joined nearly every club that caught my interest. For the first time in a very long time, I actually liked myself. My classes were stimulating; my high school had given me an excellent foundation upon which to build. Thus I shone academically, in large part—at least in the beginning—because most Montana students came from tiny towns with even tinier high schools. They experienced Missoula as a culture shock. I had graduated in a class of more than nine hundred students. For me college was a piece of cake. Doing well in the beginning gave me confidence, something to build on in the coming years. I loved all of my history classes, of course. And I got at least an inkling of something called "historiography"—although I didn't call it that, indeed I didn't even know the word existed—during my sophomore year, when I enrolled in the U.S. history survey course. A lecture on what I now recognize as the "Turner thesis" piqued my interest. The argument seemed so compelling, indeed so romantic. But, I idly wondered, did everyone agree with this perspective? Curious, I screwed up my courage and visited my professor during his office hours, asking him if there might be another approach. Of course he was thrilled to have a lowly undergraduate ask such a question. He pulled book after book from his shelves, piling them onto my outstretched arms, urging me to return to his office to discuss my opinions once I had digested the issue. So *this* was history. It wasn't just facts and dates and events. There was no right or wrong answer. History was open-ended. I was hooked.

As I continued with my studies, my vague, poorly-thought-out assumption was that I would somehow defy the odds and land a job teaching at the high school level. I didn't even consider college teaching. That was simply not a part of my universe. At the start of my junior year, however, my favorite professor nonchalantly asked me where I planned to attend graduate school. My response surely stunned him. "What," I asked innocently, "is graduate school?" Needless to say, I learned the answer to that question very quickly. A whole new world was about to open up for me. Most appealing, if I went to graduate school, I could put off any decision about "what to do with my life" a bit longer. I liked school. It was the one thing I knew I could do. Why not just keep on doing it for a while? And yes, I am ashamed to admit it, I figured if I met the right man—which somehow still hadn't happened even though most of my friends were getting "pinned" or engaged right and left—then I would *never* have to make those decisions. Somehow, without me thinking much about my future at all, everything seemed to be falling into place.

Amazingly—or perhaps not, given the climate of the times—I never considered the possibility that my status as a woman could be an obstacle to my endeavors. I was politically active as an undergraduate. I was heavily involved in the university's fledgling antiwar movement. I was aware of and supported the civil rights movement. As a result, I knew that African Americans experienced discrimination in every conceivable way. I had no sense, however, that this was true for women. Although I saw no evidence of it, I just assumed that the academic world—unlike the world of business—operated on meritocratic principles. If I studied hard, I would achieve my goals. I don't know why it did not occur to me that throughout my academic career, I had no female role models. I never took a class from a woman historian at the undergraduate level. As a graduate student I took a couple of courses from one woman, a visiting professor, there only because the "real" professor was on sabbatical for the year. I knew that Ivy League schools were the domain of men. Had I been looking for a job in the "real world," I would have turned to the "help wanted" pages of any newspaper and would have seen job listings categorized by gender, the lower-paying, dead-end positions going invariably to women. I was aware of all that—vaguely—and yet it never dawned on me that when I went to graduate school I would be entering a man's world.

Why, I sometimes wonder, was I so ignorant about my prospects as a woman entering a profession dominated by men? I was ignorant at least in part because my aspirations—like the aspirations of many women of this era—were so modest. If I thought of doors closed to me, I thought much more in terms of class than gender. (Those girls' schools, for instance, that society viewed as a substitute for Harvard and Yale were beyond my reach because my parents could not afford to send me there. And I knew I wouldn't fit in with those girls even if I somehow enrolled in one of the female Ivies.) Even when one of my (male) professors warned me that I would find it difficult to achieve even my modest goals, merely because I was a woman, I shrugged. Surely his advice didn't apply to me! And so, totally clueless, I proceeded.

And at first my unfounded faith in academia was rewarded. I took the GRE and predictably utterly failed the quantitative section and scored very high on the verbal portion. (My major professor at Iowa once told me the members of the department burst out laughing when they saw my scores, wondering if two different people had taken the exam.) Two professors at Montana walked me through the process of applying for admission to graduate school. They told me where to apply and how to seek fellowships. I did no research. I didn't contact anyone in the history departments to which I applied. I planned to major in American intellectual history, but I had no idea who my major professor would be at any of those schools. I was flying blind. Somehow, it worked out. I was accepted at Berkeley and Harvard with no offer of a fellowship from either institution. The University of Iowa and UC Santa Barbara both offered me a lucrative (for the time) National Defense Education Act (NDEA) scholarship. A product of the Cold War, NDEA fellowships were a response to what appeared to be the superior educational achievements of Soviet youth. We were being beaten by the "godless Communists." Passed in 1958, the act's purpose was "to strengthen the national defense and . . . to meet critical national needs for other purposes." Clearly my grant was for "other purposes"! Until 1962, recipients had to sign a disclaimer indicating that they did not support the overthrow of the U.S. government. Fortunately, I did not have to sign this disclaimer, although I did recognize the irony that someone like me would receive a stipend designed to strengthen America's military might. The fellowship lasted for three years. The first year, I received $2,000, plus tuition; the second year, $2,200; the third, $2,400—all tax-free. This seems like very small potatoes these days, but I lived on that fellowship, did not go into debt, and had enough money to buy a steak now and then and to drink plenty of beer!

It never occurred to me to borrow money to go to a "better school." And there was no way my parents could help me meet my graduate school commitments. My father was a schoolteacher who worked nights at the post office to help make ends meet. My mother was—as were all the mothers I knew—a stay-at-home mom. My father had struggled to put me through college—a gift I am ashamed to say I took for granted. He was already saving money to pay for my two younger brothers' college education. He would not, could not, help me pursue a graduate school career. For this, I was on my own. I needed to support myself, and the NDEA fellowship allowed me to do just that. I decided to go to Iowa—my professors told me this was the best place for me, and I deferred to their wisdom even though I would have preferred to have gone to California rather than return to the Midwest—a boring place I had always been eager to flee.

In fact, Iowa turned out to be an excellent choice. Although I didn't know it at the time, it was one of the few American universities that wholeheartedly welcomed women. This can be explained, at least in part, because so many professors at Iowa were brilliant but were themselves vulnerable in some way. Many were Jews at a time when this remained a roadblock at many institutions. My own major professor, Sydney James, had briefly been a member of the Communist Party and was hounded for years—first by Harvard where he received his PhD, and then by the House Un-American Activities Committee (HUAC). Although the faculty did not include a single woman when I first enrolled there, it readily accepted women graduate students, giving us some of the best fellowships available. It also admitted students who were not "to the manor born." Very few of my cohort were wealthy; they had not attended the "best schools." A couple came from truly impoverished circumstances. These were people with whom I was comfortable, and whom I grew to love and respect. Like me, they felt lucky to be where they were. They never took their position for granted. And they were truly noncompetitive. I have heard my colleagues talk about the mean-spirited and cutthroat competition they faced in graduate school. Fortunately, that was not my experience.

I was totally unprepared for graduate school. I didn't really have a clue about what I was getting into. I should have had some inkling of my ignorance when I audited a summer school class at the University of Montana, right after I graduated. I talked briefly to the visiting professor who taught the class. I proudly informed him that I was going to graduate school at the University of Iowa that fall. "Ah," he said, "then you will be studying with Stow Persons?" "Yes," I replied, although until that moment I had never heard of Stow Persons! "And of course you have read his book?" he asked. "Yes," I lied again. Who knew that he had written a book? Who knew that most professors wrote books? Not me! Clueless again.

But off I went. The first thing I did upon arriving in Iowa City was to register for classes. I knew how to read a course catalogue. I had never consulted my academic advisor at Montana. I figured I could do this on my own. I noted that Stow Persons was, indeed, teaching an intellectual history course. But I had taken intellectual history as an undergraduate. Surely it would be cheating to take the course "again"! So I didn't enroll in a lecture course taught by the person I assumed would be my major professor. That was mistake number one. Mistake number two caused me considerable trauma. As an undergraduate, I had generally taken three or four courses per quarter. I somehow assumed that graduate students should take *more* courses than undergraduates. After all, we were smarter. So I blithely enrolled in five classes. I didn't find out until halfway through my first semester that everyone else was taking just three. By then, it was too late. I suffered under a huge course load, managing, somehow, to get all As, but vowing never to make *that* mistake again.

I was also baffled by the library. Montana's small library still operated under the (even then) antiquated Dewey decimal system. Iowa had long since switched to the Library of Congress classification. I still remember wandering through the stacks that first day, looking at more books than I had seen in any one place in my life, totally bewildered as I tried to decipher the meaning of these new strange letters and numbers on the spine of each volume. I felt as though I was entering a foreign country. And in some ways, I was.

Still, good fortune was on my side. I easily passed the French proficiency test—I had taken three years of French in high school and another three years in college. Just as I prepared to add German to my repertoire, the History Department changed its language policy; one language—not two—would be required of all American history students. The department also decided that a few first-year students would be exempt from writing a master's thesis. Instead, we would begin studying for our PhD comprehensive exams immediately, bypassing the MA entirely and proceeding more quickly toward the PhD I was one of those who received this benefit.

What was an advantage from one perspective, however, was a bit daunting from another. My plan—such as it was—upon entering graduate school was quite modest, and as it turned out, exceedingly unrealistic. Simply assuming that an MA would prepare me for a job that would be relatively easy to get, I thought I would get a master's and teach in a small liberal arts college—preferably one in the Northeast. I had no idea that I would, or should, publish anything. I did not see myself as a "scholar" at all. I would be Miss Chips and nothing more. And that would have made me very happy. Now, it appeared that I would never receive an MA. If I did not pass my comprehensive exams, if I did not go on to get a PhD, I would leave Iowa with a BA and a lot of credits. I'd boxed myself in. But I tried not to think about that—or anything else—too much.

I settled down, met new people, made friends, attended classes in the daytime, and the bars at night. This was an exciting time to attend any major American university. There were efforts to unionize all graduate students. Antiwar protests were heating up. In the spring of 1970, after the Cambodia "incursion" and the killings at Kent State and Jackson State, life became especially tense. (Ironically, the death of student protestors at Jackson State University, a Historically Black College in Jackson, Mississippi, passed almost—if not completely—unnoticed by me or most of my peers.) There were demonstrations every night and a boycott of classes during the day—all of which activities were supported by virtually every history graduate student—and in the end, the entire university shut down for the semester. In the midst of all this, I was vaguely aware that at least in one way, my status as a woman was an advantage. I did not face the draft. Most (but by no means all) of my cohort were men who worried constantly about that possibility. President Nixon had abolished the student deferment. All age-eligible men were thrown into a lottery, and when a man's number came up, he had to make a decision. Would he simply accept his fate as inevitable? Would he flee to Canada? Would he refuse his orders and end up in jail? These were very real issues that every young man faced in these years. Murphy Richardson, later to be my husband, received his draft notice in 1970, during the demonstrations against the Cambodia invasion. He went to his physical, but, as he happily told me upon his return to campus, he failed—his poor eyesight did him in. Another history grad student actually cut off his thumb to avoid the draft. And a third spent some time in jail when he refused to be inducted. This was serious business, indeed. While I went blithely about my business without worrying about such—literally—life-and-death issues, every young man had his existence consumed by the specter of the draft.

But for me, life was pretty easy. I was poor, of course, but then everyone I knew was poor as well. We all lived in dimly lit, poorly ventilated apartments, furnished courtesy of Goodwill. Most of us—especially the unmarried students who had no spouses (mainly wives) to support them—had no televisions, no cars, and, of course, no computers. I had a Smith Corona manual typewriter, a gift for my high school graduation, which was my most prized possession. All of us studied in the daytime and early evening, partied hard on the weekends, planned for "the Revolution" that was right around the corner, and thought about the future as little as possible.

After using up my maximum three years of the NDEA fellowship, I received two more years of fellowship money from the History Department. This time I had to earn my keep as a teaching assistant (TA), giving me my first chance at becoming "Miss Chips." I loved it. This, I quickly decided, was truly my vocation and my purpose in life. My second year as a TA was especially rewarding. The department developed an alternative to its traditional Western civilization course, giving graduate students the option of being instructors of record, and creating a new course in conjunction with a professor. Those of us who took this route were responsible for everything: lectures, discussion sessions, book assignments, papers, and exams. A number of us chose "Revolutions" as our topic. We began with the "bourgeois" French Revolution and moved on to topics that included the Russian, Chinese, and Cuban revolutions. Frankly Marxist in orientation, the courses were fun to teach, and I learned a lot. Whether the students learned as much as the instructors did, was and is debatable! Ironically, my experience with this course actually helped me land my first one-year job. I convinced the Ripon College search committee that I was able to teach a similar course aimed at freshmen. Note to job applicants: within reason, you can teach *anything* if given enough time—and with enough desperation on your part.

I spent more time preparing for my classes than I should have. But I did manage to study for my comprehensive exams. I had long since abandoned American intellectual history as a major field, in favor of American colonial/ Revolutionary history under the guidance of Sydney V. James. I was—of course —nervous as I faced the ultimate showdown. A large group of graduate students had taken comps the semester before I took the plunge, and a couple of them had failed one or more of their exams. So I knew it was definitely possible to flunk. Still, I was not fully into panic mode. I played mental games with myself so that I could remain (relatively!) calm. I refused to curtail my social life or my "important" political activities. I put in many hours as a volunteer for a child-care center (which we called Free University Child Kare—you figure out the acronym), organized by a few graduate students. My rather lame strategy was that if I didn't study *too* hard, I would be able to tell myself that I wasn't *really* a failure if I had to retake some or all of my exams. Failing would somehow be less embarrassing if I hadn't actually tried; moreover, I would have the energy to begin the process again. Once I had actually passed my written exams, I faced the dreaded oral. For me, this was scarier in some ways than the written exams had been, but I convinced myself that unless I totally blew it, the department would not fail me, even if I deserved it. They had, I realized, spent a lot of money on me and had given me excellent fellowships. If I failed, they would have to admit that they had made a terrible mistake. Somehow, I didn't think they would be courageous enough to do that.

In fact, my oral exam was pretty easy, made even easier by its comic beginning. As I walked into the exam room, three professors, behaving like traditional gentlemen, stood up, then awkwardly sat down, while the seated professors stood up instead before sheepishly returning to their seats. I realized that they were more nervous than I was! They still were not really used to dealing with women graduate students. They didn't know quite how to behave. I figured they were afraid that I would cry if they were too hard on me. And they were not. Most asked me softball questions. The whole thing was over in forty-five minutes, and I had now earned my ABD (all but dissertation).

When I had entered graduate school, the possession of an MA coupled with decent recommendations were enough to enable an applicant to secure a position in a small (and not especially prestigious) liberal arts college. But between 1967 and 1970 (when I passed comps), someone had moved the goalpost. Now, everyone said, the possession of a PhD would be sufficient to secure that same position. That being said, it became apparent even to me that I had to write a dissertation. I had no idea what my topic might be. Scholars in early American history had recently become enamored (for a blessedly short period of time) with "numbers." Demography was all the rage. Town studies blossomed. This—clearly—was not for me. I went to Syd James for advice, and he readily obliged. He asked me first where I would like to live. Did I like warm, sultry climes, or would New England winters appeal more to me? New England, I said without hesitation. In that case, he suggested that I concentrate on Newport, Rhode Island. He, himself, was working on a book on Rhode Island history and had contacts in Providence, where the Rhode Island Historical Society was located. And because the British army had destroyed so many of the town's documents during the American Revolution, a traditional demographic study of my town was virtually impossible. It sounded like a plan. It might not have been *my* plan, but I didn't really care. I was used to following orders.

I began reading secondary works, and some of the primary sources that were available in print. (There were obviously no troves of documents on the internet to consult in those days.) But it was clear that I would have to go to Rhode Island to delve into the real sources. That, of course, required money. The nationally available research fellowships that exist for aspiring PhD candidates these days simply did not exist back then. Nor would I get more financial help from the History Department. My time there had run out. Luck, once more, was on my side. I received a call from my father, who told me that a "social studies" position had opened up at Proviso East High School—the school from which I had graduated in 1963, a school that I had been very glad to leave behind forever. But they paid well—$11,500 for one year, which seemed like a fortune. So I arranged an interview, took the Greyhound back home, and was hired. I secured an inexpensive apartment and began my "career" as a high school teacher—never bothering to tell anyone that I had no intention of remaining in my position for anything *but* one year.

My decision was ultimately the right one. But my experience proved to me that while I might be a decent teacher at the college level, I was not cut out for the rigors of high school. Discipline was unpleasant. The students were (of course!) immature and not particularly interested in history. I had a few who were wonderful, and truly engaged, and I still feel guilty for not giving them the attention they needed and wanted. For me, I was simply counting the days, saving every penny I had, so that I could leave for Providence at the end of the year.

I handed in my resignation in June, and in July I was headed to a city I had never visited and knew nothing about. Syd knew someone who rented rooms in a house located within walking distance of the Historical Society, and I signed up for one room sight unseen. Murphy soon joined me, renting a room next to mine. Rooms they were. I had a tiny little kitchen next to my tiny bedroom/living room. Everyone in the house shared the same bathroom.

It took us very little time to figure out that some of the occupants of the house were, well, rather strange. One young woman, a Brown student, introduced herself immediately, only to ask us if we heard car horns from the street in the middle of the night. No, we assured her, we did not. Well, she said, they were honking at *her*, trying to frighten her (and evidently succeeding). "They" were either the CIA, the FBI, or members of the Mafia—we were never quite sure which—and had been following her from house to house for some time, for what reason neither we nor she could figure out. Much to our relief, she soon left the Barnes Street establishment. Another occupant on the first floor was more unnerving. Every day when I went in or out of the house, I had a feeling that I was being watched. On occasion, if I looked quickly, I thought I saw someone's eyes staring out at me, however briefly, through a crack in the door of the ground-floor apartment. I told Murphy about it, but I was half-convinced that my imagination was playing tricks on me. We put it out of our minds. Until the day the police arrested the man who occupied that first-floor room. He had begun starting fires in his wastebaskets and had then paraded around the yard totally naked. Obviously, my sense that something was wrong with this guy was right on target! After that, things settled down, and we established a routine.

I walked to the Historical Society every weekday, taking voluminous, handwritten notes on my trusty 3" x 5" notecards. At night, I went to Brown's Rockefeller Library—which charged me fifty dollars per semester to enter its hallowed halls!—to read eighteenth-century newspapers on microcards. On the weekends—and once I had finished with all the relevant newspapers, every night, as well—I began writing my dissertation. To say that I was a little frightened—especially in the beginning—would be a gross understatement. I had not written an MA thesis. I had never seen, much less touched, documents such as the ones I encountered in Providence. I didn't really know what I was doing, what I was looking for, what questions to ask. And I couldn't help wondering if I could actually *do* this. What if I hated it? What if I didn't have the talent for writing a dissertation? I needed that dissertation—it was, as we cynically called it in those days, my "union card." It would get me the teaching job I so desperately wanted. Without it, I was sunk.

Once the wonderful librarians at the Historical Society realized that I was a serious scholar, not a genealogist, they were eager to give me all the assistance I needed. They helped me find documents and allowed me to rummage freely through the boxes of merchants' letters and invoices, ministers' sermons, the odds and ends, the bits and pieces of "stuff" that the Society owned. Toward the end of my stay, I took the bus to Newport, visiting the much smaller Newport Historical Society. I also found documents at the John Carter Brown Library and the Rhode Island State House, which had a decent collection of eighteenth-century probate records. Most days, I found that I actually liked what I was doing—something of a relief, something of a surprise. It was a bit of a grind. I knew that I had just one year's worth of money to do everything that had to be done. And so, although Murphy and I went to an occasional movie or play, we led a very quiet existence. I was determined to get the dissertation researched and a decent rough draft written by the end of the year. Which is exactly what I did.

In June 1973, Murphy and I packed up our few belongings, loaded them into the bowels of the Greyhound bus, and headed back to Iowa City. We got an apartment. Murphy got two jobs—one as a "stacks reader" at the university's main library, the other as a study hall supervisor at the local junior high. I got a job as a clerk-typist at the university's Institute for Agricultural Medicine. By this time, the women's liberation movement was in its early, halcyon days. For some reason, one of the grievances women seized upon at the time was the then common practice of having secretaries make coffee for the boss. During my job interview, I was assured that I would *never* have to make the coffee! A nice gesture, to be sure. And an indication that I would be treated with respect. Which I was. I typed (and usually rewrote poorly worded) letters, organized the Institute's library, did a lot of Xeroxing, and answered the phone. At night, I went home and typed the final copy of my four-hundred-plus-page dissertation, struggling to fulfill the exacting standards set by the Graduate School. Most people I knew hired someone else to type their dissertations—or had their wives type them. I had no wife and was much too cheap to pay someone else to do what I could do very well, so I failed to follow that wise example. Consequently it seemed as though I typed all the time—for other people during the day, for myself at night. When I dragged myself to bed, I couldn't get my fingers to stop moving. But I did it.

Finally I was ready to defend the dissertation—an old-fashioned study of the merchant community in Newport, Rhode Island from 1720 to 1765. When I consulted Syd about the makeup of my dissertation committee, he insisted that I include a new member of the department, someone who had arrived in Iowa City the year I was in Providence. That someone was Linda K. Kerber—the only woman in the department. Linda was there—despite her excellent credentials—at least in part because her husband, Dick, had been offered a prestigious position at the university's medical school. Syd, exercising his usual good judgment, was one of Linda's champions. She was a superb scholar, although she was not yet THE Linda Kerber. She was not even a historian whose work focused on women or gender issues. Indeed (unbeknownst to me), she had just embarked on her research for her iconic *Women of the Republic,* which would not be published until 1980. From my self-centered perspective, Linda was simply an unknown factor—something that made me a little uncomfortable. But Syd—unusually for him—was insistent. I continue to bless him for that.

In fact, the dissertation defense went off without a hitch. And as soon as it was over, I headed back to my job, becoming Dr. Clerk-Typist. Nothing had changed. But now I had my union card—surely that college job was within reach. Not quite. Someone had moved those damned goalposts yet again. It was 1974, the time when the bottom fell suddenly and precipitously out of the job market. No one, at least no one in Iowa's History Department, seemed to have had any idea that this was about to happen. Nor was anyone in the department prepared to help us deal with this new and dispiriting reality. Most of our professors had obtained their jobs through the "good-old-boy network." They had obtained their degrees at a time when there were relatively few graduate programs, everyone knew everyone else, and when any institution had an opening, faculty members simply called their friends and asked for recommendations. Often lucky candidates were hired sight unseen. Thus none of Iowa's professors had any experience with the job market as it played out in the 1970s.

Today's sophisticated graduate students would be shocked at our lack of preparation, not to mention our pathetically sparse vitas. In those days, when graduate students went to the (relatively few) history conferences, they were expected to be seen, not heard. We did not give papers. We seldom even asked questions of those professors whose presentations we came to observe. Very few graduate students published in the (again) sparse number of journals in their fields. No conference, not the AHA, not the OAH, had sessions dedicated to helping graduate students navigate the challenges of the job market or the rigors of finding a publisher. Nor did students have the benefit of mock interviews. We walked into our first interviews (usually conducted in someone's hotel room) with no idea about how to conduct ourselves or what we might expect. I still remember my sense of absolute panic when one interviewer asked me what my *next* project would be. Next project? I was happy to be done with *this* one. We all did our best, scurrying around, scouring the AHA *Perspectives* looking, usually in vain, for a job opening for which we might be qualified. Or we went to the AHA, scanning the bulletin boards, looking for a last-minute job announcement. We were all—men and women, star students or mediocre aspirants—flying blind. We were all clueless.

I actually managed to snag a couple of interviews for one-year jobs (we didn't call them VAP [visiting assistant professor] appointments in those days) and got an on-campus interview and then a one-year job at Ripon College, a small liberal arts college in Ripon, Wisconsin—just the sort of position I had always envisioned. Admittedly, I had envisioned a permanent job, not a one-year gig. Still, I was delighted. It was something. Definitely a start. The teaching load was rigorous: three classes a semester, each of which met four times a week. I would teach "both halves" of the American history survey "Colonial America, Revolutionary America"—and my course on revolutions, the only class for which I had lectures prepared. I had to wing it with the others, often finishing the latest lecture just an hour or so before class began. Needless to say, I had little time to revise my dissertation with an eye to publishing it or to carve an article or two out of what I already had. I taught my classes, socialized with the other young, peripatetic members of the faculty, wrote long letters to Murphy, who had decided to remain in Iowa City, and looked for job openings. I still did not notice that all of my interviews were conducted entirely by men. Nor did it register that I was the only woman in Ripon's History Department—and that the person whose position I took for the year was a man.

The Ripon College job ended—as promised—in the spring of 1976. I had no prospects for the coming year. So I did the intelligent and responsible thing: I decided that Murphy and I would spend the summer in London. This might be, I reasoned, the only time in my life when I would have enough money to cross the pond. So off we went, finding, with the help of graduate student friends, a flat near the University of London. We had a lovely time until our money ran out, and we had to return "home" to Iowa City. There we were confronted with a phenomenal housing shortage. We stayed with friends, moving from one apartment to another when we felt as though we had worn out our welcome. I applied for unemployment benefits, which were excruciatingly slow in coming. We spent all of our time looking for an apartment. We faced a couple of insurmountable obstacles. Because we had no car, we had to live within walking distance of a grocery store. And we were not married. This was a seller's market. Landlords were choosy. They interviewed potential tenants, and when they found out we were unmarried, they simply refused to rent to us. We could have lied, of course, but we were afraid that we would be "found out" and kicked back into the streets.

Finally, we simply gave up. We decided to return to Providence. There I could think seriously about ways to turn my dissertation into a publishable manuscript. And we could find a place to live! Murphy left first, securing an apartment in fairly short order; I followed him as soon as my first unemployment check arrived. And so I found myself once more on the Greyhound bus, arriving in Providence thirty-five hours later, hoping I would somehow turn my life around.

I did some more research, began revising the dissertation—although I had no real idea about how I would turn a dissertation into a book manuscript. I could have asked Linda or Syd for help, of course, but I didn't want to display my ignorance. And they evidently assumed I knew what I was doing. I did manage to publish an article in *Rhode Island History.* My first publication! It felt good. I applied for whatever job I heard about, even a couple of high school positions that opened up in the area. I remember one on-campus interview at a small boarding school in Massachusetts in particular. The interviewer informed me, with some embarrassment that he was looking for an "older, more motherly type," although this was not part of the job description! Just as my unemployment checks were about to expire, I once again ran into a bit of luck.

The University of Mid-America, located in Lincoln, Nebraska, was developing a class taught via a radio program centered on the work of Henry Steele Commager. Commager would lecture once a week. Two historians would develop background material, reading lists, and study questions to accompany the lectures. The interview went well, and I got the job. It was temporary, of course, but temporary looked very good at the moment. I left for Lincoln, leaving Murphy behind. There was no point, we thought, in having him travel to Nebraska when I planned to be there for just a few months. I didn't even mention Murphy's existence in my job interview. I later found out to my chagrin that when I first received my job offer, I could have asked for money to bring Murphy to Lincoln for three or four visits. That, I was told, was typical practice in the business world. Who knew? I was grateful for the job and didn't want to do or say anything that would give people an excuse to hire someone else. I enjoyed my brief time in Lincoln, and to my surprise actually liked writing. But our "team" kept running into difficulties with Commager, who was something of a "consensus historian" and who resisted any of our references to other historians, especially to those associated with the "New Left." Finally, the university sent me to Washington, D.C., to talk to him about our project in person. We ironed a few things out. And Commager regaled me with delightful stories of his own rebellious youth, even as he appeared to reject the views of the "rebellious youth" sitting right beside him.

Just as the project was winding down, I began to get on-campus job interviews—they were all for one-year jobs, but jobs they were. And in the space of one week, I got two offers. The one I accepted was at Western Connecticut State College (West Conn) in Danbury. Murphy went to Danbury to get us an apartment; I finished up my work in Lincoln, and we arrived in Connecticut in the fall of 1977. We soon realized that we needed a car. Danbury was spread out; it had no public transportation. I had finally learned how to drive the year I was in Ripon and even had a driver's license. We *would* have a decent salary for a year. Maybe we could afford it! We took a cab to the local Toyota dealer (Toyotas, like Volkswagens, were the cheap cars in those days) and decided upon their least-expensive model—only to find out that we could not buy the car because we had no credit rating. Neither of us had a credit card. We had never borrowed money. What we saw as an indication of our fiscal prudence, the real world saw as unacceptable. For all practical purposes, we did not exist. We mentioned our dilemma to Ellen Rosenberg, a professor in the Anthropology/Sociology Department. Without so much as a hesitation, Ellen offered to cosign for the loan. I was so clueless at the time, I had no idea how unusual or gracious that offer was. She didn't know us. She knew we would be in Danbury for just one year. We could easily have stopped paying for the car, leaving her to pay for a vehicle she would never own. We took advantage of Ellen's generosity and bought our first car.

Teaching at West Conn was delightful. I taught undergraduates and, for the first time, graduate students (mostly high school teachers who were seeking raises or promotions). Most of the undergraduates were first-generation students who did *not* take their classes for granted. Many were single mothers, struggling to exist on welfare and student loans. They eagerly soaked up information and always wanted more. They were not all brilliant, but their attitude toward learning made teaching them an absolute pleasure, something I hated to abandon. At the end of the year, I faced joblessness once again. So when the head of the department suggested that I stay on and teach a couple of courses as an adjunct, I was more than happy to do so. Better yet, one member of the department was slated to retire, and the department chair indicated that once he was gone (yes, as usual, all the members of the department were "he"), I could expect to be hired as a tenure-track professor. It seemed too good to be true. And it was.

I did what I needed to do, teaching a couple of graduate classes each semester and securing a job as a desk clerk at the local Howard Johnson's motel to help make ends meet. I applied for other jobs (just in case), but while I got a few nibbles and secured a few on-campus interviews, I always came in second. It was enough to make me think I was competitive, but not enough to get me any closer to my goal—a tenure-track position anywhere under any circumstances. Still, I was reasonably confident that I would remain at West Conn, and I would have been thrilled to do just that. Unfortunately, the college was not a democracy. The president of the institution—a woman as it turned out—was something of a dictator. When the position I thought was mine opened up, she decided not to fill it. Instead, she gave "my" position to the Department of Criminal Justice—which she thought (perhaps correctly) would draw more students than I would. I was once more facing a bleak reality. No job. No book contract. No future.

Yet again, I was lucky. Syd James had a year's sabbatical for the 1979/80 school year. And the department chairman at Iowa asked me if I would like to take Syd's place for the academic year. Would I? Of course! So we packed up our still meager possessions and returned once more to Iowa City. It was the first time we had moved without the benefit of a Greyhound bus. But we still managed to get all of our possessions in that one small Toyota. This time, we had no problem getting a decent apartment. No one seemed to care that we weren't married. Maybe things had improved. A bit. Still, I did have that feeling that I was running in place. I was back in the same town, encountering many of the same people on the same streets that I had known when I first arrived in town in 1967. I was now a colleague in the Department of History instead of a lowly graduate student. And everyone treated me well, even listening to me when I occasionally spouted off in department meetings. But it was strange. And I was in fact about ready to give up. This had been going on way too long.

I made something of an effort to revise my dissertation, rewriting, tightening, and getting it ready to submit to yet another press. But my heart wasn't in it. I went to the AHA in New York, not really expecting to succeed where I had failed before. As soon as I arrived at the conference hotel, I went to the bulletin board (yes, a *real* bulletin board, where notices of last-minute jobs were tacked up in random fashion) and noted that the University of Mississippi was looking for an early American historian. I submitted my pathetic vita to the proper authorities, and the next day, I received word that one member of the department would grant me an interview.

Mississippi. I could not help but think, as I headed for my appointment, that it would be ironic if I got this particular job. Once upon a time, when I had not known how very tight the job market was, I had filled out a form at the University of Iowa's placement office. The form asked me to indicate which areas of the country I would most like to go to (New England and the Pacific Northwest), and which places I would refuse to go to under any circumstances (the Deep South.) I had long since modified my form to indicate that I would go absolutely anyplace, but I still did not see the South—especially Mississippi—as a place that was high on my list. But a job was a job.

In fact, I received an invitation for an on-campus interview. And for once, I was not clueless, thanks to the excellent advice of Linda Kerber. Linda was the first person to teach me how to think strategically about job interviews—and indeed about everything else in the profession. I had been flying blind, doing everything on my own, not really thinking the whole process through. I gave my job talks, answered questions, tried to be charming—although that was a bit of a stretch!—and hoped for the best. It never quite worked. Linda gave me the first practical advice I had ever received. She told me to obtain a copy of the University of Mississippi catalogue, get a list of the names of the members of the History Department, and check out the publications of each member. What a novel idea! She also called the chair of the Search Committee—who fortunately happened to be a historian of the New Republic, and thus was familiar with Linda's work—to put in a good word for me. So *this* was how intelligent job searches were conducted. Who knew?

In fact, the on-campus interview was almost fun. The members of the faculty did everything they could to make me feel at home. They even asked a single woman who taught at the Law School to join us for cocktails the last night I was in town, just to prove to me that there *were* some single women on campus (I, of course, said nothing about Murphy's existence) who managed to survive in a university dominated by men. I also discovered that the History Department was the first at the university to hire members from outside the South. Moreover, it was peopled by staunch liberals, and while it had no tenure-track women in its ranks, it did have one African American.

This seemed like a place I could like. Even the weather cooperated. I had left Iowa in a snowstorm, and in Oxford the sun was shining, the flowers were blooming, and I was charmed.

Indeed, I felt so comfortable that I almost forgot that this was a job interview. My last night in Oxford, we all met at the Holiday Inn bar. Most members of the department showed up, as did their wives. The whole affair turned into a party. No one had told me that job candidates should avoid drinking alcohol—or at the very least, they should judiciously sip—during their interviews. We all drank too much. Me, included. Toward the end of the evening I was talking to someone, waving my hands in the air as is my wont, and I knocked over a full glass of scotch into the lap of the department chair. I can still see the horrified look on his face. At the time, my faux pas did not seem to be a big deal. As I remembered the incident in the following days, however, that look seemed to grow more horrified, the size of the glass grew exponentially. I was sure I had blown it. This, I thought, had been my last chance to do what I desperately wanted to do. It was over. I returned to Iowa City and made an appointment with the university's job-placement advisor, obtaining advice on career possibilities outside of academia. I was prepared to move on.

Instead, much to my astonishment, I got the call. The job was mine. The chair offered me time to think about the offer, but I accepted it right then and there. I didn't want to give him a chance to reconsider. I had no idea that one should negotiate a little—ask for a higher salary given all my years in the trenches, ask for moving expenses. I was ready to move to Oxford, Mississippi. Once again I would be the only woman in a department of men. One woman, Jan Hawks, a University of Mississippi PhD who was the dean of women, had a "courtesy appointment" in the department, but she was not eligible for tenure and never would be. Everyone did all they could to make me feel at home. I found out later that the department had a long-standing tradition: the newest member of the faculty had to take minutes at department meetings. Robert Haws—who had been a member of the Search Committee—immediately recognized that this tradition might be problematic. Wouldn't following the usual practice lead me to believe that I was being treated like a "secretary" and not a member of the faculty? And so he volunteered to take the minutes himself, not letting me know that I was actually being treated as a special case.

I loved the members of our department. I was a bit taken aback by our students. I often felt as though I had stepped into a time warp. Women students wore dresses, gobs of makeup, and daubed on so much perfume that I was afraid of being asphyxiated whenever I stepped into a crowded elevator. Far worse, however, they were politically conservative! I had always promised myself that no matter how far to the left the next generation of students moved, I would support them. It never occurred to me that students in the age of Ronald Reagan would move to the right. It was a shock—a shock I eventually realized that professors throughout the country were facing. But no matter. I had a job.

Now that I actually had that long-awaited tenure-track position, I had to worry about getting tenure. At first, I was not especially concerned. Most members of the Department of History—the people who would be deciding my fate—had published little or nothing over the years. They had been operating under a 4–4 teaching load (reduced to 3–3 when I arrived) and were not rewarded monetarily or in any other way for turning out even the most brilliant monographs. Their primary task, what they got paid (not much) to do, was to teach. Indeed, one of my colleagues told me early on that when the department voted on tenure, its members awarded it to people they figured they could tolerate sitting next to at faculty meetings for the next few decades, and little more. This, I thought, would be a piece of cake. Finally I would be "Miss Chips."

True enough, the department chair said something about expecting some level of publication from its newer members, but like so many aspiring academics, I heard what I wanted to hear. I already had an article, with another one on the way. Wouldn't that be enough? Moreover, I looked carefully at the university tenure guidelines—no department had its own criteria written down at that time. Those guidelines indicated that applicants would be judged on the usual triad of publications, teaching, and service. Moreover, if anyone was "outstanding" in two of those categories, they would be granted tenure. Yes! I could do this. I threw myself into my new life. I spent hours preparing for my classes; as one of the few women in the university, I was sought after to serve on virtually every committee. I quickly became a member of the Faculty Senate. I even obtained recognition as a teacher, becoming the first recipient of an "outstanding teacher award" sponsored by the College of

Liberal Arts. I made a few more desultory efforts to secure a publisher for a dissertation manuscript that was now six years old. No one wanted it. Town studies were out of fashion. And the sort of town study I had written had never really been *in* fashion! Syd and Linda liked it, but no one else did. Still, I figured my position was reasonably safe. Admittedly, whenever I received my annual review from the tenured faculty, I noted that the department sternly warned me to cut down on my service activities. But I ignored the warning signs. I wasn't doing all *that* much, I told myself. And I somehow managed to see the warnings as a backhanded compliment! Clueless yet again.

And then the sky fell in. I now recognize what happened as a true blessing. At the time, it seemed like an unmitigated disaster. The university hired outside reviewers to evaluate select departments in the College of Liberal Arts. Ours was one of those departments. The end result of the evaluation was predictable. We were a "nice" department; everyone got along; we took our teaching seriously and did it well; but we were woefully lacking in publications. Still, we had potential. If the university was willing to spend a little money on us, and if we developed more rigorous standards, we could, indeed, be a fine department. The university responded. It designated history and three other disciplines as "excellence" departments. It gave us money to hire two new assistant professors. It also created a slush fund upon which faculty members could draw in order to conduct their research. In return, we devised new, "tough" (i.e., normal) standards for tenure and promotion. Teaching and service mattered less. A book—not a mere article or two—was the key to job security.

Everyone was excited. I pretended to be pleased as well, but in fact I was in panic mode. What did this mean for me? I had three years left before I had to face the music. And I had no book prospects. I had to do something, and quickly. Thus, for the first time in what passed for my academic career, I began looking for a topic of my own, on my own. I had just finished rereading Pauline Maier's stunningly beautiful *The Old Revolutionaries,* which analyzed the life and views of five supporters of the American Revolution. Perhaps, I thought audaciously, I could write a companion piece to her book, telling the stories of five loyalists with an eye to figuring out just why they had made the choices they did. I began looking for "representative characters" and stumbled almost immediately upon William Franklin, loyalist son of Benjamin

Franklin. I never got around to identifying my other four loyalists. Franklin's story was fascinating—indeed I still can't quite figure out why scholars ignored it for so long. The documents were there. The university would pay my way to the various archives. And so I began. I spent a summer going from one city to another: Philadelphia, of course, home of the American Philosophical Society and the Historical Society of Pennsylvania; Newark, New Jersey, and the New Jersey Historical Society; Boston; New York; Washington, D.C.; and even the Clement Library in Ann Arbor, Michigan. It was a slog. Research is exciting, even, I was forced to admit, fun. But it is also lonely. I longed for someone to talk to. Today, with email, and even Skype for those people who are adept enough to use it, it is much easier for travelers to stay connected with the "real world." But in the early 1980s, those options didn't exist.

By the end of the summer, I had enough "stuff" to make a book possible. But I didn't have a lot of time. I proceeded with something approaching a strategy. First, I published an article on Franklin, "William Franklin: His Father's Son," with the *Pennsylvania Magazine of History and Biography*, which actually won an award offered by SEASECS (the Southeast American Society for Eighteenth-Century Studies). I also secretly applied for another job. One of my former colleagues had accepted a position at a small liberal arts college in Pennsylvania, and he informed me that his department was looking for an early American historian. I applied, got an on-campus interview, and received a job offer. It was not a job I particularly wanted. I sensed that the president of the college ran the institution with a very heavy hand. But it was a job, and it might be my salvation. I informed the department chair of my situation, and he immediately convened the tenured faculty. The department made me an offer. Because the tenure guidelines had been put into place three years after I arrived on campus, I would not be held to the standard that subsequent assistant professors would face. If I completed a book-length manuscript that the department thought *would* be published, I would receive tenure. Relying on that promise, I began to write.

I finished the manuscript and turned it in just as my tenure clock was about to expire. I was fortunate (lucky yet again!) to have the support of Winthrop Jordan, who had become a member of our department in 1983. He procured a couple of outside readers from U.C. Berkeley, who indicated that the manuscript, with a bit of tweaking, was, indeed publishable. I figured I was home free. But some members of the department began to have second thoughts. They weren't convinced that the manuscript was good enough to meet their new standards. The final vote was not inspiring. Half the department abstained; the other half voted in my favor. The department chair also supported me. At least, I told myself then (and now!), no one had voted against me. But still. As my dossier moved up the ranks, I held my breath. The Liberal Arts dean decided in my favor, as did the dean of the Graduate College, and ultimately the chancellor. It had been an excruciatingly painful experience, but in the end, I had survived.

I scarcely noticed that I was the first woman to have received tenure in the Department of History at the University of Mississippi. Nor was I unduly unhappy to work in a department peopled entirely by men. To me, this was normal. I was pleased when the department hired a woman in 1985, and yet another in 1989. I had a number of women friends in other departments—English in particular. And I was active in supporting the new Women's Center, headed by Jan Hawks. Jan had loved her work as dean of women, but unfortunately for her, this was a position whose time had come and gone. As something of a consolation prize, she had become the first director of the Sara Isom Center for Women in 1982. The center focused more on teaching and service than it did on scholarship—a focus that jibed with my personal interests. I saw myself as a feminist and an activist, not as someone whose scholarship had anything to do with women's history. I had not taken—indeed, I had not had the opportunity to take—a single course in women's history at either the undergraduate or graduate level. When, during my many failed job interviews, I had been asked if I could teach a women's history course, I perversely responded with a firm negative. This from someone who had blithely agreed to teach a course on the Chinese Revolution! Somehow, I resented being put in a stereotypical box. Why did people think I could teach a course on women just because I had a vagina, not a penis?

One thing, however, had changed. I had discovered—I am surely a very slow learner—that I actually *liked* doing research, writing, and even publishing. Once again, Linda Kerber—who had been my mentor for so many years—stepped in. She read my manuscript on William Franklin, decorated it with many smiley faces, and suggested that I send it on to Oxford University Press. I was stunned. I had never aimed that high, but I obeyed. To my amazement, I received a book contract. And I began looking for a second project. Luckily, my timing was perfect. The papers of Judith Sargent Murray, an eighteenth-century essayist, poet, and dramatist who had published a number of essays defending her belief in the intellectual equality of men and women, had just been donated to the Mississippi Archives in Jackson. I knew a (very) little about Murray, enough to know that scholars of women's history had been fascinated by her feminist leanings. One of my graduate students had actually written a seminar paper on Murray, relying—as did everyone—on her printed work. I now had the opportunity to be one of the first scholars to read her voluminous correspondence and attempt to write something of a biography. This meant, of course, that in spite of myself, I was about to become a historian of women.

What took me so long? The more I read—of the secondary literature, of Judith's own writing—the more fascinated I became. Everything was new; everything was different. I had enjoyed doing research on and writing about William Franklin—and even about Ben, in a little book I published with Bedford Press. But I was totally immersed in my work on Judith Sargent Murray. I looked forward to each new day, as I read letter after letter, piecing together a life that often seemed like an overly dramatic soap opera. I obtained two contracts for books on Judith: one, a short book aimed at college audiences for Bedford, the other, a full-length biography for the University of Pennsylvania Press. In the process of doing my research, I became so intrigued by women's history—all sorts and varieties—that I developed a course on gender, "Masculinities and Femininities in American History," which quickly became one of my favorites. And I discovered—for the first time, I am shocked to say—how much I wanted, even needed, a community of women scholars with whom I could talk about my work. I had a very difficult time organizing the book. Franklin's life had been so neat and clean, dominated as it was by the major public events in the Revolutionary era. It organized itself. Judith's life was messy. A strict chronological narrative, discussing the many private and public experiences of her daily existence, would be tedious in the extreme and would be of little value to any reader. The third section of the book was especially difficult. I wrote it and rewrote it. (At least by this time I was composing on a computer, instead of a Smith Corona, so that the rewrites were not quite so daunting.) How I longed for a group of women scholars who could help me figure this out—or who would at least listen sympathetically to my tale of woe. I am still not pleased with the third section. But it had to do. I did it on my own, and the end product suffered, as a result.

I found out, more or less by accident, just how valuable a community of scholars could be. In the summer of 2008, Elizabeth Payne, who is a colleague of mine at the University of Mississippi (yes, we are finally regularly hiring women!), and Betsy Jacoway—the inspiration for this collection of essays—organized a group of women scholars who taught at various venues in the Southeast—Arkansas, Mississippi, Louisiana, and Tennessee. I was invited to join the group. Some of us were old hands; others were just getting started. Eventually, we called ourselves the Delta Women Writers. We meet twice a year, devoting an entire weekend to one another and to our scholarship. Four to six of us submit our papers to the group in advance. We spend all Saturday analyzing, criticizing, and praising each paper. No one comes away from those sessions without having learned a great deal about the craft of writing. I only wish this group had existed as I was struggling to organize my Judith Sargent Murray book.

The Delta Women Writers is a wonderful, supportive group whose contributions to the scholarly careers of its members are truly phenomenal. But the friendships we have formed have been even more meaningful, at least to me. I look forward to each meeting, not just because I will learn a great deal from these fine, perceptive scholars, but because I want to touch base with people I care so much about, people I truly love. I might add, that the Delta Women Writers have helped me so much, that I can—almost—say that I am no longer clueless.

AN UNTIDY LIFE IN ACADEME

GAIL SCHMUNK MURRAY

Even as a child, I liked to organize things: toys, books, clothes in the closet. My mother, a child of the Great Depression, took pride in keeping a beautiful house, entertaining regularly, and making sure her children practiced manners and decorum. Although I resented the Saturday household chores she expected me to fulfill, I still inherited her desire for order and organization. She had grown up in the same small German immigrant community where she still lived, a time and place when one's home was a reflection of one's character and status. The flower garden, the public rooms, the private spaces—all were kept clean and beautiful by the housewife. My community fit the stereotype of the 1950s Midwest family. I embraced that sense of order and compliance.

During college, other students borrowed my notes for their completeness and clarity. (One charming fellow borrowed an entire semester of "Social Change" notes and returned them after the final.) In graduate school, boxes of 4" x 5" notecards from every research project I undertook nestled in a series of color-coded file boxes. Like my mother's, my homes were ready to receive guests at any time, and I took pride in not having household help. Orderliness represented a life under control. A neat, clean, tidy life—until it wasn't. Sometimes life cannot be ordered, and therein lies the tale.

I was not one of those precocious youngsters who knew early on that she would become a writer or an archaeologist or the first woman in space. My rural Ohio world—vast in terms of the flat acres of wheat and corn—was small in its ethnic and cultural diversity. Besides political party, the major divisions in Oak Harbor were Catholic/Protestant and farmers/townies. We were a homogeneous bunch. As a child, I traveled out of state only twice on short family vacations. The only employed women I knew were school-teachers, sales clerks, or secretaries. I never gave much thought to a career, although I did think librarians must surely have the best jobs of all.

Attending four-year college was not part of my family tradition. My father went to a General Motors' engineering program immediately out of high school but left to enlist in the air force in 1942. My mother started nurses training after high school, only to drop out after watching her first surgery. She worked at a local defense plant until she married my father in 1943, while he was still in flight school. He died in a plane crash in Burma in 1945, just months before the end of the war. I was less than three months old. My mother struggled with this grief, moving in with her in-laws for a year until her father-in-law died from a heart attack. I was the only grandchild in two loving extended families, all living within a few blocks during my entire childhood. My mother remarried when I was four, and although my stepfather legally adopted me, they agreed to honor my father by keeping the Schmunk surname for me. Though I was unaware of it, I'm sure the name marked me as the "war orphan" in that small town. I simply thought I was lucky to have extra grandparents and great-grandparents living close by. Throughout my childhood, I was well loved and cherished.

I would realize only later what a profound influence my father's brother, Uncle Paul, had on my future career. At age twelve, Grandma Schmunk and I visited him, his wife, and new baby in Albuquerque as he was finishing a PhD in American studies at the University of New Mexico (UNM). The cross-country train trip enchanted me, and the stark beauty of the mountains and deserts made elementary social studies books come alive. The UNM campus was huge, and the multistory library, with more books than I could have imagined, stood in such contrast to the little, white reclaimed house that served as my hometown library. Uncle Paul introduced me to a wide range of books, classical music, and horseback riding. I returned home thinking, "I'm going to college."

Certainly, my small high school (eighty-eight graduates in my class) encouraged students to attend college and offered the basic curriculum necessary. However, the school system in this farming community also put equal emphasis on practical subjects. Many girls in my class took courses in secretarial skills and home economics. For boys, there was woodworking and an active Future Farmers of America chapter. My favorite period of the day was band, my favorite extracurricular activity was theater, and my favorite subject was history. We had no guidance counselor, and I don't recall any teacher encouraging me toward a specific field of college study or discussing the merits of large public versus small private colleges. Many of my friends planned to attend Bowling Green State University, the closest public institution to home, and a few others went to nursing school nearby. I wanted to be different, do something more exotic like Uncle Paul out in New Mexico. My parents encouraged this dream, for unbeknownst to me, they had been saving the government stipend I received as a war orphan for just that purpose. So during my senior year, Mom and I toured several private, liberal arts colleges in Ohio. Mom preferred the church-affiliated ones and drew the line at the "hippies" she saw at Antioch College.

Marietta College, on the Ohio River and as far from my hometown as one could get and still be in the state, sealed the deal with a hefty scholarship, and I enrolled in the fall of 1962. I was drawn to subjects that weren't offered in my high school: sociology, biblical studies, German, and psychology. I pledged Tri-Sigma Sorority, after being rejected by my first choice, and I joined the tiny marching band. I both admired and was awed by my professors (one sociologist was even a woman.) I did well academically and made several close friends. Dormitory life felt like pure freedom after living at home, even though we freshmen women had to sign out when we left the dorm, be in by a certain hour, and were forbidden to entertain male visitors. At least I could move about the campus and town independently without feeling that everyone knew me and would offer full accounts of my activities to my parents.

In my sophomore year, I unexpectedly found myself president of my sorority, the smallest and newest on campus, when the president-elect failed to return to campus that fall. (Never spoken of openly, she had become pregnant and had dropped out to get married.) As part of the fall homecoming festivities, each sorority prepared a skit that presented the sorority's candidate for homecoming queen at the fraternity houses. The men then chose the winning contestant. Our skit featured a French theme, "Gigi," and at the finale, I presented each fraternity chapter president with a bottle of champagne.

A nice French touch, perhaps, but unfortunately for me, it violated the "no alcohol on campus" rule. Even an unopened bottle was *verboten*. The next day the dean of women summoned me to her office for a stern rebuke. I had committed a minor offense, but as someone who had *never* broken a rule or run afoul of any authority figure, I was embarrassed and humiliated. For the first time since I had gone off to college, I called home crying. My parents, I think, were amused (being no teetotalers) but comforting. I, however, was done with Marietta College. When the dean offered me a paid position as dorm monitor for the next year, I smugly told her no, I had decided to transfer colleges.

The college's overreaction to an unopened wine bottle was only part of the stimulus to transfer schools. Course offerings were so limited in the two-person Sociology Department—my intended major—that I turned to Uncle Paul for advice. He was by then a professor and founder of the American studies program at the University of Wisconsin–Whitewater, and we settled on the University of Michigan–Ann Arbor for its stellar academic reputation. I was dazzled by the variety of course offerings. I knew only one other student enrolled there, but I believed the anonymity of a large university would be a welcome change from small-college life. My parents supported the move, as it brought me much closer to home, though giving up my scholarship for out-of-state tuition surely cost them financially.

I loved everything about the University of Michigan. Instead of two sociology professors, I could choose from over a dozen. I did not transfer my sorority membership and found I could meet a greater variety of people through classes and the campus Methodist student fellowship. (I didn't know about "cultural diversity," but I was drawn to it. My first summer there I lived in the Quakers' International House.) My otherwise supportive parents did, however, object to my sociology major. "What can you do with that?" was my stepfather's persistent question, until I gave in and cast about for an alternative. One of my professors advised that, as I already had courses in economics, political science, and history, I could easily convert those credits plus my sociology courses into a social studies major. Michigan offered this concentration in the College of Arts and Sciences, so I did not have to transfer to the School of Education. By adding some educational theory, curriculum development, and student teaching I was able to graduate just one semester late.

By August 1966, I had an A.B. *cum laude* and a State of Michigan teaching certification in social studies and German.

In addition to awakening my intellectual and cultural curiosity, those two years at the U of Michigan honed my personal values and shaped my political views. I was there when Tom Hayden served as editor of the campus newspaper, the *Michigan Daily*, and when anti-Vietnam War protests and teach-ins were regular events on campus. I joined an interdenominational study group that met for weekly discussions of contemporary theologians and political activists such as Paul Tillich, Dorothy Day, and Reinhold Niebuhr. One weekend we traveled to Chicago to learn about community organizing from disciples of Saul Alinsky, author of the famous "12 Rules for Radicals." I attended a "teach-in" on Vietnam and volunteered to tutor minority elementary students. All these activities honed my social consciousness and laid the groundwork for the volunteerism that would shape my postcollege decades. The whole atmosphere of university life—personal, social, and intellectual—stood in contrast to the farming community where I had grown up. My parents were none too pleased when I came home with a Japanese boyfriend, denounced U.S. foreign policy in Vietnam, and claimed marijuana was no more harmful than alcohol.

By my senior year, I knew I was not ready to leave college. Thanks again to Uncle Paul's encouragement, I applied to the Rackham Graduate School at Michigan in his field, American studies, and was accepted. Also during my senior year, I fell in love. Patrick worked at the university as the assistant director of Religious Affairs (a title that prompted many jokes when we announced our engagement). Looking back, I now see we came from vastly different backgrounds and our courtship was far too short. We were engaged before Christmas and married by May. My parents thought that, at thirty-one, he was too old for me and that we hadn't known each other long enough. He had no siblings, and I never met his elderly parents until the wedding rehearsal. Nonetheless, we went ahead with the wedding, rented a tiny apartment near campus, and I finished my summer courses for graduation. Before I could begin graduate school in the fall, my husband received an offer to join the Philosophy Department at Arkansas State Teachers College (ASTC) that his graduate-school friend chaired. The dean was promising that ASTC would add religious studies (Pat's field) soon, and to sweeten the offer, he said that a master's program in history was about to be approved. It never occurred to me not to support my husband's career by moving south with him. I naively believed I could simply do my graduate work at ASTC, not realizing the vast difference between the University of Michigan and an Arkansas state teachers college. The promised MA program turned out to be a master of science in education instead. What could I do but enroll anyway, take history courses almost exclusively, and settle into married life? I was one of the few grad students who wrote a thesis rather than take additional coursework, and it was my first foray into primary source research. Limited though my research was, I loved the archives. "The Depression Comes to Arkansas" began with the devastation of the 1927 flood and analyzed the economic and social history of the early 1930s. With encouragement from my graduate advisor, Foy Lisenby, I pared the thesis down to an essay for the *Arkansas Historical Quarterly.* I was laying the groundwork for my eventual career, but it would take another twenty years before it came to fruition.

I graduated in May 1968, two days before our first child arrived. The small hospital in Conway, Arkansas, provided no childbirth classes, all mothers were anesthetized, and only medical personnel entered the delivery room. After Patrick drove me to the hospital, our doctor explained that first labors often lasted many hours and suggested my husband go home. As Pat was eager to watch the televised debate between Democratic presidential candidates Robert Kennedy and Eugene McCarthy, he agreed. We had both worked on the McCarthy campaign earlier that spring, typing letters to all the Arkansas delegates to the nominating convention. He had just settled in to watch when he was called back to the hospital—our daughter had arrived. It was hours before I was awake enough to see her, and I have no memory of the birth at all.

We had three children in our first ten years of marriage. I never sought paid employment, but my inclination to organize and oversee things kept me busy in the community and the church. I amassed many volunteer hours working on local political campaigns, the League of Women Voters (LWV), and the Arkansas Human Relations Council, and I was president of the American Association of University Women (AAUW). I was invited to attend a grant-funded course for young adults interested in running political campaigns. We became foster parents and kept several newborns. I joined a few other faculty wives in a "consciousness-raising group," reading Susan

Brownmiller, Robin Morgan, and Gloria Steinem. I was busy and happy. Pursuing further education seemed neither feasible (no nearby PhD-granting institution) nor affordable. Life was busy enough.

However, by late 1976, my life had taken two dramatic turns. Patrick changed careers, leaving academia for the Episcopal ministry. Although I supported his career change, leaving close friends of ten years to move into an uncertain future was lonely and painful. As we pulled out of the driveway with two cars, three children, a dog, and a trailer, tears streamed down my face. We relocated to Fayetteville, a thriving university town in northwest Arkansas, and Pat began two years of pastoral internship leading to ordination.

Without the college as home base, the only opportunity for making friends was through the parish at a time I particularly needed friends. Our third child, Erin, had been born just three months before the move to Fayetteville and had been diagnosed with a heart defect and hypotonic muscle tone. At four months, she was not gaining enough weight or meeting developmental milestones. Friends from the Conway consciousness-raising group came to visit, both with some medical training. They tried to prepare me for unsettling news when our pediatrician sent us to Arkansas Children's Hospital in Little Rock for days of testing. Yes, Erin was significantly developmentally delayed, and no, they had no etiology for her condition. They ventured no prognosis about what she might or might not be able to achieve physically or mentally. An aloof pediatric neurologist simply said, "Take her home and love her." Providing Erin with daily stimulation activities while parenting the other two children and navigating the new role of clergy wife occupied me completely. Quite suddenly, my future felt not just unpredictable; any sense of a managed, controlled life felt out of reach.

New challenges followed when Pat's two-year internship in Fayetteville ended. We moved to a small parish in Russellville, Arkansas, a town of fifteen thousand with little in the way of cultural activities or social activism. My friends were either members of the congregation or parents of my children's friends. Good people all, but I found myself reverting to the messages in my head from small-town Ohio layered with the expectations of being judged as a clergy wife. The messages carried my mother's voice: "Don't leave the house without fixing your hair and makeup," "Never leave beds unmade or dirty dishes in the sink," and "Keep the house tidy at all times." Because I was also the pastor's wife, I never missed a church service, I entertained frequently, I participated in Diocesan women's meetings, I volunteered with a child-abuse agency, and I had dinner on the table every night at six. It was a full-time, unpaid position.

In our third year there, Dr. Gene Boyett, a professor of history at Arkansas Tech University and a church member, put me in touch with the chair of the Social Sciences Department, who offered me an adjunct position teaching one survey course in Western civilizations. I was twelve years away from graduate school, having had almost no background in classical or medieval history. I accepted anyway. And how I loved prepping and teaching. I even managed to stay a few days ahead of the students, and I'm sure I learned much more than they did. The other faculty could not have been more gracious or helpful, and I enjoyed the three semesters I taught there. I especially appreciated the seriousness with which other department members treated me and the help they provided.

Then my husband accepted a new appointment to a parish in Jonesboro, Arkansas. Decamping just before Christmas, we arrived with the three children too late to buy a Christmas tree but excited to be living in a larger town. The position of clergy wife was less intimidating this time around, but the congregation was older and more conservative. I found it harder to make friends. By the next fall semester, I delighted in landing an adjunct teaching gig at Arkansas State University (ASU). This larger history department included several female colleagues and many publishing scholars. Again, I wasn't well prepared, as ASU offered a course in world civilizations rather than Western civilization, so preparing materials on ancient India, the Far East, and Africa was bit like cramming for exams. Again, the faculty there were generous with their time, sharing slides and books and essay topics.

Gradually my confidence grew, and colleagues in the department encouraged me to think about pursuing a doctorate. The closest PhD-granting institution was Memphis State University (MSU), a ninety-minute drive away through cotton and rice fields. By then, my three children were all in school, the youngest in special education classes. I dipped my toe in the water and signed up as a "special student" in the spring of 1984. I chose a three-hour seminar on the philosophy of history, less for its content than for the fact that it met only once a week on my husband's day off. I later learned that this course was one of the most challenging in the doctoral program and one most students saved for their final semester.

Sometimes ignorance pays off. This class changed the way I thought about history, both as a discipline and as a process. Most of my undergraduate and master's courses had presented history as if it were the accumulation of information that scholars had carefully wrung from the documents and cultural artifacts of the past. But this seminar wasn't about data collection at all. We examined what historians across centuries and nationalities had understood history to be: its purpose, its craft, its methods, its audience. When we came to the modern era, we studied "schools of history" as reflections of the major intellectual and cultural questions of the day. I found myself amazed that the same set of documents could produce such widely varying interpretations. So, this was what the study of history could be! Professor Major Wilson structured the course around weekly writing prompts. What did a particular historian (or school of historians) assume about his subject? What new questions did he ask? (Yes, we read only male historians.) What unconscious biases were evident? Those short papers amounted to dialogues between the student and the historian, whether Immanuel Kant, Leopold von Ranke, or Fogel and Engerman. As he scribbled in the margins, Dr. Wilson entered the conversation with elaborate comments and insightful questions. Over the next five years, my first graduate professor became my model for scholarship and for teaching, as well as my major advisor and friend.

I continued teaching at ASU and enrolled in another graduate seminar at MSU that fall. Professor Robert Frankel never let on—although I'm sure he realized it—that I was completely ignorant of the many aspects of Tudor-Stuart Britain that he sought to elucidate. While he worked patiently to ferret out the emergence of individualism in seventeenth-century England, I was trying simply to keep the players straight and figure out why "individualism" mattered. Again, I was learning that doing history was an intellectual, interpretive process, not a memorization feat. I read while doing laundry, cooking, eating breakfast. And the more I read, the more I was drawn into the world of ideas, a world much more exciting than diapers and vacuuming. I decided to apply to Memphis State for admission as a regular graduate student.

Other than the two professors with whom I had already studied, I knew only one other member of the History Department, Paul Ropp. He had taught

Chinese history at ASTC when I lived in Conway, our families had become friends, and he arranged for me to meet with the graduate advisor at Memphis State. The interview began with a few questions about my academic credentials and background. When he discovered that I used to be an avid Cleveland Indians fan, he called another (male) professor down to the office, and they proceeded to quiz me about teams and players from the 1950s. I held my own, but was this an interview for the PhD program or Baseball Trivia? I was too naïve to realize I was but a pleasant diversion for the afternoon. When we finally got around to discussing in which area I might concentrate, I told him that, in teaching world civilizations for several years, I'd become fascinated by the medieval period. "Ah, then you need to meet our medievalist," he said and sent me upstairs to meet Professor Marcus Orr. I later learned that Orr was a polarizing teacher; either you became devoted to his Socratic method or you avoided his courses at all cost. After some discussion of my adjunct teaching, he explained that before I could work with him, I would need to master medieval French and Latin, develop a passing knowledge of Greek, and brush up on my undergraduate German. No doubt these are standard courses for any medievalist, but at age forty-two with a commute and a busy family life, mastering several languages sounded like an impossible obstacle course. Call me lazy, but that was all the incentive I needed to decide I would rather study United States history.

The graduate school took my application under advisement and decided that, since my MSEd was eighteen years old, I would need to take the standard GRE as well as the history portion before being admitted. I studied like a fiend, being especially fearful of the math and logic components. As I recall, my score was acceptable but not outstanding. The History Department asked me to sit for an interview with several professors. I recall that Wilson and Frankel attended, as well as the new department chair, Joseph Hawes. Each interrogator started with a basic historical event or question and then drilled down until I was at a loss to respond. Most questions related to the two courses I had already taken, but one stands out for its minutiae: "When Freud visited the United States in the early twentieth century, whom did he most wish to see?" I stumbled and managed to guess correctly on my second try: William James. I was approved on a conditional basis and enrolled in two courses for the upcoming term.

By choosing a Tuesday-Thursday class and a Wednesday seminar, I could drive to Memphis on Tuesday mornings and return to Arkansas Thursday nights. A fellow graduate student let me sleep on her couch two nights each week. I chose courses that fit that midweek schedule, the "History of Childhood in America" and "Reformation Europe." Again, I lucked into another opportunity. In the "History of Childhood," I wrote a short paper about teachers in rural Ozark communities, based in part on my mother-in-law's experience in the 1930s–1950s. Professor Hawes encouraged me to submit the essay to the annual Arkansas Historical Association Meeting, and the following year I attended my first professional history conference to present that paper. I began to believe I might do this doctorate thing after all. I remember wishing I could share my excitement with Uncle Paul, who had died in his forties, well before I began the PhD program. How, I wanted to know, do I bring both parts of my life together: holding a faculty position and being a clergy wife and mother? Even he had not been a role model for that.

I received support and encouragement from most of the Memphis State faculty. Several urged me to apply for a graduate assistantship, which carried in-state tuition plus a salary of one thousand dollars a semester. However, it also required a full-time, three-course, enrollment. Taking another big step in the fall of 1987, I enrolled in three courses and became Hawes's grading assistant in a large U.S. survey. As this meant spending most of the week in Memphis, I rented a cheap apartment, bought a mattress, and set up a card table for a desk. I was in the throes of self-discovery, heady with graduate school, and to all intents and purposes, living a marital separation though I never named it as such. The two younger children remained in Jonesboro with their father, the oldest was away in college, so that I was an academic four days a week and a clergy wife and mother over the long weekend. I thought everything worked and everyone was happy. Such was the illusion of a controlling person. I could not admit that the whole family system was fraying.

The intensity of that tumultuous year has blocked out most of my memories of it. Weekends consisted of a blur of household tasks, church activities, and catching up with the children. There were football games and concerts, church retreats and meetings. I must have sometimes returned home during the week for children's doctor appointments or school meetings, but I don't remember them. I know I confined all my studying to the days I was in Memphis, creating a bifurcated life. I'm sure my friends in Jonesboro found me distant, driven, and frenetic. I have no recollection of how the younger two children were doing in their respective schools. My oldest was attending college in Memphis, angry at me for disrupting the family and worried about her younger, intellectually disabled sister. I learned later that she did confide her confusion and unhappiness to some faculty members, women who later became my colleagues when I began teaching at Rhodes College.

What I recall best about that year was the feeling of joy that washed over me as I saw the Arkansas-Memphis bridge loom on the horizon as I headed east across the Mississippi and toward the campus. Memphis and the university felt like home. I liked not having to pack school lunches or cook dinner for five; I liked eating in bed and reading late into the night. But there was also the guilt. I had briefly attended a few sessions of marriage counseling the previous year but began to visit the therapist alone to work through my conflicting emotions over moving away and abandoning my children for most of the week. In therapy I explored how growing up in a family where expressions of anger were not allowed and where compliance and proper behavior were rewarded had led me to repress my ambition and resentments. Over the last few years I had not shared my feelings of being stifled and angry with a husband who was often overwhelmed and depressed. I was contemplating divorce from a good but unhappy man. All I knew to do was leave.

The following year I filed for divorce, rented a larger apartment in Memphis, enrolled my youngest daughter, Erin, in Memphis public schools, and moved my share of the household goods to Memphis. Years later, my son told me that my asking him to help me load that furniture and drive the U-Haul to Memphis had made him very angry. I had left him to face his senior year with a clinically depressed father. Only in retrospect can I appreciate the pain this caused. At the time, it only felt like freedom.

Although Memphis State was my only option for PhD work when I started, it turned out to be a good program for a forty-something woman reclaiming herself. Most of the doctoral candidates were nontraditional students like myself. They included, among others, two high school teachers, an auto mechanic, a homemaker, and a librarian. We knew what we didn't know, we didn't compete, we scraped by with little money, and we had a variety of life experiences behind us. Most of the faculty accepted the unevenness of our undergraduate preparations and provided encouragement and support.

And then there were those who didn't. For example, I did a research paper in a business history course on the rise of Memphis's largest employer, Federal Express. The professor returned my paper with a big "A" on the front and nary another mark or a comment, thus providing no help in how I could have deepened my research (I had done no interviews), improved my analysis (there was little), or sharpened my writing.

On the whole, the doctoral program was structured around traditional political periods and nation-states, with more political and intellectual content than social history. By contrast, I found myself drawn to social history topics courses like "History of Childhood" and "Material Culture in Twentieth-Century America." My favorites, I think, reflected my attempt some twenty-five years earlier to do graduate work in American studies at Michigan. Toward the end of my coursework, Dr. Elsa Barkley-Brown arrived on a one-year appointment. Only later, as I became active in the Southern Association for Women Historians (SAWH), did I begin to read her work, hear her conference papers, and realize what I had missed by not taking a course from her.

The history doctorate had few requirements: "Philosophy of History" (my introduction to the graduate program), "Research Methods" (library and computing skills), and three primary-source research seminars. The remaining course hours, many of which also contained undergraduates with shorter reading lists, were drawn from whichever courses fit to create a major and two minor fields. After I became active at professional conferences, I learned that graduate students often used such research seminars to develop chapters of their dissertations. No one ever suggested such a strategy to me, and I had yet to define a research topic. I think most of us in the program chose seminars based simply on when the course was offered or who was teaching it. My research seminar in the early national period of the United States included studying the then-current debate over early America's "republican values." We read Drew McCoy, whose work centered on the ideological underpinnings of republicanism as it was understood in the post-Revolutionary era, and Joyce Appleby, who argued for republicanism's essential pragmatic and capitalistic foundations. To compare these two interpretations, I chose to use early American children's books as evidence of the transmission of these republican values. Children's books were then available in the Shaw-Shoemaker microfiche collection, an experience no younger historian has to face thanks to digitization. I wrote and rewrote that research paper, as Ed Skeen took me to task for passive voice, clunky phrases, and insufficient evidence. The paper improved. On his prompting, it found a home in the *Journal of the Early Republic*. I had my first national, peer-reviewed publication, and later, part of a chapter in my first book.

With Skeen and Wilson offering a course titled "The U.S. to 1865," my choice of concentration fell easily into place. Choosing two subfields proved more difficult. The British legal and educational system had intrigued me ever since I had spent a semester in London as an undergraduate. But after two semesters of British history, and despite excellent professors in each, I found most British historical writing plodding and sterile. I minored instead in the two fields that seemed closest to my love of early America: Early modern Europe and the modern United States. In Wilson's course on Jacksonian America, the antebellum reform movements that rumbled through the United States between 1820 and 1850 intrigued me, especially as they provided urban women a noticeably public role. No doubt my volunteer hours in the League of Women Voters and the American Association of University Women in Conway influenced my attraction to these women and their benevolent organizations. When I read Gertrude Himmelfarb's *The Idea of Poverty* in a course on Victorian England, I wondered how assumptions about the poor underlay American women's benevolence efforts.[1] A dissertation idea took shape. As I continued exploring secondary sources, I realized that, with the exception of one dissertation, the existing scholarship exclusively drew on northern and urban materials.[2] Barbara Bellows's work drew heavily on Charleston. I proposed a comparative study among several southern cities, looking at the extent of white poverty and the public response to it. The fact that I had taken no courses in southern history dissuaded me not at all. I had a lot to learn.

My coursework complete, I sat for comprehensive exams in the spring of 1989. Although the department had a computer lab of bulky Zeniths with a cumbersome software program called WordStar, graduate students still wrote their comprehensive exams by hand over a four-day period, seated in a small, windowless room. I passed. I then chose a dissertation committee, wrote a proposal (no defense was required), and was cleared to begin the research. The summer found me doing archival research in New Orleans. Passing comps also qualified me for a teaching assistantship in the fall. I taught two sections of the early U.S. survey with about thirty-five students in each. The textbook and readings book were predetermined by the faculty, but teaching assistants (TAs) could add other readings. As I had as an adjunct in Arkansas, I thoroughly enjoyed teaching history, but now I had a vision of the kinds of questions I wanted to raise in students' minds as they encountered the reading and writing assignments.

I expected to continue as a TA for a second year as I worked on the dissertation, but in early summer I got a phone call from Rhodes College, the four-year liberal arts college across town where my daughter was a junior. They were looking for an adjunct for just one U.S. survey and had called someone at MSU for a suggestion. The "old-boy network" worked in my favor, and I was offered the spot. I was thrilled: the class would be limited to twenty-five or fewer, and I could choose my own books and readings, including fiction. It was a rich experience, and I loved the liberal arts atmosphere at Rhodes, the curricular freedom, and especially the keen students.

The following year, I returned to MSU to accept a full-time instructorship, which meant four classes a semester, leaving little time to finish the dissertation. That fall, Joe Hawes and I married. Though we had violated no university policy in dating, he deemed it best to resign as chair of the department. Only later could I fully appreciate what he gave up so that I could finish my PhD without suspicion of favoritism. I submitted my dissertation, "Poverty and Its Relief in the Antebellum South: Three Cities," in 1991. Nervousness prevailed as I prepared for my dissertation defense. Several persons on the committee were people I had not studied with: the new woman's historian and the longtime southern historian. I wasn't sure what to expect, and none of my graduate student friends had yet gotten to that stage. While Wilson pushed me to develop my theory more carefully, and Skeen again helped rework my prose, I got no specific advice on how to turn this research into a book manuscript. In fact, one member of my committee provided no feedback on either the proposal when it came or on any of the chapters as he received them. Then at the oral defense, he questioned my inclusion in the research design of New Orleans as a "southern city." My unflappable, supportive advisor helped diffuse the objections, and the dissertation committee signed their approval. Earlier that year, I had taped a monthly writing schedule to the wall of my home office, and when I graduated, my daughter presented me with that schedule, nicely framed. In writing the dissertation, she seemed to say, I had followed an orderly path.

By my May graduation, I had neither applied for any positions nor been on any job interviews. I expected to spend the next academic year as an instructor at Memphis State and to work on expanding my dissertation research to include additional southern cities. I had also signed a contract with Twayne Publishers for a book on American children's literature, part of their History of Childhood Series edited by Joe Hawes and Ray Hiner. Their original choice had failed to produce, and I had a start on the topic with the article in the *Journal of the Early Republic*. But once again the unexpected happened. I received a call from the chair of the Rhodes College History Department, Kenneth Goings. One of his faculty had resigned at the end of term, and he was looking for a one-year replacement. He apologized for the lateness of the offer and the low salary of thirty-two thousand dollars (much more than MSU would have paid), with fewer and smaller classes. How could I refuse? I headed across town in August with my newly minted PhD in hand to assume a 3–3 teaching load. All my classes had twenty-five or fewer students. I had stumbled into a dream job. And I had a book contract.

As a one-year appointee, I was not involved in departmental decisions. I assumed they would advertise a tenure line in U.S. history and the competition would be fierce. Instead, the department offered me a second one-year visiting appointment. I was on the job market during my two "visiting" years there and went on two campus interviews at state universities with large history departments. At the first, I was told my research agenda (two book proposals, one under contract) was "too ambitious" and that I could never accomplish that while teaching four courses a semester at their university. At the other, I was asked by a male faculty member what I had been doing in the twenty years between my master's degree and my PhD. I heard in that question a critique of my failure to follow a traditional academic path. Neither university offered me a position. I felt caught between a rock and a hard place.

Rhodes offered a third one-year appointment, during which time I won an NEH summer workshop grant to attend "Jeffersonian America," a six-week program coordinated by two major scholars, Peter Onuf and Robert Gross. Participants represented a range of American studies fields: philosophers, linguists, literary critics, historians, and material culture experts. We spent two weeks each at William and Mary University, the University of Virginia, and Historic Williamsburg. Though I had hoped to find a wealth of colonial children's literature for the book I had under contract, there was little time for archival research in the packed schedule of speakers and field trips. I did, however, gain a wealth of information for teaching "Colonial America," and getting an NEH also made me a more attractive and credible scholar to the Rhodes administration. They offered me a three-year, non-tenure-track contract beginning in the fall of 1994. Had administrators forgotten that I had been hired without a national search? I was naïve about the academy, so it didn't occur to me that they didn't need to offer a tenure-track slot to someone who would probably stay in the position anyway to avoid a long-distance marriage. I'm sure the administrative position rested on a perceived need for hiring flexibility, but hindsight suggests I was a captive hire.

In addition to teaching and advising, the department asked me to participate in "Search for Values," a two-year humanities requirement. Many faculty avoided joining the program, as it pulled one out of her disciplinary silo and required teaching primary texts well outside one's discipline. I had no graduate training in the ancient world, philosophy, or art history. But seeking to increase my employability and value to the college, I joined the "Search" staff, teaching two semesters of the four-sequence course. I came to appreciate this multidisciplinary program and benefited from the program's endowed resources: attending interdisciplinary humanities conferences and twice traveling abroad with other faculty to visit sites and museum holdings critical to the "Search" program's material.

In 1995, the Rhodes administration announced that to keep the college "nimble" in its hiring, new faculty would be offered long-term renewable contracts (LTRs) rather than tenure-track lines. My three-year contract was converted to a six-year LTR, but I was not given credit for the four years I had already taught at Rhodes; I started over. LTR contracts carried higher starting salaries and a full year's paid sabbatical following a successful sixth-year review. The review process was largely identical to a tenure review, handled by the same committee. Many faculty members complained that departments would not be able to compete for the best scholar-teachers without the possibility of tenure, but those of us converted to, or hired with, LTRs had little choice but to go forward or leave. I persevered.

In every other way, Rhodes proved an excellent place to begin a career. I found the students inquisitive and well-prepared. Faculty worked hard on innovative teaching and assigned heavy reading loads. The college provided handsome, competitive summer research grants and ample conference travel funds. There was no summer school teaching to divert one from research and writing. Especially supportive was a group of female faculty who had begun gathering quietly on Friday afternoons several years prior to my arrival at Rhodes. They originally dubbed themselves "The Grouse Club," not because of the obvious need to complain about paternal administrators or imperious male colleagues but rather because they enjoyed sharing Famous Grouse Scotch! Some years later, they renamed the group after Saint Beatriz da Silva, the foundress of the Order of the Immaculate Conception, an ironic send-up to the Presbyterian pillars of the college. For its members, Friday afternoons at 4:00 became a time for sharing teaching tips, getting advice on committee service, learning the ins and outs of campus culture, and sharing laughs and fears. In a predominantly male faculty, the lounge where Beatriz met became a sacred space. As members came and went, brought out books, achieved tenure, and reared children, the group remained a significant part of my support system for twenty-some years, fading away only when women were no longer minorities in departments and on committees.

I also appreciated the History Department's support of topics courses I proposed, all of them in areas of social history. The "History of Childhood" was the first, drawn directly from my graduate school work, as was a course on antebellum reformers. I introduced an upper-division course on southern women's history after many fruitful conversations at Southern Association for Women Historians conferences. Disappointed that the course drew only white women, I changed the name to "Black and White Women of the South" and drew a diverse constituency to what became my most popular class. When the college began to cultivate community outreach and "service-learning" classes, I introduced "History of Poverty in the U.S.," sent students to volunteer at various social agencies, and joined the small urban studies program.

I was in my ninth year at Rhodes when I became eligible for the sixth-year review conducted by the Faculty Tenure and Promotion Committee (TPC). They read letters from tenured faculty in my department, evaluations of scholarship from outside reviewers chosen by the dean, visited classes, and examined mandatory student survey scores. The TPC sent its recommendation to the academic dean and the president. I knew I was a popular enough teacher and I had more than adequate service to the college on faculty committees, designing advising workshops, and advising the History Department's student honorary, Phi Alpha Theta. I had published the requisite book, *American Children's Literature and the Construction of Childhood,* a peer-reviewed essay drawn from my dissertation, and some encyclopedia articles. Still, I worried that I wasn't good enough.

My contract meeting with the dean began with a long, friendly chat about various college issues and committees. I remember thinking, "This is going very well." Then, he looked down at his desk and informed me that I had "failed to meet the numerical expectation on the Student Instructional Rating Survey forms" (SIRS). My score, he said, just below the norm the president expected. That was it: I was not approved for renewal. However, the dean went on to say, since the rest of my portfolio was "solid," the college was willing to grant me one additional year in which to "bring up your teaching score." Leaving the dean's office in a daze, I ran into a member of the TPC. I told him I had just come from my review meeting with the dean, and he beamed and congratulated me—until I told him I had failed. The expression on his face clearly indicated that this was news to him. The TPC had obviously approved; the dean and the president had the final say.

Over the next few weeks, I talked to several senior faculty who agreed that the one-year extension was most irregular. The *Faculty Handbook* had no such "do-over" provision, nor did it have any absolute SIRS score to be achieved. (In fact, the faculty often held meetings to explain to new hires just how complicated and difficult the SIRS results were to interpret.) Friends urged me to formally appeal through the Faculty Appeals Committee. However, I thought a personal approach might be less aggressive. I asked for a meeting with the college provost, planning to show him that the handbook description of teaching performance did not specify a quantitative measure. Before I could begin speaking, he informed me that the one-year extension described by the dean was now "off the table." Instead, the college would grant me a year's sabbatical, but then my employment at the college would be over. I suspect the college lawyers had weighed in, pointing out that violations of the *Faculty Handbook* might prove difficult to defend. Best I just be gone.

I was plunged into despair. I felt I had lived the nightmare that is not uncommon among female faculty: one is unmasked and found not actually to have earned a PhD. I considered where I might find work outside the academy—a library? High school? Macy's? But first, the hectic last month of the semester—research papers returned, letters of recommendation written, final exams—demanded my energies. In the midst of that activity and a month after our initial meeting, the dean called me in for another appointment. After some uncomfortable small talk, he announced that "the college had reconsidered" my case. I was approved for a sabbatical year, after which I would return with a six-year LTR contract. He refused to offer any explanation about this reversal, saying only that "your department chair will be notified."

I have never uncovered the reasons for the college's reversal. My department chair claimed he did not know what had gone down, though I suspect he and other senior faculty may have personally argued with the dean on my behalf. I do know the president was about to retire, so it is also likely he wanted to leave no legal loose ends for his successor.

The sabbatical had given me time and space to process the ordeal. For someone who follows rules and convention, yet fights for the underdog, I felt vindicated by my restoration to the faculty. However, the affair disrupted my sense of security, control, tidiness. I compensated by plunging into something I could control on sabbatical: my research and how I used my time. I packed a carton of books and traveled to China with my husband, Joe, who had won a semester's Fulbright teaching grant. The rigors of acclimating to living and traveling in China and of presenting guest lectures on U.S. topics to Chinese students and at university conferences kept me from dwelling on the Rhodes experience. I also read heavily and crafted a course on the American Revolution. When I returned to campus after a year away, I found an upbeat atmosphere under the new president and no rehashing of my experience. Since tenure reviews were never publicly announced, only members of the TPC, my department, and my friends were aware of the roller-coaster experience I had had. As the years went by and I met each year's new faculty cohort, I simply was another associate professor to them. Within two years, the administration discontinued offering LTR contracts to new hires, and all persons currently holding such contracts had the opportunity to convert to tenure-track lines. By 2002, I was a tenured associate professor.

Four years after my return, the department chair stepped down, and a new dean offered me the position. I became the first woman to chair the History Department, an irony that did not escape me. I had never expected to assume any administrative duties, but the time was right. I had just finished editing a collection of essays on white, female civil rights activists in the South. I was ready for a new challenge. Two female colleagues, each of whom had chaired her department, worked with me to develop a calendar of annual deadlines for college reports, tips on course scheduling, and other helpful information for chairs—a guide that had never existed. They explained budget intricacies and provided moral support as I learned the ropes. I found that I enjoyed setting goals, chairing department meetings, conducting new-faculty searches, and writing recommendations for colleagues. But I learned to dread the voice at the office door saying, "Got a minute?" which was usually prelude to a long discussion. I served as chair for four years, with a semester off for another sabbatical, and decided not to accept a second term. I was ready to get back to sustained writing, conference papers, and tinkering with courses, all difficult to sustain while being chair. Teaching "Black and White Women of the South" had led me to engage the amazing life stories of how African American women navigated work, cultural, and social spaces. I used that experience to create a digital document collection on African American female civil rights activists and began collecting more oral histories of Memphis activists.

An invitation from Betsy Jacoway to join a regional writing group for women historians came exactly when I needed the impetus to bring more of my Memphis research to light. Along with five other women, I presented at the first gathering of the Mid-South Writers' Symposium at the University of Mississippi. This writing group, now known as the Delta Women Writers (DWW), has grown to twenty members whose residences span the Mississippi River delta from Newport, Arkansas, to New Orleans. All are practicing historians and represent three generations of scholars. Nearly everyone in the group can claim a book, a scholarly essay, or a conference paper that has profited from the input of the DWW. Unlike our own college environments, where we are usually the only "expert" in our field, in DWW we benefit from women who work in the same or a similar field. Between paper sessions, during meals and late-night talk sessions, we share personal and professional frustrations, hobbies, book lists, and family stories. We have become sisters in a very real sense, with all the accommodations, squabbles, and inside jokes that every family has. Several of us have now retired from teaching, but not from writing, and DWW brings us into the academic world again—but with a critical audience that is brilliant, receptive, and generous with their comments.

I continue to write since retirement, more for pleasure than publication. I miss the stimulation of the classroom, but not the daily pressures, the grading, the committee work. I appreciate having more control over my time for reading, friendships, and community volunteering. The engagement with the poor that I began studying and critiquing as far back as that master's thesis in 1968, the dissertation in 1991, and a book in 2004 is now something I can do rather than something I study. There is satisfaction in feeling that my life is more under my control, while knowing at its core, life is always untidy.

NOTES

1. Gertrude Himmelfarb, *The Idea of Poverty: England in the Early Industrial Age* (New York: Knopf, 1984).

2. Barbara Bellows, "Tempering the Wind: The Southern Response to Urban Poverty" (PhD diss., University of South Carolina, 1983). She expanded her work in *Benevolence among Slaveholders: Assisting the Poor in Charleston, 1670–1860* (Baton Rouge: Louisiana State University Press, 1993).

THE HIVE

BEVERLY GREENE BOND

I put off this exercise in writing my life story because I never thought it had the excitement or drama that one would expect from an African American woman who was born and raised in the segregated South and who now teaches at the university she reluctantly attended as an undergraduate. The first person to actually suggest that I write about my life was Anne Firor Scott, and when she suggested this, I knew she had no idea how ordinary my life has been. Do quiet, ordinary women write compelling narratives about their lives? Probably not, but this is for Anne, who thought I could.

Figuratively speaking, I was raised in a cluster of beehives dominated by strong, protective, and supportive queen bees. Mine was a world of movement and purpose-driven activity. The queen bees—my grandmother, mother, and two aunts—coexisted in their clustered hives under the direction, of course, of the one real queen (my grandmother). They nurtured the individual personalities of their daughters (and sons) and prepared us for a preordained future as guardians of our own hives. Our hive-world was not a gender-exclusive, female-only world, but it was clear to us from a very early age that it was a matriarchal society. My father and grandfather were always present; uncles and male cousins were in and out. But it was the women who seemed to dominate in decision-making and discipline. I also grew up in the racially segregated urban South during a time of monumental change, change that would remake the world into something the women in my personal hives had not anticipated, but for which they prepared me all the same.

I am the product of a close-knit two-parent household. My parents married too young but managed to stay together, despite some turbulence along the way, and raise five children. My family of clustered beehives included my maternal grandparents: my grandmother, "Mother Dear" to her three daughters but just "Dear" to all her grandchildren, and my grandfather, "Daddy" or "Daddy Dave." My grandparents were the honey that kept our extended family glued together. I also come from horizontal and vertical lines of educators; in fact, I think of teaching as our "family business." My childhood was spent on a street where Dear and Daddy Dave (and my Aunt Jerry and her daughter, Kay) lived directly across the street from us. We knew all our neighbors on the street, around the corners to other streets, and for several blocks. This was a community where kids rode bicycles to their friends' houses until sunset on Saturdays and in the summer. I attended a church where people sat in the same pews every Sunday, and my sisters and I playfully put handkerchiefs over our faces and counted the ceiling lights when we were bored by the minister's long sermons. Perhaps we thought the handkerchiefs made our misbehavior invisible to the rest of the congregation but especially to Mama and Dear.

My mother, like her mother and other neighbors, was active in the civic club that kept the neighborhood informed about politics and political choices. I remember my family and my neighbors voting in local, state, and national elections, although I was unaware of the poll tax requirement until I came across that requirement in my college textbooks. In fact, I was seven years old before Tennessee eliminated the poll tax and a sophomore in college before the Twenty-Fourth Amendment made this restriction on voting rights unconstitutional for the nation as a whole.

I attended the same neighborhood schools from second through twelfth grades. Students were expected not only to graduate (as most probably did) but to go on to college, trade school, or the military. I took piano lessons from a former opera singer, Florence Cole Talbert-McCleave, until it was obvious that I really had no musical ability. I was a Brownie and a Girl Scout, took a variety of classes at the YWCA and the YMCA; and went to Girls State with other young black girls from across Tennessee. Of course, I noticed the absence of young white girls and women in all of these activities, but, since this was the South, I knew why they were not present. I never thought I missed out on anything because of their absence. This was just the way of life in the segregated South, and, other than the merchants who owned and operated most of the stores in our neighborhood, white people just weren't involved in our daily activities. But later in my life, when I met white women from other neighborhoods of Memphis, I discovered that we had actually lived "parallel lives" in mid-twentieth-century Memphis.

We had traveled in identical imaginary vehicles down parallel roads toward similar destinations in the same city. We all went to the Malco movie theater on Main Street in downtown Memphis, but the white girls (and boys) sat on the main floor, and I sat in the balcony. We all went to the Overton Park Zoo, but whites could do so any day except Thursday; blacks could only go on Thursdays. We all loved the fabled Beale Street. Black Memphians frequented the churches, stores, professional offices of black doctors and lawyers, and the cafés and nightclubs on the "Main Street of Black America."

But, in the 1950s, our parallel tracks began to merge, some vehicles collided, and all of our lives changed. Black and white Memphians had to figure out how to reconstruct their lives in the old spaces, but without Jim Crow looking over our shoulders to make sure we stayed in our places. The changes of the 1960s were big on a national level, but it would take a decade for them to impact the life of a little black girl living in Memphis, Tennessee. My school was still segregated immediately after *Brown v. Board of Education;* signs in stores still indicated which water fountains and bathrooms were for "negroes" and which were for "whites"; we still sat in the balcony of the movie theater—unless we went to the theaters that catered only to black audiences or to the drive-in movie. We knew about the *Brown* decision and understood what it could do to our world, but change was so slow we thought it was happening in another world.

However, I do remember some subtle developments. For example, my mother suddenly decided to limit our playtime with the daughters of the white family who operated the small neighborhood laundry. The laundry was on the other side of an alley that separated our house from a strip of businesses along Highway 51, or Bellevue Boulevard. The little white girls used to come over to play in our backyard while their parents worked. One day, soon after the murder of Emmett Till in 1955, my mother and grandmother decided that those play dates had to end. My little brother, Michael, was about three years old. He was a handsome child (even to his older sisters, who generally considered him a nuisance), and our little white playmates may have acknowledged his beauty a little too openly as they cuddled and cooed at him. Mama decided that she didn't want her son looking into their faces and thinking that what he saw was something to be admired. So there was an abrupt end to the interracial play dates—no arguments, no discussion, just the end. I would understand later that it wasn't the whiteness of their skin (we had friends and relatives who were "whiter" than these girls); it was what that whiteness meant. This ended my first relationships with white girls on a more or less equal basis. After all, these little girls crossed the alley to play in our yard with our toys on terms set by my mother and grandmother. My sisters and I had no interest in making the reverse trip to spend the day in a hot laundry.

I came of age in the 1960s. My life story is not that of a radical advocate for civil rights, but race is an important part of the story, particularly gendered race relationships. My life story centers on developing, on a personal level, the ability to speak to, work with, trust and befriend white women across a color line that was shifting away from my first across-the-alley relationships with the laundry owner's daughters. My sisters in the Delta Women Writers and other friends probably think I've always possessed these capabilities, but these are not natural qualities for someone who grew up when and where I did. In many ways, my cluster of family hives experienced lives that were very typical of African American families, but not in the ways that most white people might assume. Or maybe, because this is my story, my foremothers' stories just seem normal and ordinary to me.

I was born and raised in Memphis, Tennessee, and my father's family has probably been in the state for two centuries. They came to Tennessee, like scores of other African Americans, as slaves from North Carolina and Virginia. My paternal great-grandparents were born into enslaved families in Haywood and Hardeman Counties, and it's unlikely that they were freed before the Emancipation Proclamation and the Thirteenth Amendment. I know these paternal great-grandparents only from a faded photograph my paternal grandmother occasionally took out of her quilt closet, from a hand-colored photograph of her father that my uncle gave me, and from another photograph of both of these ancestors that mysteriously found its way into my own closet decades later.

My sisters and I were too young to really appreciate the stories that my grandmother may have shared with us about her family. All I can really remember is that my grandmother thought her mother was part Indian. Was this true, or was it an example of the myth of Indian heritage many African Americans pass down to their descendants? My sisters and I were much more interested in the myriad cats that called my grandmother's house their home than in listening to her family stories. There were so many cats that we just called all of them "Cat" or "Kitty." Although I can live with not becoming personally acquainted with "Cat" or "Kitty," I deeply regret not listening to Grandmother's stories or visiting and paying more attention to my grandmother's younger sister Mattie. Aunt Mattie was the family "historian" and keeper of records, many of which seemed to have disappeared after her death. I missed an important opportunity to know about the personal impact of slavery on these women's lives, the postslavery experience, and the impact of migration from the eastern seaboard to western Tennessee.

Grandmother and her siblings were the first generation of her family born in freedom, and they seemed, like many of their generation, determined to live lives that may have eluded their ancestors. For a photograph taken in the late nineteenth or early twentieth century, the daughters in the family chose the long-sleeved, high-necked blouses and beautifully coiffed hairstyles of "respectable women" of the period. Several of the sisters also chose teaching as their careers. My grandmother operated a small community nursery school on the lower level of my uncle's house, and my Aunt Mattie taught in the Memphis City Schools in the 1960s.

My father, the youngest of seven children, was born late in my grandmother's life, and I'm sure she thought he married much too early. His first three children (all girls) were born before he was twenty-one years old. I can still remember my father's oldest brother affectionately calling my daddy "Ju Baby" (his name was Julius) when Daddy was in his fifties. My sisters and I weren't the first grandchildren in the family, but we were about a generation younger than most of our paternal cousins. My sisters and I got the cats, Grandmother's front yard full of cacti, photos of relatives we'd never really know, day trips to visit Grandmother's brother and his family on their farm in Brighton, and passed up opportunities to hear and understand the family stories.

I was much closer to my mother's family. Her younger sisters were teenagers when I was born. I even remember my maternal great-grandmother as a sweet-tempered woman who could catch a chicken, wring its neck, pluck the feathers, and prepare it for dinner—all without batting an eye. My mother's father always centered me in this side of the family by telling me that I looked just like my great-grandmother. The older I get, the more I see the facial resemblance, but that's where it ends since slaughtering chickens for dinner will never be part of my skill set.

My grandmothers were very different women, but they raised their children (my parents) to understand and acknowledge a similar set of middle-class values. Both my grandfathers were present in and worked to support their families, but it was the women who ran the households, meting out heavy doses of love and discipline. Both women were from the rural South, but by the time my parents were born, both families were urban, or at least what passed as "urban" in some sections of Memphis and Shelby County, Tennessee. In both families, hard work and education were extremely important. My paternal grandfather was a carpenter and brick mason, and my maternal grandfather was a Pullman porter who later became headwaiter at a Memphis hotel. My paternal grandmother ran the little nursery school, and my maternal grandmother was a seamstress. Their labor provided some income for their households and kept them out of service in white households.

I also grew up in a neighborhood surrounded by African American educators, a situation that had advantages and disadvantages. My friends and I sometimes visited one of our teachers and graded papers for her. This, of course, gave us an inflated sense of self-esteem and sent a few of us down the road to a future where we would be in charge of our own classrooms. On the other hand, no instance of misconduct ever escaped the notice of my mother or grandmother. Since my grandparents lived directly across the street from us, if we walked home with the "wrong" friends, or if we were even a few minutes late getting to our porch, Dear was waiting. She stood watch from a tiny window in her bedroom closet, waiting for us to walk up the driveway to our back porch. "Wrong" friendships could mean many things but were usually associated with how acquainted my grandmother was with the friends, their parents or relatives, the church they attended (or whether they went to church at all), or their demeanor as we strolled home from school.

Until I was in junior high school, my mother was what is now referred to as a "stay-at-home" mom. But she was a "stay-at-home" only because she couldn't find the right job, one that suited her ambitions, her thirst for knowledge, and our family's need for extra income. My parents could easily have become statistics in some sociological study of the dangers of teenage marriage. They had known each other most of their lives and attended the same south Memphis elementary school. In 1943, when they were in high school, they sneaked across the Mississippi River Bridge to Arkansas (probably with the help of one or two of my father's four older brothers) and got married. Their secret was safe with the brothers but was soon revealed when my mother couldn't hide her pregnancy from her mother. I'm not exactly sure of the sequence of events that followed this revelation, but my father enlisted in the navy for the duration of the World War II, while my mother stayed home awaiting the birth of my older sister. Like many African American men serving in the pre-1948 navy, my father was a cook on a ship in the Pacific and even made it to Japan after VJ Day.

My mother visited him in California, probably in the late summer of 1945, and I was born nine months later. I was named "Beverly" (for Beverly Hills) in honor of that California vacation. I was born eighteen months after my older sister, and my younger sister was born eighteen months after me. Neither of my parents had completed high school before they married and the babies started coming along. But in the early 1950s, my parents got their GEDs, and my mother decided to go to college. Her two younger sisters had finished their degrees, and she knew that she had to get her degree. By 1956, she was twenty-eight years old, married, with five children. She wanted to be sure that her children would be able to go to college. She was not satisfied being a full-time housewife, and our family needed a second income. But she did not have the temperament to work in anybody's kitchen or do domestic labor for another family. My mother was also one of the smartest women I have ever known, and her thirst for knowledge had a profound impact on her children. We both loved to read, and later in my mother's life she and I often shared books. One of our favorites was Toni Morrison's *Son of Solomon.* My mother died in 1988, and as I went through the books that she always kept stacked by her bed, I found her copy of Morrison's book. She had highlighted some of the same passages I had highlighted in my own copy. I think my daughter has my mother's copy, and possibly mine as well, among her books, and I wouldn't be surprised if she had added her own color-coded highlights in the same places as my mother and I.

My father went to work for the U.S. Postal Service after he left the navy, and my parents and grandparents built almost identical houses on opposite sides of Gill Avenue near the intersection of South Parkway East and Bellevue Boulevard. My mother and grandmother single-handedly painted their houses and probably did much of the yard work in the early years. Except for a few white residents, the neighborhood was, like most Memphis neighborhoods, segregated. White merchants owned the drugstore, laundry, groceries, restaurants, and other businesses that lined Bellevue Boulevard (renamed Elvis Presley Boulevard in 1971). A beautiful city park with an elaborate, modern baseball diamond was located at the corner of Parkway and Bellevue, but, although the neighborhood was almost all black, the park was for the exclusive use of white Memphians. Black residents included the owner of a bank and insurance company, doctors, lawyers, educators, and businessmen and businesswomen, but socioeconomic class did not trump race in mid-twentieth-century Memphis. However, although our neighborhood schools (Hamilton Elementary and Hamilton High School) were segregated, we had some of the finest teachers (all of whom were black) in all of the Memphis schools, people who were committed to seeing their students excel and preparing us for the future.

But in the 1950s and 1960s, no one could predict what that future would look like. The walls of segregation were just beginning to crack, but the structure still stood firm. This was the era of *Brown v. Board of Education,* the desegregation of Little Rock Central High School, the Montgomery Bus Boycott, the Civil Rights Acts of 1957 and 1960, and the election of John F. Kennedy. Yet it was still possible for me to ride the #4 Walker Avenue bus from a corner near my home all the way downtown to shop in the segregated department stores on Main Street without having to sit in the back of the bus. Few, if any, white patrons boarded the bus as it made its way downtown, so no one demanded that I get up and move to the back.

Of course, when I got downtown, I couldn't sit at the lunch counters or try on clothes in the department stores except on the rare occasions when my grandmother accompanied me to pick out something from one of the stores that allowed her to shop unimpeded. How was this possible in Jim Crow Memphis? The only answer I could ever fathom was that she was Effie Gary Franklin, a beautiful, proud woman who knew fashion (she was a seamstress) and commanded respect. There may have been more to it than that, but there were also other women like her in my community, so that's the answer I chose to remember.

The "etiquette" of Jim Crow dictated that I could get a drink of water from the public fountains if I participated in an essential ritual of segregation and drank only from the ones designated for "colored." The downtown library was segregated until sit-in demonstrations and a lawsuit forced desegregation of all the city's libraries in 1960. Until then, African Americans used the small branch library that had been opened on Vance Avenue in 1939, or the library at LeMoyne College, the city's Historically Black College. There were no black policemen until 1948, and the first African American patrolmen were confined to walking the beat on Beale Street.

The church I attended (First Baptist Church Lauderdale) was on Mississippi Boulevard next to a large black-owned funeral home (T. H. Hayes and Sons Funeral Home) and in the same neighborhood as the Vance Avenue Library. Less than a mile south of my church but still on Mississippi Boulevard was Fire Station No. 8, the segregated quarters of the men hired in 1955 as the city's first black firefighters. I was nine years old at the time. The Memphis Fire Department was not fully desegregated until 1966, the year before I graduated from college.

Our annual church picnic was held every summer at T. O. Fuller State Park. It was a beautiful wooded park reserved for African Americans only. Indian remains had been discovered at Chucalissa (on or near the grounds of Fuller Park), but in the 1950s and 1960s I could only visit that archaeological site on specific days set aside for Negroes. That would have seemed pretty normal when I was growing up since we could only visit the zoo one day a week, but never the grounds of Overton Park adjacent to that zoo. The Pink Palace Museum, which housed an actual shrunken head, was also off-limits except for one day a week. I can describe these situations dispassionately because they were so much a part of the norm for African American life in Memphis from the 1940s through the early 1960s that I think most children assumed that everybody lived with these kinds of limitations. My extended family of parents, grandparents, aunts, uncles, cousins, and my community also created safe spaces in this segregated world where children could grow up doing all the things children normally do. But we knew that this tightly constricted environment was not all there was to life. To a great extent, white people just weren't a part of our world, and we didn't miss them as much as we missed what we eventually realized they were holding back from us.

I was eight years old when the *Brown v. Board of Education* decision was handed down, but I can honestly say that this momentous Supreme Court decision had absolutely no immediate impact on my life in segregated Memphis. No bolts of lightning or claps of thunder signaled a new day. In fact, I don't even remember my parents' and grandparents' reactions to the decision. My "School Day" photograph from that year just shows a little brown-skinned girl, with braids to her shoulders—one bent at almost a right angle by some force of nature. I was nearing the end of third grade, and I'm sure I had more important things to think about on that day in mid-May—like the impending close of school and summer break.

I had started school when I was four years old simply because I refused to stay home with my baby sister and little cousin while my older sister Paul went to SCHOOL. I didn't really know what went on in school, but I was not going to hang out with the babies. I insisted on joining my big sister and, rather than stir up one more crying child, my mother enrolled us both in Lutheran Cooperative School. We remained at that small private school until I'd completed first grade, then we both transferred to Hamilton Elementary. Of course, at that point there was no way they were going to have me repeat first grade, especially when I was sure I knew as much or more than the other second-graders. I soon discovered that I was not the only "underage" student in my class or in any of the other classes. This seemed a common remedy for precocious children and an easy way to get them out of their parents' hair.

Working hard in school was never a problem for me because I loved the whole learning process. Since the local libraries were segregated until I was in high school, in elementary school I could usually be found at the front door of my house waiting for the "bookmobile" (the mobile library) to come down our street. I understand exactly what Oprah Winfrey meant when she described books as her "pass to personal freedom." Like Winfrey, I learned to read at an early age, and where she "discovered that there was a world to conquer that went beyond [her] farm in Mississippi," I learned that I could travel beyond my south Memphis neighborhood to anywhere in Tennessee or beyond. I could stand beside Johnny Tremain during the Revolutionary War, help George Washington Carver experiment with peanuts in Alabama, or explore the lives of Chinese peasants in a Pearl Buck book.

My youngest brother was a toddler when my mother decided it was time to get her college degree. My grandmother took charge of both of my younger brothers, and my mother took the bus over to LeMoyne College several days a week. She loved going to college, and more importantly, her children all learned to love the education she was receiving. We were introduced to classical music when she took a music appreciation course and to the world of great books when she took literature courses. My mother graduated from LeMoyne College in 1961, the year before my older sister finished high school. My sisters and I helped her set up her first classroom at Georgia Avenue Elementary School and were rapidly introduced to a world with which we were totally unfamiliar. The school was about a block from our church, but we only knew the church grounds on Sunday mornings, the funeral home next door, and the Church of God and Christ on the corner. It was a rough neighborhood of housing projects, pockets of extreme poverty, and children who really could see no reason for compulsory school attendance. The architectural design of the newly constructed school where my mother taught provided for two entrances for each classroom, one directly to the outside, on each of the two floors. As we decorated Mama's classroom for her new students, my sisters and I were treated to a chorus of neighborhood children loudly proclaiming (in words we may have heard before but never from children) how much they hated school and the teachers. I knew this would not be a good year for my mother, but, because I knew my mother very well, I could also predict that any of those children who was lucky or unlucky enough to be in her classroom would learn to love school or would happily spend a lot of time in the principal's office.

My older sister graduated from high school the following spring and spent 1962–63 at Tennessee State University in Nashville. I spent my senior year at Hamilton High dreaming of how I was going even farther from Memphis, maybe to Atlanta or to Washington, D.C. I even had a plan to get a scholarship to Spelman College or to American University. But reality intervened.

My parents and grandparents had a major educational objective for the eight grandchildren in the family. Each of us had to get at least a bachelor's degree; then we could go on for higher degrees on our own. Because my sister and I would probably be in college together for the next three years, we both had to attend the less expensive Memphis State University and, hopefully, finish before my younger sister completed high school. That was definitely not a part of any plan I had imagined. I don't remember what I said or did when I realized I was heading to the recently desegregated, predominately white (which really meant a few hundred black students in a sea of thousands of white students) school in east Memphis. But to say that I was angry and disappointed doesn't come close to describing my state of mind.

Memphis State admitted its first black students just four years before my freshman year. My sister and I had to ride the bus from our south Memphis neighborhood, where there were very few white people to make us move from our preferred seats behind the bus driver, to east Memphis, where the many white riders made it impossible for us to get those "good" seats on the reverse trip back home. In fact, even after the buses were desegregated, we could still expect to encounter white bus riders who took aisle seats and put their packages in the window seats to block us from taking those seats. Of course, that tactic didn't last long because there was no way I was going to stand in the aisle on a bus trip to or from a place where I did not want to be. I was going to take a seat even if I had to step on a white foot to get to it.

When I started in 1963, some of the initial restrictions on black students at Memphis State had been eliminated. When the school was desegregated in 1959, black students were only allowed to take morning classes, could not live in the dormitories, and could not use the cafeteria or the student center. They were accompanied by police escorts, had to leave campus promptly after their classes, and had to sit in a special section at basketball games. However, by the mid-1960s, the cafeteria (Tiger Den) was a popular hangout for the growing contingent of African American students. It was a haven from the oppressive and unrelenting racism of the institution (Kappa Alpha Fraternity still held its "Old South" days, and their pledges dressed up as slaves), the site of what seemed like twenty-four-hour-a-day card games, and the place where many romantic relationships began. But Memphis State University in the fall of 1963 was not a very welcoming place for a young black woman. I learned very quickly that the only real haven from racism on this "desegregated" college campus was among the books in the library tower or in some classes—if you were lucky enough to find them.

After four years of focusing on science and math courses in high school, I decided on my first day of college life that I never wanted to see another microscope or slide rule again. I was pretty good at English grammar (thanks to brilliant high school teachers like Bethel Hunt and Martha Flowers), and books, fiction and nonfiction, had always been special for me; but I decided that history was my real love. My first or second day of college, I found myself standing outside a classroom where the legendary Dr. Marcus Orr was holding his world history class. Of course, I didn't know he was legendary at the time. I opened the door to what seemed to be a sea of white students occupying every seat on every row except one that seemed to be reserved for me: center, front row. This was truly the worst nightmare of a college freshman seeking anonymity.

But somehow I made it to my seat and immediately tried to hide. Dr. Orr was doing class introductions, and, beyond our names, he was asking random students to describe their ethnic origins. I just knew he wasn't going to ask me that question since the answer was so obvious, but my day couldn't get much worse, and he did single me out. When I finally raised my head up, whispered my name, and said something (which I can't remember) to acknowledge my racial identity, I realized that his question had actually forced me to claim my right to a place on this campus. He was a very intimidating person, and over the next few days I became more acquainted with the reasons for his "legendary" status. Marcus Orr was a wheelchair-bound paraplegic as a result of a World War II injury. He was a brilliant man and a great teacher. I had ignored warnings from other students (black and a few white) to steer clear of the History Department if I ever planned to graduate. After the first semester, I decided to major in European history, and I took every course Marcus Orr taught. By my senior year, I was determined to pursue a graduate degree in history, but with a focus on America, not Europe.

By my senior year, I was on track from quiet, serious, unattached student to quiet, serious, unmarried adult. All my friends were married or moving in that direction, but I was still spending most of my time with the books in the library tower at Memphis State University. My most important extracurricular activity was my sorority, Alpha Kappa Alpha (AKA), and it wasn't even on Memphis State's campus. The first black sororities and fraternities were chartered on the MSU campus the spring before I arrived (Phi Beta Sigma in March 1963) and the fall of my freshman year (Delta Sigma Theta in December 1963). But I had my heart set on AKA because my aunt and a cousin were members, so I joined the chapter at historically black LeMoyne College. That gave me an extracurricular affiliation—but on another campus.

So, even with a growing number of African American students on Memphis State's campus, my campus life remained academic. Other than some lectures and Phi Alpha Theta (the history honor society) activities, my after-class college life usually involved eating a quick lunch in the Tiger Den, studying in the library, or heading over to LeMoyne for sorority activities. And, while I was sure I was going to graduate school, my mother was equally sure that I was going to teach for a few years. She made it clear that I needed to prepare for this obvious career choice, so I majored in history but minored in education. In the fall 1966 semester (my senior year), I added student teaching to my list of activities, and I was assigned to Melrose Junior High School.

Although I had lived with or been close to educators all my life, and worked with a master teacher for a few months, I don't think I was ever happier than when that semester ended. I sensed that junior high school students were not among my favored groups of people and hoped that, when I became a teacher, I would be placed with any other age group. I also met my future husband at the end of that fall semester. He was sitting with a group of young black veterans who were planning a party for early January, and they invited me to attend. They actually pretended that the party was to celebrate one of their birthdays. The veterans weren't able to pull off the party because they had planned to have the party at the American Legion hall, but they were informed that they couldn't use the facility since the party would be racially integrated. But the man who had invited me to the party asked me to go to the movies instead. So that was how I met and began dating my future husband, Geraldus "Fuzz" Bond. In the spring of 1967, Fuzz became one of the first African American men to live in a campus residence hall—seven years after MSU desegregated. He was from Brownsville in rural Haywood County (about sixty miles from Memphis), three years older than me, a recent army veteran, and could easily be mistaken for white. But he was unapologetically black, and living and matriculating on campus during a very turbulent period.

Fuzz had applied for campus housing when he was admitted to Memphis State in the previous fall, but he was rejected, allegedly because there were no rooms available. Black women were already living in the residence halls, but with black roommates and on specifically designated floors. For several weeks, Fuzz commuted to campus more than a hundred miles (round-trip) from Brownsville to Memphis. Then he met a white friend from Brownsville on campus who asked whether he was still making the daily drive. When Fuzz told him he was and why he had to do this, the friend responded that he lived in a residence hall where almost a whole floor was unoccupied. So Fuzz went to the Residence Office and applied in person. He was assigned a room almost immediately, but the receptionist inquired whether he'd applied before. She was a little stunned when she pulled his records to verify he was a student and realized that he was black. She brought the administrator of Housing into the conversation, and he asked Fuzz if he knew why he'd been denied a room. Fuzz said yes, but "I want you to tell me why." The conversation shifted to his status as a veteran, and the administrator apologized, noting that the "times" were changing but not fast enough, thanked Fuzz for coming in, and told him that he could have a room on any floor in the dorm. But he was not assigned a roommate until the Fall 1967 semester, and that roommate was a young black man.

I received my BS degree in the spring 1967 semester at the same ceremony my mother received her MEd. The next school year she was assigned as a reading specialist at two different schools. It was a rigorous assignment but very appropriate for a woman who loved books. The end of that semester also put a temporary end to my own graduate school plans. My older sister graduated from Memphis State in the spring of 1966, but my younger sister started college the following fall. She had chosen our mother's alma mater, LeMoyne College, over Memphis State University because she wanted a smaller campus environment. If I went to graduate school as I had planned to do, we would both be in school at the same time for at least a year. So, my plans were temporarily sidelined.

I got a pretty good score on the National Teacher Exam, graduated *cum laude*, and was offered a teaching job at recently desegregated Kingsbury

Junior High School. Teaching eighth-graders was definitely not one of my career goals, but I didn't have a choice, and some people actually thought I was lucky to be assigned to a white school. The only "luck" I could see was that I was assigned to Kingsbury with one other black teacher, Dorothy Jean Jones, one of my sorority sisters from LeMoyne College. For the students, their families, and many of the faculty and staff, Dorothy and I were the first black women who had ever entered their educational spaces as anything other than custodial help. Some of them had a lot of adjusting to do over that school year.

I did as well, but it didn't take long for me to reaffirm my conviction that I did not want to spend eight hours a day, 180 days a year in close spaces with thirteen- and fourteen-year-olds. I remember driving into the parking lot for Parents' Night in the fall of 1967 and thinking that, if the number of cars in the lot was any indication of the level of parental commitment, then Kingsbury Junior High might not be so bad. But, as I walked through the halls past the almost empty classrooms to my own classroom, I realized that the parents weren't necessarily there to demonstrate how committed they were to their children's education but to see the "Negro Teacher." At that point, I knew that my first teaching experience was going to be as interesting as my mother's first year at Georgia Avenue—but for completely different reasons.

Every day, I drove from a black south Memphis community that was caught in the social, political, and economic turmoil of the civil rights movement, to teach the children of white north Memphians, who had no idea of how the decisions they made impacted the lives of my friends and neighbors. Many evenings, my best friend (who was teaching at an all-black junior high school in south Memphis, near the school where my mother had been assigned four years earlier) and I would compare our situations. My students had everything they could possibly need to guarantee their academic success; her students were constantly in need of even the basics. By the early spring of 1968, her students were living through a sanitation strike that involved some of their fathers; my students didn't know or care what was going on because it was, except for the garbage that might have been piling up on their streets, completely outside their frames of reference. And then Martin Luther King Jr. was shot on the balcony of the Lorraine Motel, and both of these Memphis worlds collided.

I also experienced my first friendships with white women during this first teaching experience. These women were my colleagues at Kingsbury Junior High, one the principal or assistant principal and the other, another young first-year teacher. Dorothy and I were visiting the latter's apartment when we heard the news about King's assassination. Our friend lived in a white neighborhood that seemed thousands of miles from our own homes in black Memphis. As the three of us absorbed the news of King's death, Dorothy and I also had to figure out how we'd get back home. There were scattered instances of looting and violence soon after King's death was announced, and a curfew that had been imposed after a march that turned into a riot the previous week was reimposed. Governor Buford Ellington ordered four thousand Tennessee National Guardsmen into Memphis, and, within a few days, grim-faced bayonet-carrying troops (all white and many very young) stood beside tanks that lined the highway in my neighborhood. The same was probably true for Dorothy's neighborhood, but not for much of white Memphis. I had not participated in the demonstrations and marches before King's death, but I did join the April 8 march to City Hall to demand that Mayor Henry Loeb end the sanitation strike. My young students were particularly excited about this and even believed me when I said I could point to myself among the forty-two thousand marchers pictured in a local newspaper photo.

But their excitement over this historical moment was not enough to keep me at Kingsbury Junior High. I can't remember exactly when I decided to return to graduate school at Memphis State—maybe as soon as I started my teaching assignment. I applied for admission to the MA program in the History Department and asked to be considered for an assistantship. I knew I'd need the assistantship to convince my parents that this was a feasible plan because, although I was going to continue living at home, I had purchased a car soon after I had started teaching, and now I had to figure out how to pay for it. When my admission and assistantship were approved and I told family about my plan, they seemed as relieved as I was. This family of teachers had probably already figured out that I was not cut out for eighth-graders.

I met my third white female friend, Catherine Pickle, in MSU's graduate program. Catherine was an older student who had decided to enter the program full-time. She was brilliant, funny, sincere, and one of the first white people from Mississippi that I had ever considered befriending. I lived about fifteen miles from the Tennessee-Mississippi state line, and though my maternal grandparents and great-grandparents were from Mississippi, I never considered crossing over into that foreign country. After all, it was where countless blacks, including Emmett Till in 1955 and civil rights activists James Chaney, Andrew Goodman, and Michael Schwerner in 1964, had been murdered. But Catherine and I became good friends, and her friendship probably prepared me for a lifetime of friendships with other white women. While some may assume that gender can be a natural mortar cementing relations between black and white women, this is seldom the case, especially when history (not the discipline but the reality) comes into play. Catherine's was a friendship based on mutual trust, respect, and a lot of honestly answered questions about race.

For my MA focus, I had shifted from European history to American history, and my particular area of interest seemed to be narrowing more and more on the African American experience, although that was not an official field in the department's program at the time. There were courses in African history and African American history by 1968–69, and I wrote more than a few papers in my other classes on topics related to the black experience. I'm not sure they realized it at the time, but Catherine Pickle, Anne Trotter (the professor I was assigned to as a graduate assistant), Bob Brown, and Marcus Orr were my departmental mentors during this time.

When I completed my MA, the question of employment came up again. This time I accepted a position in social studies at LeMoyne-Owen College. But I also taught a course in African American history at Christian Brothers College and U.S. history at Memphis State. The combined salaries from all three institutions almost enabled me to support myself, but expenses were less of a problem since I lived at home until Fuzz and I married in 1970. By fall 1971, we had a baby daughter (Julia), my position at LeMoyne had ended, and Fuzz's job had transferred us to northern New Jersey.

We lived with Fuzz's sister and her family in Teaneck, New Jersey, for several weeks before moving into our apartment in neighboring Hackensack. Although I knew nothing about northern New Jersey or neighboring New York City, by January 1972, I knew I needed a job. Teaching at a college or university was not an option, because I knew that I would need a doctorate to be competitive in that job market. Every week, I combed through the newspaper advertisements for jobs teaching in public schools or working at publishing companies, and one day I spotted a listing in the *New York Times* for a teaching position in black studies at Teaneck High School. I couldn't believe my luck since Teaneck was the only place I was really familiar with in New Jersey or New York. Of course, I think the Teaneck Board of Education thought they were pretty lucky too. I had BS and MA degrees in history with much of my graduate work focusing officially or unofficially on African American history. I also had the equivalent of about three years of teaching experience. However, I soon discovered that my Tennessee teaching license was insufficient, and I had to complete some additional courses at a local college. But I got the job. The position had become available in the middle of the year because the regular teacher resigned and the permanent substitute decided to quit as well. That should have been a clue that this might be a difficult assignment, but I needed a job, and it was a high school and not a junior high. I started teaching at Teaneck High School in February 1972, and I taught there for fourteen years.

Teaneck was a typical suburban community with a significant black population; most came from other parts of the Northeast (particularly New York City), but others came from southern states or were the children of African Americans who had come north decades earlier. Teaneck had voluntarily desegregated its schools in the 1960s by developing a plan that created six neighborhood elementary schools, two junior high schools, and one high school. The town's population was ethnically mixed—white, Jewish, Italian, Irish, African American, and, by the 1980s, Middle Eastern, Hispanic, and Ethiopian. The school system made one fruitless attempt to move me to a junior high position, but I told my supervisor that I would teach anything (even high school courses that I was not certified to teach) rather than teach junior high students. My daughter was in junior high at that time, and, after living in the same house with her, I absolutely knew that I could not spend twenty-four hours a day with that age group. It takes a special kind of teacher to successfully interact with this age group, and I knew I wasn't one of those teachers.

Teaneck valued education and offered an incentive to encourage its teachers to continue coursework at any of the colleges or universities in the area. The town paid our tuition and did not require reimbursement as long as we completed the courses with passing grades. Teachers also advanced along a pay scale that rewarded us for accumulating credits beyond our degrees. I enrolled at Columbia University's Teachers College almost as soon as I started teaching at the high school. I initially planned on working toward an EdD, but, after about three years, I decided that this was really not the degree I wanted. The EdD in social studies education would signify my expertise in this particular area of teaching, but it would not satisfy my interest in American history, particularly the African American experience. So, in 1976, I accepted my MEd and settled into what I thought would be a long career teaching high school. I met some wonderful professors along the way, and during one of my summer breaks I spent six weeks on a Fulbright Study Abroad Program in Kenya. A few summers later, I participated in a NEH program in African literature at City College. I even thought about entering Columbia University's PhD program in history or entering Rutgers University's Law School with a friend. I'm not sure what I planned to do with the latter degree since, as my brother-in-law noted, I was a confirmed classroom teacher.

Then, after fourteen years in the Northeast, Fuzz's company seemed to remember where we were and decided to transfer us back to Tennessee, or so I thought. The reality was that although Julie and I were happy in New Jersey, there wasn't much opportunity for career advancement for Fuzz as long as he stayed there. In late 1984, he accepted a transfer back to Memphis, and we began making plans to return to a place we once called home but had only visited for the past fourteen years. He moved in with his parents in Brownsville in the winter of 1985 and commuted to Memphis for the next six months. He was responsible for finding us a house in Memphis, while Julie and I managed the sale of our house in Teaneck, closed out the school year, and made the long road trip to Memphis.

I got a teaching position at Germantown High School, and we managed to agree on a house in the same community. There are always pros and cons in any move, and while this one offered an opportunity to be closer to the family "hives," we had a teenager who had grown up in the Northeast and left friends she had known all of her life. We had left a racially divided southern city in 1971, and learned to navigate in a northern suburban community where diversity was accepted and celebrated. I had a circle of friends and neighbors for whom differences in race and ethnicity were positive, not negative, attributes. Fuzz and I had raised Julie to celebrate these differences and to be proud of who she was. Now we were moving to a suburban community with a small African American population in a place where race still mattered.

Fuzz settled into a new position with his company, and I settled into my new high school. I taught world history and American history my first year at Germantown High, and then I was asked to teach some Advanced Placement (AP) American history courses my second year. Although Teaneck High School had offered several AP courses, I had never taught them. I pulled together every bit of information I could find on the AP American history curriculum and received a lot of help and advice from my friend Catherine Pickle, who was now working as a social studies supervisor for Memphis City Schools. I was ready for the challenge when that school year began, with one small adjustment. Julie had registered for the AP American history course with several of her friends before she left for a six-week study program in Japan. After careful consideration, I had her switched to a regular class. Of course she was not happy when I told her about this, but I knew that I could not work with my smart but temperamental teenage daughter in an intense and demanding new preparation.

I also decided to start taking classes at Memphis State University. The History Department had added a PhD program, and I wanted to test the waters and see if I could still think on a graduate level. I knew many of the faculty from my previous degree work, and my graduate coursework enriched my AP classes. I began taking one or two courses per semester in women's history, history of childhood, and African American history; then I applied for admission to the PhD program. I had not been in a history program in over a decade, and many of the fields and focus areas were new to me, but I just kept plodding along.

I took a few summer classes to prepare for the required language exam (for me, in French), which was administered by Dr. Bob Brown, who had been my undergraduate advisor in the 1960s. I was actually his first advisee when he was new to Memphis State University. I worked with Dr. Dalvan Coger on a minor field in African history. I had studied African history with him in the 1960s, and memories of his class had motivated my decision to do the Fulbright to Kenya in 1976. I also met new professors like Dr. Peggy Caffrey, my professor in women's history, who became my dissertation advisor; Dr. Ed Skeen, whose courses in the early national period framed my understanding of gender in the early 1800s; and Dr. Joe Hawes, who taught me children's history, served on my dissertation committee, and accompanied me and several other graduate students to our first meeting of the Southern Association for Women Historians (SAWH).

I meandered through the PhD program with a strong student cohort who tutored me in courses like "Labor History" that I needed but did not have time to take. I thought I was the only student in the program who was teaching full-time (three AP American history classes and two regular American history classes) in a public school system, but I discovered that there was at least one other. By the time Julie graduated from Smith College in 1995, I was nearing the end of my PhD program.

I had chosen to research and write on African American women in nineteenth-century Memphis. No other scholar had tackled this topic because most felt there were no available sources. One of my fellow graduate students, John Dougan, had written a paper on why free black people chose to remain in nineteenth-century Memphis. I decided to center my study on the women in these households. I reexamined the records John had used, focusing on how many of these free black households included women (enslaved or free), how the free black women had become free, and what they did socially and economically as free black women in this urban setting. Then I moved my focus back to enslaved women in the city and the surrounding rural hinterland, and forward to refugee and freedwomen in Civil War and Reconstruction Memphis. There was no single treasure trove of documents, but the women were there. They were in court papers, wills, census records, deeds, and other public records. They were in planters' diaries and journals, in the records of the Freedmen's Bureau and the missionary societies, in African American church records, in newspapers, and in other secondary sources.

I defended my dissertation in early 1996, and, as I was working on revisions, a friend who was also preparing to graduate in the spring of 1996, and some members of my dissertation committee, including Peggy Caffrey, Joe Hawes, and Ken Goings, suggested that I apply for a tenure-track position in nineteenth-century African American history that had just opened up at Memphis State University, now the University of Memphis. I didn't even know the process for applying for a university-level position since the only jobs I had applied for in the previous twenty-five years were in public education. I also fully understood that, with three degrees from Memphis State/University of Memphis, I had next to no chance of getting this position. I liked my job at Germantown High, was tenured in that position, and had not planned to leave even after I received my doctorate.

So, I was probably the calmest applicant in the job pool. Then I made the top three candidates, and I started to worry a little. I came for the interviews and calmly presented a chapter from my dissertation. Ken Goings had suggested that I be sure to mention that I could, of course, teach courses in African American women's history since that was what my dissertation was about. I didn't get the customary lunches or dinners with the department members, probably because I already knew most of them, but I met Janann Sherman and a few unfamiliar faces. In many ways, applying for a job is easy when you don't think you have a chance of getting it.

Then the department chair called to offer me the position, and I went into real panic mode. What was I going to do now? Fuzz and I talked it over and weighed the pros and cons. I had worked for eleven years in the Shelby County Schools, was tenured, and my salary was pretty good. I had taken a pay cut when I moved from the Teaneck (New Jersey) Public Schools to the Shelby County (Tennessee) Schools, but I was nearing the top of the pay scale again, especially with a terminal degree almost in hand. The university teaching load was lighter, three/two classes instead of the five/five classes per year in a public high school. The students were probably about the same, especially in the survey classes, since my AP courses were considered college level, especially if my students earned high scores on the College Board exams for the field.

Then I called on my next group of advisors for guidance. First, my brother in-law, Dr. Andrew Bond, who had been teaching at Tennessee State for decades and was also dean of Allied Sciences at Meharry Medical College. His point of view was that there really was not any question what I should do: I should accept the offer. I consulted my aunts, the current queen bees since the deaths of my grandmother in 1986 and my mother in 1988. Although my father had died in 1990, I knew that he and my grandfather would think that whatever I decided to do would be the perfect decision. My aunts, both former public school teachers, also thought I should accept. I think one pointed out what I was thinking all along but had not mentioned. Accepting the university position meant that I could do what I really enjoyed doing, research and writing. So, I joined the History Department at the University of Memphis in the fall of 1996. I immediately gained a best friend and a sister from another mother, Janann Sherman.

Jan and I became colleagues with offices on opposite sides of Mitchell Hall's first floor, until she moved upstairs to the chair's suite a few years later. We traveled together to history conferences and to interview job candidates (and twice to South Africa), coauthored or coedited four books, went to theater and musical performances, and enjoyed the company of her amazing husband, Charlie. Jan and Fuzz even went to a country music concert together. I wasn't invited since both of them knew I wasn't a fan of this music genre. I learned from Jan, my mentor/advisor/friend Peggy Caffrey, and many other women I've befriended at various times in my life, that real friendship can't be restricted to race or ethnicity. Jan's famous potluck dinners for her "December Babies," "April Babies," job applicant meet-and-greets, and other occasions brought together friends and colleagues from across Memphis and the University of Memphis. Our family's current queen bee, my aunt Jerry, has welcomed Jan into our hive, and I'm certain Mama, Dear, Aunt Peggy, and my other female ancestors would have done the same.

But the friendly collegial relationships and social activities sometimes masked deeper challenges that I faced in the first few years of my transition from public school to university culture. First was the challenge of shifting careers at a time in life when many people are considering retirement. My PhD hooding was less than one month after my fiftieth birthday. Another challenge was the transition from student to colleague. I had known and worked with several of the History Department's faculty as an undergraduate and graduate student. Now I was junior faculty, but still faculty. I served on committees, sat in meetings, mingled at social activities with men (Jan, Peggy, and I were the only tenure-track or tenured female faculty for many years) who had known me for decades. I made it through this transition, but as I worked on several search committees, I often wondered which of my colleagues might have been opposed to hiring me for some of the same reasons they opposed hiring other candidates.

A third challenge was overcoming a tendency to agree to any and all of these "service" requests: Would you like to serve on the search committee for this tenure-track position? Can you coordinate Tennessee History Day and/or the High School Scholars' Seminars? We need you on the General Education Subcommittee for U.S. History Survey, the Advising Committee, the Honors Committee, the Arts and Sciences Recruitment and Retention Committee, the Arts and Sciences High School Counselors Day Committee. My natural inclination, born of many years of service in public school settings, was to say "yes" to these requests, especially since I knew that service was also one of the three components of Tenure and Promotion (T&P) at the university. In public education, you only have to make it through three years of teaching and evaluations and show up on the first day of your fourth year to make it to the coveted tenured position. On the university level, you must show evidence of service to the department, your college, and the university; be an adequate to exceptional teacher; and be a productive scholar. After twenty-five years in high schools, I had the teaching component well under control. The first year, I was assigned a U.S. history survey, which went pretty well, except for the students who thought I included too much material on African Americans and women. I overdid the service, and I still haven't completely figured out how to say "no," but I'm working on that.

Although I relished the opportunity to dig deeper into the experiences of nineteenth-century black women in Memphis, the research component of Tenure and Promotion was probably the most difficult to master. With lots of help from Jan Sherman, Peggy Caffrey, Joe Hawes, and Ken Goings, I learned how to do book reviews, write articles for journals and encyclopedias, and present conference papers. I made some revisions to my dissertation and sent it out to academic presses for review, but my own monograph on black women in nineteenth-century Memphis is still in the works. It's taken me quite a while to understand the stages and timetables of publishing, from developing a book proposal to responding to the manuscript reviewer's comments. The keys to the latter are in the writer's confidence in herself and her work and in understanding when to let her work go. I usually tell my PdD advisees, "Don't bring me any more sources," when they fall in love with the research process, or "You are the expert" just before their dissertation defenses. But I sometimes can't take my own advice. I encourage my students to be confident and assertive when I know they're ready to do so, but I agonize over my own work.

When I attended my first workshop to guide tenure-track faculty through the Tenure and Promotion process at the University of Memphis, each of the panelists advised us to join a writing group. It sounded like a great idea, but I was new to this whole university culture and had no idea how to find a writing group. I worked with a few other tenure-track women from across the university for a few semesters, but we were more of a support system than a writing group. We shared problems and difficult experiences as most of us successfully navigated the T&P process, but we rarely, if ever, read and commented on each other's work.

The idea of a writing group continued to intrigue me as I circulated my work to a few trusted colleagues for review. Then, Jan Sherman invited me to a meeting of the Delta Women Writers (DWW). I met brilliant, confident, funny historians who were working on a variety of topics across the spectrum of American and global history. These women take their own writing very seriously and actively encourage each other to do the same. The DWW are brutally honest and question each other about things that seem to elude us as we put pen to paper (or computer key to digital paper). Then we have fun over lunch and dinner and travel home to refine our work into the articles and books that are a tribute to our process.

Every writer should have a writing group, but I'm not sure they'll be lucky enough to find one or form one like the DWW. I've learned a lot from this group, and the lessons go beyond having what I write make sense to an audience. I've also learned the value of constructive criticism and of trust and friendship that goes beyond the boundaries of race. The queen bees in my ancestral hive might have been amazed by the composition of this interracial, intergenerational beehive of female writers, but they would have celebrated its existence.

IN PURSUIT OF THE DREAM

ELIZABETH JACOWAY

I was born in Little Rock near the end of World War II to a beautiful, capable mother and a brilliant, introverted, Harvard Law–trained father. Mother was president of the Junior League and a founder of the Arkansas Arts Center while I was growing up; Dad was a prominent attorney from a fine old family of lawyers and politicians. We were not wealthy—very few people in Little Rock were at that point—but we were "comfortable," as they say.

We lived in west Little Rock in an area called "the Heights," and my brothers and I attended the best public schools in the city, all segregated. We and our peers were the hope of the future for our Depression-era, World War II–hardened parents, and the expectation that we would "succeed" was a palpable force in all our lives, though success for little girls was measured in different ways from that for little boys. It was clear to me that I was supposed to marry well, join the Junior League, have beautiful children, decorate a distinctive home, entertain often and well, and help my husband become a federal judge. It didn't happen, to my eternal gratitude and relief.

Instead, after two years at lovely, rigorous Randolph-Macon Women's College in Virginia and two years at the University of Arkansas—where I majored in sorority life—my father insisted that I go to graduate school and get a master's in teaching, just in case my future husband died young and left me with children to feed. I chose the University of North Carolina, praise the Lord! In my first independent decision I marched across the campus and asked the history department chairman if I could register there. He asked me what my GRE scores were; they were good; and I became a graduate student in history. Somehow I wandered into a seminar with George Brown Tindall that changed my life.

George Tindall dressed elegantly and looked for all the world like any one of the gentlemen I had known growing up, and so his appearance deceived me, and I didn't hear how radical his ideas were compared to those of my father and his peers. Before I comprehended fully what was happening to me, I had realized with blinding clarity that I had grown up in and benefited from a racist world, I had lived through one of the most important domestic crises in our nation's history, and I hadn't thought about any of it. For someone who had always thought of herself as "smart," this was untenable.

At Christmas I went home and told my dad I was going to write my master's thesis about the Little Rock desegregation crisis; he lost no time in correcting me, saying, "No child of mine is going to stir that pot!" This was just ten years after the events of 1957, and Dad was still practicing law there. Of course he was right, as I would learn to my sorrow even fifty years after the crisis; stirring that pot would make lots of people unhappy, in Little Rock and elsewhere. Nonetheless, I encountered in Chapel Hill a world of seriousness and high purpose that I had not imagined possible, and I began to dream of joining that world, and of pursuing the excellence that I saw modeled all around me.

After completing my master's thesis under Joel Williamson—George Tindall had gone to Vienna on a Fulbright year—I married Gus Burns, a fine young historian who was a socialist and an atheist, and we moved to Gainesville, Florida, where he taught southern history at the university there. The marriage was a mistake from the start. He had not visited my home until the day before our wedding, and he was appalled by the social milieu out of which I had emerged. After the rehearsal dinner we sat in the car outside my parents' house and we both cried. We gave it our best shot for seven years, and then I became the first person in the history of my family to divorce.

My first year in Florida I taught junior high social studies forty miles away, in a little school that had just integrated; it became clear to me within a matter of weeks that there had to be an easier way to make a living. The following fall found me back in Chapel Hill pursuing a PhD in southern history, working under George Tindall and Joel Williamson. Two years before, Joel had put me to work on a master's thesis using some papers that the Southern

Historical Collection had just accessioned in 1967; nobody knew what they contained, and Joel told me years later that he had thought it would be an innocuous pursuit for "a cute little girl from Little Rock." To my great good fortune, those papers turned out to be a gold mine, and I was able to reconstruct critical parts of the story of Penn School on St. Helena Island, South Carolina.

Penn had started out as a freedom school during the Civil War; then, at the turn of the twentieth century, a group of northern philanthropists had taken it over and made of it an "experiment" based on the Hampton-Tuskegee model of industrial education. Immersing myself in the extensive correspondence between the school's directors and its Board of Trustees, I came to realize that these wealthy northerners were hoping to eradicate what they called "the Negro problem" in this country (and in their cities) by demonstrating that their ideals of "character" and "service" could be instilled in the African Americans from the isolated sea islands of South Carolina and Georgia. I became completely captivated by the story I was reconstructing, and it didn't upset anybody in Little Rock (though it did upset the historian August Meier, who was heavily invested in the idea that industrial education of the sort taught at Penn School was nothing more than a ruse to keep African Americans in menial positions). In short, I learned my craft while working on a fascinating, important story under the tutelage of two of the giants of the southern historical profession, and then LSU Press published it as my first book. Pretty good for a cute little girl from Little Rock.

My first Southern Historical Association meeting was at Hollywood by the Sea. I was *very* young, and very out of my element. I listened with tears in my eyes as James Silver talked about "Mississippi's closed society," and I knew that race in America was something I had to understand. I had no idea what to wear for such an auspicious occasion, but since the program said there would be a "cocktail party," I took clothes that would have been suitable at the Little Rock Country Club. Wearing a yellow satin blouse and black satin lounging trousers, a glamorous scarf tied around my head, I rushed up to Forrest McDonald and said, "Oh, Dr. McDonald, I have just read *We the People!*" He turned away from the conversation he was having and said in the most casual manner possible, "You wanta fuck?" My husband, ever the gallant gentleman, said I should have responded, "No thanks, I just had one."

Given the standards of that era, I never dreamed of being offended. I mostly thought it was funny, if confusing, and I took away from it something like, "Well, there are boors in this high-minded profession just like everywhere else." I also made a mental note that fancy party clothes would be a detriment to my desire to be taken seriously as a budding scholar.

After Hollywood by the Sea, the Southern Historical Convention became an annual event for me, though it was never quite as exciting after that. Its warm collegial feel attracted me, as did the amazing papers that sent me home each time with dozens of inspirations. I made new friends every year and grew accustomed to meeting and visiting with major figures such as Anne Scott, John Hope Franklin, and Winthrop Jordan.

Back in Chapel Hill, I had an intense two years of coursework, flourishing in seminars under Joel Williamson, George Mowry, and Don Matthews. Don liked a paper I wrote for him and encouraged me to submit it to the *Journal of Southern History*. In rejecting it, Sanford Higginbotham wrote, "You and your graduate student friends think you know everything." It didn't even occur to me to wonder if he would have said that to a man. Don's encouragement of me was the first real affirmation I had had in the professional world; on my paper he changed my name from "Betsy" to "Elizabeth" and wrote, "If you are going to be a professional, you must present yourself as one." It was a small thing for Don, but for me it was a watershed moment.

The coursework done, I spent several months studying with two other graduate students for the PhD oral exams. Too soon, it was time to face five older, male professors in a seminar room in Hamilton Hall. On George Tindall's instructions, I met him in his office before the ordeal began, where that lovely, ironic southern gentleman told me to "just think of it as a rape. Just lie back and enjoy it." This was hardly comforting, and I went into those exams feeling thoroughly addled. Somehow I passed.

While I wrote my dissertation, by hand, on legal pads, using the 5" x 8" cards on which I had recorded all my research, I sat in on a few courses as an auditor. Jane DeHart Matthews taught the best of these, on women's history, and it was my first exposure to a new way of thinking about—and asking questions about—the past. I should have taken her teachings to heart and written more about the two white women who ran Penn School, but my conceptualization was already in place, and I was in a hurry. Supported entirely by my husband, who was also repaying his student loans on a meagre salary, I lived in a series of hovels and one lovely upstairs apartment, I ate on the "meal plan" at the university cafeteria, and through the whole time I wore two pairs of jeans, two turtleneck sweaters, and a Japanese army jacket my brother had sent me from Vietnam. I looked like a hippie, but I didn't know what I was. It was a happy time with lots of graduate student friends and a monkish devotion to reading, thinking, and writing. George Tindall provided no direction, perhaps not expecting me to finish, and so I crafted my own approaches and conclusions, apparently to his great surprise.

The dissertation behind me, I accepted a job teaching at the University of Florida in a lower-tier program for freshmen and sophomores. (The history department wouldn't consider me because the university's nepotism policy dictated that husbands and wives could not teach in the same department.) My salary was $9,400. For a year I taught sections of a course called "American Institutions" (religion, politics, and culture), and sections of a dreadful course titled "Comprehensive Logic." Fortunately, the second year the college created a new department they named Behavioral Studies, and they let me develop a course I called "The Search for Southern Identity" (where I became a master of Wilbur J. Cash), and another one called "Race in America." The dean even allowed me to put together a speaker series on southern history, and I invited Eugene Genovese, Sheldon Hackney, Winthrop Jordan, and Numan Bartley to campus, where they all spoke before standing-room-only audiences. The dean was no more amazed than I was. [*Note to young scholars: be bold.*]

I also divorced Gus Burns and persuaded my father that since he had retired, he should now allow me to write about the Little Rock crisis. He agreed, and I applied for a grant from the National Endowment for the Humanities to begin that project. To my astonishment I was awarded the fifteen-thousand-dollar grant for a senior fellowship for "Independent Study and Research," which gave me a year to do nothing but travel and read primary documents. I resigned my job at Florida, accepted a position in the history department at the University of Arkansas at Little Rock, and set out in January 1976 on an odyssey that took me from Little Rock to Chapel Hill (to organize my thoughts) and then from Boston (Brooks Hays Papers) to Madison, Wisconsin (Daisy Bates Papers), to Abilene, Kansas (Eisenhower Presidential Library) to undertake the primary research that George Tindall had insisted must precede any exploration of secondary materials. By the end of that year I had my project well in hand, I had completed two dozen interviews, and I had developed ideas for an edited volume on southern businessmen and desegregation that would announce my ownership of the territory of the Little Rock crisis, but that would keep me off the hot seat until my thinking and research had become more firmly developed.

Just as I was leaving Chapel Hill, degree in hand, the department there hired Jacqueline Dowd Hall, whom Joel Williamson described to me as "a real fox." In visits back to the campus I heard great things about her and her Southern Oral History Program, but nothing I heard impressed me more than her extensive critique of one of my female friends' dissertations. Her comments were rigorous, penetrating, and encouraging, and I was simply dazzled. I had never seen work treated with such seriousness and thoroughness. When I finally met her I was probably tongue-tied, so I was deeply flattered when she asked me to conduct interviews for her program with Daisy Bates, mentor of the Little Rock Nine; Edith Mitchell Dabbs, wife of James McBride Dabbs, who had helped me with unfailing generosity with my Penn School book; and Vivion Brewer, founder of the Women's Emergency Committee to Open Our Schools in Little Rock.

Back in Little Rock, I took over the UALR Oral History Program and used a dozen Junior League volunteers to pursue a project on "the Southern Lady in Little Rock." Those interviews have sat in a library somewhere on the campus for forty years, untouched, and they would make a great little edited volume for someone to attempt. I also taught two sections each semester of "World Civilization" (including explorations of the Gupta and the Tang, about which I knew nothing), and a section of southern history. It was a load that would have staggered Atlas, and I did nothing but work. For a while I did not notice that my colleagues in the department were cool to me; with no time on my hands and no need for caffeine, I failed to participate in what apparently were obligatory coffee breaks during which departmental dynamics were established. Finally, one of the secretaries confided to me that when I had been hired only one position had been advertised, and yet the department had hired two southern historians, both Little Rock natives from prominent families. The buzz in the department was that we had been hired only because of pressure (and perhaps monetary contributions) from our powerful friends. When word of this (not from me) got back to the other fellow they had hired, he resigned. My reaction, as always, was to work harder.

It did make sense to me now, however, why no one in the department had complimented me on having been invited to deliver my first conference paper at the Southern Historical Convention. I spoke about Penn School, and one of the commentators was very enthusiastic about my work. The other one, a black scholar I thought was "old" (he was probably about fifty), felt that my analysis of my "Yankee missionaries" was way off base, since everyone knew that the purpose of industrial education was to prepare African Americans to be skilled laborers. The audience participation was very encouraging, and I left the conference feeling affirmed and excited. One of my new colleagues had attended the session, and apparently he returned to Little Rock and told the other members of the coffee klatch that I had been creamed. Ah, well. I have always wondered what those people thought when I won an NEH grant and headed out for a year of study and research.

Another new hire in the history department was Tony Freyer, a legal historian who had studied under Stanley Katz at Indiana. Tony brought Katz to Little Rock to speak, and the older scholar asked if I would introduce him to Daisy Bates. Katz had taught the Little Rock crisis for years, and he was enchanted by Mrs. Bates. Shortly after that he invited me to speak to one of his seminars at the University of Chicago, and he treated me royally to a fine meal and a great hotel. He also suggested that I invite Tony Freyer to join me in writing a brief legal history of the Little Rock crisis, which I did.

One of my good friends from graduate school and the University of Florida, David Colburn, and I cooked up an idea at the Southern Historical Convention one November to edit a book together. We were both working on the role of the businessmen in our respective cities—Little Rock and St. Augustine, Florida. We recruited several other scholars to write about the businessmen in the cities they were studying, and we made important new friends in our field. I delivered a draft of my chapter as a conference paper at the Organization of American Historians' annual meeting in New York City, where Elliot Rudwick eviscerated me. (His close friend August Meier had not appreciated my challenging of his thesis in the Penn book, soon to be released.) Embarrassed and absolutely devastated, I returned to my hotel room and thought about jumping out the window. Thankfully, my soon-to-be new husband sent flowers, and sanity returned.

In a lovely ceremony in my parents' living room, I married the first boy who had ever kissed me when I was twelve, the first boy to say "I love you" when I was eighteen, and the first boy to break my heart, my old friend Tim Watson. He was everything my parents had hoped for, a handsome lawyer from a fine old family in the Arkansas delta. I moved with him to Newport into the home he had just built, and at the age of thirty-four we set out on an adventure. Within three years we had produced two children, Timothy and Todd, and I had produced two books.[1] Life was good. At the Southern Historical Convention in Atlanta in 1979 I was eight months pregnant, and longtime SHA secretary-treasurer Ben Wall commented in my direction, "Now that's how I like to see my women." I liked it too. I liked everything about my new life.

As soon as I found myself pregnant with my second child, I wrote Tony Freyer that we would not be able to do the little legal history we had planned. He responded that he was going to write it anyway, and he soon produced a book titled *The Little Rock Crisis*.[2] I felt that I had been scooped, and I thought my days as a historian were over. Fortunately, George Tindall came to Little Rock to speak, and he admonished me: "That's not your book! Write *your* book!" So I kept on reading and conducting interviews.

I gave a paper about Harry Ashmore at the Arkansas Historical Convention that brought me to the attention of Willard Gatewood, who had just been named a distinguished professor at the University of Arkansas. He commented to some of my former UALR colleagues in the lobby, "Gentlemen, *that's* what a conference paper is supposed to be like." I would love to know what they thought about that! I gave another paper at the Mid-America Conference on History in Springfield, Missouri. The other presenter was an impressive young woman I had never heard of before named Darlene Clark Hine. We have been friends ever since. [*Note to young scholars: keep in touch with the people you meet. Some of them will rise to the top of the profession.*]

In 1978 the fledgling Southern Association for Women Historians invited me to stand in for Jacqueline Hall and talk to their annual meeting about the Southern Oral History Program. SAWH president Martha Swain called to invite me on my wedding day, and I was in such a good mood I would have said yes to anything. The meeting was held in St. Louis concurrently with the Southern Historical Convention, and I have no idea what I said. Whatever it was, Martha liked it, and she persuaded the SAWH Executive Committee to invite me to serve as president the following year. This began a relationship that has been a major interest of mine from that day to this, as SAWH has remained very dear to my heart. Its work in mentoring younger women, as well as in recognizing and rewarding the work of women and women's history have substantively changed the climate in which women historians work in the South. Many, if not most, female historians had had experiences similar to if not worse than mine, and the field was ripe for an organization that would address these concerns, usually in a ladylike manner.

My new friend Jim Jones was a program officer at the National Endowment for the Humanities and also a native of Arkansas. He later confessed to me that he had been wishing that a good proposal to study the Little Rock crisis would come across his desk just when my application landed in his hands in 1975. He had consulted with one of his best friends, who had been one of my best friends in graduate school, and he then decided to forward my proposal to the review committee. What good fortune! They liked my proposal, and they gave me the grant. After my NEH year, Jim started putting me on panels to review other proposals, and I spent days in consultation with some of the brightest scholars in the country. On one of those trips, my little Timothy was ten months old, and all the childhood development literature I was reading told me that at ten months, babies could suffer from terrible separation anxiety. So, pregnant again, I took Timothy to Washington with me, along with his favorite babysitter, spending all of my stipend on her plane ticket. Life was getting complicated.

Back in Arkansas, I joined a group of women who were in the process of forming the Arkansas Women's History Institute (AWHI). We pulled together a talented board of scholars and laypeople who were interested in learning more about the roles of women in the development of our state. Arkansas First Lady Hillary Rodham (not yet Clinton) served on that board, though we saw little of her. This was my first opportunity to work closely with Elizabeth Payne, who had just moved to Arkansas, and who has been one of my dearest friends ever since. In 1983 the AWHI produced a book titled *"Behold! Our Works Were Good!": A Handbook of Arkansas Women's History,* which I conceptualized and edited.[3] Based on that book, we also developed a traveling exhibit, which the Arkansas Humanities Council generously managed for us. We also created the Susie Pryor Prize in Arkansas Women's History. I insisted that we make it a handsome amount, one thousand dollars, so that it would attract scholars to the study of Arkansas women; later I made the same argument when endowing the SAWH prizes. My Newport friend Kaneaster Hodges had been Governor-then-Senator David Pryor's most trusted adviser, and he raised ten thousand dollars to endow the prize—on the phone—in one afternoon.

While my boys were toddlers, I established and served as director for the Newport Montessori School. This was an ambitious undertaking that took a tremendous amount of my time, but it was one of the best things I ever did for my children, and for our community. We taught about twenty-five children a year in the little house my mother-in-law donated to us, and the products of that school have gone on to do some pretty amazing things. Maria Montessori taught that the child's intellectual foundation is laid by the age of seven, and I believed her wholeheartedly. Nonetheless, I worried every day that the Little Rock crisis was languishing on the back burner.

Longtime SAWH treasurer Judy Gentry had admonished me when I resigned my job and moved to Newport that I could sustain my relevance in the profession if I continued to publish, and I could only do that if I disciplined myself to separate my home life from my work life, or in other words, if I resisted the temptation to go put a load of clothes in the washer. That advice has served me in good stead, and I was very happy to be able to carve out a room for myself to use as my office. I took the nameplate from my UALR office and put it on the door: Elizabeth Jacoway. In the real world my name is Betsy Watson, and when people used to call and ask for Dr. Jacoway my little boys would say that no one by that name lived here. Thank goodness Dr. Jacoway *does* live here and has had the good fortune to continue to be productive.

Through the 1980s the SAWH found its footing. SHA secretary-treasurer Ben Wall had always excused his omission of women from the committees and governance of the association by explaining that women did not attend the annual business meeting, so clearly we were not interested in the workings of the organization. We made it a rule that the SAWH board would *always* attend the SHA business meeting, and soon our numbers were impressive and our interest was obvious. Years later, after women had begun to serve routinely in all aspects of SHA life, I turned to Martha Swain at one of those business meetings and said, "Where are the women?" She responded, "We won!"

In 1988 the SAWH held its first formal conference at Clemson University in South Carolina. Tim and I bundled our little boys into the car and drove over; while I feasted on the excellent papers and the hours with good friends, my men explored nearby historical sites and playgrounds. At one session I sparred a bit with Catherine Clinton, expressing the concern that we were perhaps marginalizing ourselves by focusing exclusively on women. Catherine would have none of it, saying she wasn't worried about that in the least. Of course she was right, and I needn't have worried at all. The SAWH triennial conferences have turned out to be among our most inspired efforts, along with the prizes we have endowed to encourage the study of history by and about women.

In 1979 Numan Bartley had asked me to serve on the Program Committee for the Southern Historical Association. For years after that I served on committees—Membership, Constitutional Review, Simkins Prize, and finally, Nominating. I really hoped we would nominate Anne Scott to serve as vice president and then president, but Ben Wall received the nod that year. The next year I moved up to chair the Nominating Committee, and it gave me great pleasure to be able to proffer that invitation to Anne Scott, who had done so much to pave the way for women in the southern historical profession. A few years later I served a four-year term on the Board of Editors of the *Journal of Southern History;* it was a privilege to serve with John Boles and Evelyn Nolen. And then I served a term on the Executive Council. I have always believed that service to the Southern Historical Association was a must, and I have benefited tremendously from the friendships and relationships I developed through that work.

About 1990, I learned that Wake Forest was planning a conference to honor the fiftieth anniversary of Wilbur J. Cash's *The Mind of the South.*[4] I had had a real affinity for Cash ever since a worker in the UNC bookstore had told me in my first semester in Chapel Hill that if I was going to study southern history, I needed to read Cash. As had so many before me, I found him enchanting. So I sent in my money and flew to Wake Forest for what turned out to be a rich and exciting conference. Toward the end, a woman from some department other than history walked to the microphone and heatedly chided the conference planner for not including any papers by or about women. Within a matter of weeks, Paul Escott called and invited me to submit a paper about Cash and women to be included in the conference volume, soon to be titled *W. J. Cash and the Minds of the South*. I hired someone to entertain my ten- and eleven-year-old boys for two weeks, and I sat down and wrote the paper. In retrospect, it was one of my best.[5]

As George Tindall's retirement neared, I felt the need for a *Festschrift* in his honor, to be produced by his graduate students. Most of his students agreed and wanted to participate, and four of us edited a volume titled *The Adaptable South: Essays in Honor of George Brown Tindall*.[6] About that same time Lyon College, in the nearby town of Batesville, invited me to fill in for a year for two married history professors who were taking their sabbaticals. I loved that year of teaching American and southern history, and as always, I felt tremendously energized by being back on a campus. My father died that year, after a sixteen-year death-by-inches to Parkinson's disease, as did my lifelong best friend, who had battled cancer since we were seventeen. As I neared the midcentury mark it became increasingly difficult to avoid the realization that life is fleeting. My Birthday Bunch—eleven women, most of whom started kindergarten together—became my rock as we dedicated ourselves to being a more consistent force in each other's lives. [*Note to young scholars: there are no friends like old friends. Stay in touch.*]

One of the enlightened voices during the Little Rock crisis, Vivion Lenon Brewer, died in 1982. I had interviewed her in 1976, after reading her revealing memoir at Smith College. I approached her niece (she had no children) about allowing me to edit and publish Brewer's narrative, and she agreed. I spent many hours editing, then submitted the manuscript to the University of Arkansas Press, which accepted it for publication. When it was time to sign a contract, the issue arose of what to do about royalties; I proposed that we donate them to Smith or to some other cause that Brewer supported. The family balked, and the great-niece, a lawyer, sent me a letter saying the family had decided to publish the volume privately. They incorporated all of my editing, and it appeared in print as *The Embattled Ladies of Little Rock, 1958–1963: The Struggle to Save Public Education at Central High*.[7] [*Note to young scholars: get your ducks in a row before you invest your time and energy.*]

In the mid-1990s, certain powers-that-be in Little Rock assembled a committee to plan the fortieth anniversary of the Little Rock crisis. They hoped to turn the little Mobil gas station across the street from Central High School into a museum and visitors' center. I served on that committee and was fascinated to see how many competing agendas were at work around the planning table. As it became clear to me that this was mostly aimed at providing a photo op for President Bill Clinton to open the doors into Central High for the Little Rock Nine, and for Governor Mike Huckabee to wax eloquent about how far we had come, I began to see the need for an academic conference to provide some balance for all the hoopla and rhetoric. I asked the *Arkansas Democrat-Gazette* to sponsor the conference, but they demurred, apparently leery of the leftist agenda of a group of academics. Then I asked UALR for their sponsorship; the chancellor agreed on the condition that my former chairman would be listed as a coeditor of the resulting volume, *Understanding the Little Rock Crisis: An Exercise in Remembrance and Reconciliation.*[8]

In January 1997, my seventeen-year-old Timothy popped up out of a clear blue sky in complete kidney failure. He started peritoneal dialysis immediately, which he could do at home while he slept, and we put plans in motion for me to give him one of my kidneys at the Mayo Clinic in July. All that spring I hovered, and when I wasn't hovering I was making plans for our September conference at UALR. The surgery was on July 2, forever after celebrated as our "kidney-versary." Timothy and I spent an amazingly pleasant six weeks in Minnesota while we recovered, and we entertained a revolving door of his buddies throughout that period. Elizabeth Payne came to nurse me through the surgery, good friends donated to Waiter Express so I wouldn't have to cook, and we actually had a lot of fun. Blessedly, everything went off without a hitch.

My Little Rock conference that fall made me realize that way too much time had passed without my producing the book I felt I was born to write. Plagued by insecurities and fully aware of the buzz saw I would be walking into, I planned a trip to Oxford, Mississippi, to discuss it all with Elizabeth, who was now running the honors program at Ole Miss. While she was teaching a class, Elizabeth sent me over to her church, St. Peter's Episcopal, to see the beautiful renovations they had done in their parish house. Still gnashing my teeth about whether I was adequate to the task of writing this book, I walked into the lovely, empty common room, and there it was, painted in gold lettering on the crossbeam of one wall: "Here am I, send me." I knew that message was for me. After a refreshing visit I returned to Newport, filled with a new resolve that never left me. For the next five years I worked relentlessly, organizing materials, completing interviews, sending two boys off to college, and acting like a serious scholar. My days of writing book reviews, reviewing manuscripts for presses, and delivering papers at conferences were behind me. I did continue my annual presentations about Central High to the Little Rock Chamber of Commerce Leadership Class, always in November, and my story line got better and stronger every year. I was getting ready to write.

In January 2002, the writing commenced. I had heard that Tony Freyer was writing another book about Little Rock, and I put a large banner on my wall that read, "Tony Fryer is writing!" That kept my feet to the fire. Fully aware of the pitfalls of being an "insider," and the limitations of the "fly on the wall" approach, I decided to craft my story in the way it had unfolded to me in an abundance of manuscript collections—through the eyes of one character after another. I would move my story through time chronologically, but in each chapter I would look out at the world through the eyes of a different character. Oh, it was so much fun to do! The words just flowed out of me, and the story took shape filled with all the ambiguities and contradictions I had encountered while gathering the materials over way too many years. My dear friend Jim Jones (by now the author of the much-acclaimed *Bad Blood: The Tuskegee Syphilis Experiment*) read every word, and as the chapters piled up, his criticisms and encouragement kept me on an even keel.[9] That was a happy time, as I saw the work of almost thirty years coming together in a narrative and analysis that still seemed exciting to me. I had visions of the enthusiastic reception that would greet my book, and the happiness I would feel at seeing it in print. Of course I knew that my removing of the long-accepted halo from Harry Ashmore and horns from Orval Faubus would not sit well in some quarters, but I thought that my commitment to producing a more balanced portrait of each (and of each of my other characters) would resonate with serious academics and seekers of the truth. Alas.

I completed the manuscript in early 2005 and sent it out to a few friends to critique. Three of the four gave me their enthusiastic endorsement, and I was very encouraged. I had it in a box on the backseat of my car when I went to visit my friend Sandy Hubbard at her video editing studio; I had helped her with a fine project she was producing about the Women's Emergency Committee, soon to be released as *The Giants Wore White Gloves.*[10] Sandy walked me to my car, saw the manuscript on the backseat, and exclaimed: "I didn't realize you were so close to being finished! Perhaps my brother-in-law could help you get it published." I couldn't imagine what she meant until she told me that he, Bill Whitworth, had just retired to his hometown of Little Rock after serving for two decades as editor of the *Atlantic*. Gulp! Well, yes, maybe he could help! And help me he did. He contacted his good friend Lynn Nesbit, also a Little Rock native, who ran one of the top literary agencies in New York, Janklow and Nesbit. She brought me to the attention of her superstar young colleague, Tina Bennett, who accepted me as her client. Her clients include Malcolm Gladwell (*The Tipping Point, Blink, Outliers*), Laura Hillenbrand (*Seabiscuit, Unbroken*), Eric Schlosser (*Fast Food Nation*), and others. She found me a fine editor, Bruce Nichols at Free Press, and she negotiated a contract and a six-figure advance beyond anything I had imagined. My excitement grew with each passing day, as I became convinced we were headed for the best-seller list.

My feet were effectively kept on the ground during this period by my mother's rapid decline. She lived alone in a nice retirement village in Little Rock, and as she descended into dementia it became necessary for me to make the 180-mile round-trip to supervise her caregivers three days a week. When the editing started in earnest I also had many sobering moments, as almost half of my manuscript ended up on the cutting-room floor. Those were two very painful realities, as was Bruce Nichols's insistence that we title the book *Turn Away Thy Son* in an effort to have a biblical-sounding title similar to *Roll, Jordan, Roll*, or *Carry Me Home*, two giants of the race relations genre. "Turn away thy son," from Deuteronomy 7:4, was an attempt to convey some of my thesis—that the fear of interracial sexual relationships underlay much of the racism in Little Rock and in the South—but it fell flat in that regard and just obscured the content of the book. I had titled my work "Little Rock, 1957," but I was overruled, and who was I to question my sophisticated New York editor? [*Note to young scholars: stand your ground.*]

Turn Away Thy Son: Little Rock, the Crisis That Shocked the Nation, came out to very little fanfare on January 9, 2007.[11] The person in charge of my publicity at Free Press apparently did not function. Early on the morning of January 15, I had an interview at a television station in Little Rock that I had arranged, and I returned to Mother's apartment to learn that she had just died. The book-signing party that my friends had planned for that night had to be canceled, of course. On February 14, I spoke about my book at the Clinton School before a large and receptive audience. On February 25, the *Dallas Morning News* described *Turn Away Thy Son* as "the single best history of the desegregation battle in Little Rock." On March 18, Juan Williams reviewed my book in the *Washington Post*, saying "Jacoway's version of events is a deliberate—and convincing—counter to the way the story was told by Arkansas's top journalist of the time [Harry Ashmore]." On March 18, Stan Katz (now at Princeton) reviewed *Turn Away* for the *Arkansas Democrat-Gazette*, praising the book heartily and making me look good in front of the home folks.

A very partisan, leftist weekly paper in Little Rock, *Arkansas Times*, launched a campaign against me that was an arrow straight to the heart. Furious with me for revealing some of the warts on the sainted Harry Ashmore, they equated me in one of their exposé articles with the "slime" that had formed on the walls of a jail cell. They also mocked me for suggesting that Orval Faubus was anything other than a rank opportunist and racist, which was a key part of the long-held mythology surrounding the Little Rock crisis. The facts be damned, they didn't want anyone tinkering with the "truth" as they had long understood it. I did not do a very good job of "rising above it."

It was very frustrating and nerve-wracking to have to wait for the reviews in the academic journals. I began to perceive that a profound silence had surrounded the release of my book. At the same time, my son Timothy started getting bad results from his monthly lab work, and it became clear that he was losing his (our) kidney. We began to face the prospect of having to attract another donor and endure another transplant. He was just preparing to start law school.

As I waited for the fanfare of the fiftieth-anniversary celebration at Central High, I reminded Elizabeth Payne that we had talked for a long time about starting a regional organization for women historians like the Berkshire Conference and other groups in which members encourage each other in their scholarly work, and we agreed that this was something we needed to pursue. In the spring of 2008, at the Porter Fortune Symposium at Ole Miss, we decided that the time had come to get started, and later that spring we launched the Delta Women Writers with a weekend in Oxford and papers by four presenters. That group has become increasingly important to all of us over the last ten years, and we have grown from a group of serious academics into a group of close friends. We meet twice a year, mostly in Jackson, Mississippi, and at every meeting we critique four papers that have been circulated in advance. With twenty members drawn from the Mississippi Delta area from Memphis to New Orleans, we are a diverse group in age and academic interests, and we have been tremendously successful in seeing the papers we have critiqued go on to publication in books and academic journals. [*Note to younger scholars: join a writing group.*]

In the summer of 2008, the other shoe dropped, and Timothy lost his kidney and went back on peritoneal dialysis. The hospital in Little Rock got the formula wrong, and he started having seizures. We rented a private airplane and flew him and me to Minnesota; the Mayo Clinic had been monitoring his condition ever since his transplant. Their talented medical team drew off thirty pounds of fluid in a week, and Timothy started law school, a bit late. Just at the height of the crisis my old friend David Stricklin called to say the Central Arkansas Library System had awarded me their Booker Worthen Prize for the best book in Arkansas history. This was a lovely counterbalance to the tepid review in the *Journal of Southern History*, the one journal I really cared about; reviews in the other academic journals were enthusiastic, thankfully. In the fall, the Southern Association for Women Historians awarded me their Willie Lee Rose Prize (which I had helped to establish) for the best book in southern history by a woman, which meant a great deal to me.

In the years after 2008, I pretty much stopped thinking of myself as a historian and became a gardener and, more recently, a court reporter. My book finished, I had no desire to start another one. I had two articles completed that had not made their way into the book—one about Orval Faubus's use of the National Guard and the other about Harry Ashmore—but the fire had gone out of me. A great sadness settled upon me that returned any time I thought about *Turn Away Thy Son*. It took me a long time to sort out what had happened with that book.

I had spent my adult life trying to understand the sources of racism, especially among people I knew to be good people. Following the lead of my early mentor and dear friend Joel Williamson, I argued that racism sprang from a fear of black male sexuality, which expressed itself in a determination to preserve white bloodlines by making the white woman off-limits to black men. Stating this so clearly was offensive to many people, and apparently it made many more very uncomfortable. As Melba Patillo Beals, one of the Little Rock Nine, told me at a joint book-signing event at the time, she thought my book was racist. Ah, well. As Joel used to say, you pay your money and you take your chances.

I think it is fair to suggest that the political climate of the early twenty-first century was antithetical to the tone and temper of *Turn Away Thy Son*. My goal as a historian has always been to help my readers to *understand* rather than to *judge* the past. As George Tindall instructed his graduate students in his *Ten Commandments of the Muse*, "Thou shalt not judge! Vengeance is *mine*, sayeth the Lord!" As a nation we are so caught up in angst and guilt about our treatment of our African American citizens that we are not ready to sort through the ambiguities and complexities that have always surrounded our racial attitudes. Perhaps by the time of the one-hundredth anniversary we will have made more progress in dealing with racial issues in America, but as polarized as we are now, I don't see that happening any time soon.

After 2008 I spent many hours each day searching through online programs for a second kidney for my son. He received that prize from a living donor in 2014 through an experimental program at New York Presbyterian Hospital. More transplants are in his future, probably every ten or fifteen years, but he is a healthy and successful young lawyer, as is his brother Todd. We are all grateful.

The Delta Women Writers have kept me functioning at the margins of the profession over the last ten years. In them I have found a group of congenial colleagues who all understand the special challenges that women face in trying to pursue the dream of being a serious academic. We have become a community in the fullest sense of the word; in our gatherings there is a healthy determination to be encouraging and supportive while remaining unfailingly rigorous. It is a model of scholarship and academic life I had dared to dream could be possible but had never before seen.

I am grateful for my years in the historical profession, for the experiences I have had beyond the demands of wife and mother, for the lovely people who have been my role models and friends, for the opportunities to grow and serve, and for the sheer joy of focused intellectual endeavor. It has been a glorious ride, and I wouldn't have it any other way.

NOTES

1. Elizabeth Jacoway, *Yankee Missionaries in the South: The Penn School Experiment* (Baton Rouge: Louisiana State University Press, 1980); Elizabeth Jacoway and David R. Colburn, eds., *Southern Businessmen and Desegregation* (Baton Rouge: Louisiana State University Press, 1981).

2. Tony A. Freyer, *The Little Rock Crisis: A Constitutional Interpretation* (Westport, CT: Greenwood, 1984).

3. *"Behold! Our Works Were Good!: A Handbook of Arkansas Women's History* (Little Rock: Rose, 1986).

4. Wilbur J. Cash, *The Mind of the South* (New York: Knopf, 1941).

5. Elizabeth Jacoway, "The South's Palladium: The Southern Woman and the Cash Construct," in *W. J. Cash and The Minds of the South*, ed. Paul D. Escott, 112–33 (Baton Rouge: Louisiana State University Press, 1992).

6. Elizabeth Jacoway, Dan T. Carter, Lester Lamon, and Robert C. McMath, eds. *The Adaptable South: Essays in Honor of George Brown Tindall* (Baton Rouge: Louisiana State University Press, 1991).

7. Vivion Lenon Brewer, *The Embattled Ladies of Little Rock, 1958–1963: The Struggle to Save Public Education at Central High* (Fort Bragg, CA: Lost Coast, 1997).

8. Elizabeth Jacoway and C. Fred Williams, eds., *Understanding the Little Rock Crisis: An Exercise in Remembrance and Reconciliation* (Fayetteville: University of Arkansas Press, 1999.)

9. James H. Jones, *Bad Blood: The Tuskegee Syphilis Experiment* (New York: Free Press, 1993).

10. Sandra Hubbard, prod., *The Giants Wore White Gloves: The Women's Emergency Committee to Open Our Schools* (Little Rock, AR: Morning Star Studio, 2004).

11. Elizabeth Jacoway, *Turn Away Thy Son: Little Rock, the Crisis That Shocked the Nation* (New York: Free Press, 2007).

VOCATION

EMILY CLARK

"So, you're studying to be a mummy!" Of all the many words in *Temples, Tombs and Hieroglyphs*, those tossed off by some nameless man are the ones that haunt me still. This lame pun was all that he could find to say when the book's young author revealed that she was studying for a PhD in Egyptology. A grown-up friend gave me the book in 1962, when I was eight, and it taught me two important lessons. The first was the name for what I wanted to be when I grew up: archaeologist. The second was that a woman who wanted to make a career of loving the past was going to have to contend with bad puns and worse if she didn't aim for marriage and motherhood but pursued a different calling instead. And that's what it was, as pure and simple as it was complicated and mysterious: a calling. The nuns I would write about in my first book more than forty years later call it a vocation.

My own mother was dismayed that I wanted to go to dig up things somewhere in the eastern Mediterranean. Not because she opposed the notion of putting a career first, but because loving the past was not, in her view, going to help make a better future. That was her vocation, this professor of social work who began her life on a subsistence farm in Piedmont North Carolina. Alice worked her way through college, put her two brothers through university engineering programs, and eventually, with her World War II widow's benefit, earned a master's degree in social work so that hardscrabble, bleak childhoods like hers could turn into a thing of the past. For my mother, the past was ugly and a thing to be conquered, not an object of desire.

The obituaries of the eighteenth-century nuns I studied often told of how the women faced staunch opposition from their parents, but the nuns' vocations always won in those intergenerational tussles. So did mine, but the battle lasted longer than any of theirs, and I can't blame all of it on my mother. I shared her passion for social justice, and I couldn't figure out a way for that to coexist with my love affair with the past.

The past won the first round when I began to teach myself Greek in high school in the late 1960s. There was no alternative, since the only school that offered it in my native New Orleans was the all-boys academy run by the Jesuits. Future fathers of America, lay and ordained, would enter careers for which classical languages and Homer's war stories in the *Iliad* would be a useful foundation. Why teach such things to future mummies? The parish priest of my Episcopal church was more enlightened and lent me his copy of Paine's *New Testament Greek*. Paine was a pain, but I learned my declensions and verb inflections and could soon recite and absorb the mystical opening of the Gospel According to John. Εν ἀρχῇ ἦν ὁ λόγος, καὶ ὁ λόγος ἦν πρὸς τὸν θεόν, καὶ θεὸς ἦν ὁ λόγος. In the beginning was the word, and the word was with God, and the word was God. "Archaeologist" was the word that led me toward the beautiful, difficult logos of Greek.

One of the things I delight in telling people is that I'm a high school dropout. It's cheap and childish of me, but I love the mixed expressions of surprise and confusion it provokes. It's more apt to say that I skipped my last semester of high school to start college. School was a trial, not because I didn't want to learn, but because I did. None of the succession of New Orleans public schools that I attended was truly awful, but none of them was very good, either. School was boring and uninspiring. My mother provided me with an unexpected escape hatch. I realize now that she must have seen how miserable I was and talked about it with the colleagues that she spent her days with, fellow faculty members at the Tulane School of Social Work. One of them must have reminded her that among her faculty benefits was a tuition waiver for dependents and suggested to her that Tulane just might take me for the January semester of my senior year. They did. I never donned the tacky blue mortar board of my high school for the ceremonial walk across the stage to receive my diploma. Still don't have one. I occasionally have a nightmare in which I'm required to go back to take a final semester of physical education. It was always my worst grade.

A lackluster public high school with mandatory gym class wasn't the only thing I wanted to escape. Home wasn't a happy place. My father was broken. Dazzlingly intelligent and a polymath with what must have been an eidetic memory, he read to us at bedtime from Kipling, Dickens, and Twain, never Mother Goose. He was a connoisseur of classical music and haute cuisine who played us Beethoven's symphonies on the stereo and made us crêpes suzette. Most of the time, though, he drank and he raged. He never managed to get and keep a job that could support his wife and three daughters. When I started school, my mother went to work, leaving my two younger sisters, the youngest of them seriously developmentally disabled, at home with my father. She rose before dawn every day to begin the two-hour bus journey to her job at Tulane, and returned home in the dark after another two hours of sitting on the hard, green plastic seats of the bus. She was terminally exhausted and sad but would not leave the man who married her as a war widow and gave her the children she so wanted. I left them both as soon as I could, working nights and weekends so that I could live in a dorm on Tulane's campus, a safe two-hour bus ride away from the suburban misery that continued to play out in my childhood home.

Since I wanted to be an archaeologist, not a philologist, I thought I should major in anthropology, which had classes that taught excavation and interpretation of finds. The archaeology at Tulane, though, focused on Meso-America, and I wanted to dig in Greece and Rome, so I switched to classics. I loved it. When I was offered the chance to spend my junior year abroad, the wise people in charge of placing me sent me to the University of Birmingham, which had a terrific archaeology program. There were faculty who specialized in Greek and Roman, British Neolithic (Stonehenge!), Sumerian, Babylonian, and, most fatefully, Bronze Age Aegean.

That year I was happier than I'd ever been in my short life. Now a whole ocean separated me from my unhappy family, and I was studying what I loved among people who were like me. Their politics were left wing, and they could only afford the same scruffy secondhand wardrobe that set me apart from the well-groomed coeds at Tulane. They were as likely to listen to Bach and Schubert and Mozart as to Joni Mitchell. They read Jane Austen—even the men!—but they were always ready to lay their books aside for a hike in the wild Derbyshire countryside where Mr. Darcy made his home in *Pride and Prejudice*. Most remarkably of all, I fell in love twice.

Some people fall in love all the time. At least that was the impression I got from the confessional conversations that infused the dorms at Tulane. In my first couple of years of college, I had a few short relationships with nice and interesting men. I had decidedly not fallen in love with any of them, and I came to the conclusion that it was beyond my capacities. Maybe I was too rational, I thought. Or perhaps I telegraphed my lack of interest in marrying and having children. Then again, maybe my profound insecurity and shyness kept me from letting go. There was also the risk of falling for someone who turned out to be broken, like my father. There had been sex, but definitely not love. Until Birmingham, where it crept up on me and took me by surprise. It was powerful and it was real, but it fell victim to a circumstance that I wasn't able to outsmart, something more easily conquered in movie scripts than in real life. When I returned to Birmingham after going off solo to see Greece for the first time, he broke things off. There was no room for negotiation. Fresh from the realization of one lifelong dream, the wonderful thing I'd never dared to dream made a determined exit from my life.

What looked and felt like an ending turned out to be something else. Not a confirmation that I was not the marrying kind, and not the new beginning promised by self-help books, but a passage and an affirmation. The passage was to a future that I was to shape alone, at least for a time. The affirmation was the exhilarating academic success I had that year. I took the final exams in archaeology and I got a "first," the highest result possible. The enthusiasm of my professors made it seem like archaeology wasn't just my vocation: it was my destiny. The Bronze Age Aegean archaeologist was the most enthusiastic of all. He invited me to come back to do a PhD. That year I fell I love twice, with a man and with the Minoans of Bronze Age Crete. I'd been jilted by the man, but the Minoans loved me back and held fast.

The next several years were magical. As a senior back at Tulane, I won a Thomas J. Watson Fellowship to go to Oxford, England, to study the now famous *Fresco of the Ships* that had just been unearthed from the volcanic rubble of the Greek island of Santorini. I began to work toward a PhD with the Bronze Age Aegean archaeologist. The summer after my first year, I joined the excavations conducted by the British School of Archaeology at Athens at Knossos, the capital of the Minoan civilization and home to the confusing welter of rooms and corridors that inspired the myth of the Minotaur's labyrinth. I learned to speak modern Greek, climbed the mountains that loomed over the ruins of Minoan palaces, and danced the night away to the primitive strains of the Cretan lyra.

About midway through my second season at Knossos, all the excavation teams in the vicinity were conscripted to conduct an emergency excavation of the Roman cemetery that was discovered when bulldozers began to break ground for a new medical school down the road. Ours was the only non-Greek team on the job. The motley crew of archaeologists snatched breaks together from the relentless sun in the shade of scraggly pines at the edge of the site. There we drank water by the gallon, dragged our bandanas across our sweaty brows, and swapped news of what we were finding that day in our pits. As we grew to know each other, the Greeks told us that although they were glad for our help, they thought it was time for the foreign schools of archaeology that had been excavating Crete for nearly a century to go home and dig up their own past. Greece now had its own well-trained archaeologists who were quite capable of excavating their patrimony, thank you very much. I began to realize that the Minoan past was not my future. Some other past might be, but I couldn't be part of the vestigial colonialism represented by European archaeologists who were descended from the same people who stole the marbles off the Acropolis and installed them in the British Museum.

There was also the money problem. I had borrowed money privately to support my PhD studies in England. The archaeologists that I worked with in Crete were in their thirties, and all were unemployed. They were English and had degrees from Oxford. I was an American naïf of very limited means, tenuously transplanted in England, studying for a job that didn't exist. A job that probably shouldn't exist. Late one summer, when the excavations at Knossos ended, I left Greece and archaeology for good. Much to my enduring shame, I left without a word to anyone, including my advisor.

"Now what?" I thought. My college roommate lived in Chicago—actually a nice suburb of Chicago—and she and her generous family offered me refuge. I don't think they knew that this was how I saw it, and that made their welcoming me into their home all the more remarkable. My roommate and

I eventually moved into an apartment in the city and got jobs as glorified secretaries. During my three years there, I gradually realized that if I wanted a decent job, I'd have to get an advanced degree. While I'd been studying in England, it seemed the women who came after me back home all went to law school or business school. I'd given up on an academic career, so I took the path of least resistance and decided to go home to New Orleans and get a degree in . . . social work.

The past may have been my vocation, but I needed to earn a living. Something else galvanized me. It was 1981, I was twenty-seven, and I hadn't had a date in three years. Nothing about the life I shared with my old roommate remotely resembled *Sex and the City*. I was no Samantha Jones, but I missed the company of men and couldn't figure out how to meet them in Chicago. Definitely not in the ballet classes I took twice a week. Nor at the high Anglican church I attended (across the street from the ballet studio!), where the men seemed more interested in the ostensibly celibate rector than in any of the numerous young women in the pews. The pickup bar scene terrified me, and I couldn't afford it anyway. It would be easier in New Orleans, I thought. And there I wouldn't be slipping around on ice and snow.

Back home in New Orleans, in 1981 I trained for and ran a 10K race, began a night program to obtain a master's degree in social work, had a lot of dates (most of them dreadful), and met my husband (definitely not in the dreadful category). Going home to New Orleans had been a good idea.

Social work school taught me a lot. About myself, about other people, about the slow, sometimes agonizing project of figuring out who you really are and finding a way to be true to that. Every hour was well spent, I think, but my mind was restless. I sailed through academically. I found the courses interesting but not challenging. I probably should have known this was not meant to be my path when my favorite class turned out to be statistics. Everyone else despaired. "One of the reasons I decided to go into this was because I thought there was no math!" was the student body's constant refrain. The instructor was dreadful, it's true, but it seemed to me that the math was just hard enough to make the course the challenge I'd felt missing in the other classes, and its applications to the practice of our future work was kind of cool. At some point—maybe when we were plumbing the utility of the t test—I started giving statistics tutorials during our gatherings under the oak trees between classes. Nobody failed the statistics course. I'd discovered that I was a teacher. I think it's safe to say that none of my classmates ever used the t test in their social work practice, but I did when I counted slave baptisms for my first monograph.

My dating project continued as I made my way through the social work program. It didn't go anywhere until the 1980s equivalent of Match.com intervened. Ron was the friend of friends, a married couple. I'd often go out to listen to jazz with them when I needed a break from what was becoming the chore of dating. One night they phoned me to say that they'd double-booked themselves. They'd invited a friend over for dinner and felt like they needed to ask him if he'd like to come along for the jazz. I rolled my eyes. Knowing my friends, this would be a nice, but boring guy. He *was* nice, but he wasn't boring. Our friends told us the night before our wedding that the mix-up was not an accident. Here were two unattached twenty-seven-year-olds, one a Harvard graduate, the other a veteran of Oxford. In other words, a couple of nerdy people who might get on. Ron told me that after two years with the brilliant women of Harvard, he knew he wanted to spend his life with a woman who had a brain and used it. Once he fixed on me, that was it. Affectionate, warm, and smart, he saw me as I am and loved me for it. We married in 1985, just after I finished my social work degree. He married a woman still finding her way back to her vocation. I married a man willing to stick with me on that journey.

My social work career lasted two years. I ran a program to deter child abuse and served on a slew of task forces and committees that aimed to prevent teen pregnancy, protect children, and reduce the city's drop-out rate (the irony did not escape me). I found that I was better at the policy side of things than I was at providing services to the people that the policies aimed to help. I helped draft legislation and lobbied legislators to advance the progressive politics that I believed in. I was proud of the things that I worked on during that time, but I realized pretty soon that social work was not my vocation. It was time to start looking for another job. It was 1986, and I was thirty-two.

In the mid-1980s, a job search in New Orleans still began with the classified ads in the *Times-Picayune*. One of them leapt out at me. Tulane was looking for someone to fill the position of deputy assistant to the president. The job wasn't well defined. The successful applicant had to be able to write, interact with a variety of constituencies, and generally do whatever needed doing. If the nature of the duties was ambiguous, that of the president was not. Eamon Kelly was a liberal from New York, a veteran of the Ford Foundation who was committed to making Tulane a progressive place with the explicit goal of admitting more minority students and diversifying the faculty along the same lines. Since Tulane was the city's largest private employer, his vision and leadership reverberated beyond the campus. It seemed to me that this job would give me a way to reconcile the seemingly contradictory impulses that had propelled me from one career path to another. Working for Kelly would allow me to advance social justice in a milieu thrumming with the intellectual activity I so loved.

The interview with Kelly was discouraging. He was inexpressive. There was no indication of the kind of passion that I assumed someone dedicated to social change had to have. He didn't seem very curious about me, and I felt like he was just going through the motions in the interview. There was a writing test that required me to draft a letter to a livid animal rights activist protesting Tulane's experimentation on monkeys. I wasn't keen on using animals for scientific research and struggled to write a compelling defense of the practice. I left the president's office at the end of the day convinced that I'd bombed. Maybe I had, but they offered me the job anyway.

If *West Wing* or *House of Cards* had been around, I'd have had some idea of how the vortex of activity and maneuvering into which I was thrust worked. Instead, it was baptism by fire. Everything was political. Everything took place at warp speed. Everything seemed to be life-and-death, even when it only had to do with who went onto the program and in what order for the dedication of a new building. I drafted letters for the president in response to irate parents, irate students, irate faculty members, irate alumni, and irate members of the public—such as animal rights advocates protesting primate research. I wrote speeches. I took phone calls from people inside and outside the university who were trying to get a bead on what position the president might take on some issue. I brokered peace deals between rival departments of the university and managed assorted crises and media storms.

I owe my survival in that job largely to the group of extraordinary executive women that Kelly had been smart enough to hire before I arrived. He was the first president to appoint women as vice presidents, and they and the others close to the top at Tulane made it their business to make sure that I knew that I wasn't alone and that I could do this crazy job. Each taught me and sustained me in different ways. Marcia Bromberg, the vice president for budget, phoned me on my first day and taught me how to find the secrets embedded in university spreadsheets. The head of public relations, Diana Pinckley, came to visit me bearing a copy of an article about my winning the Watson Fellowship that she had written as a young staff-writer years before. She was my guide through every one of the numerous crises that brought a clamoring press corps to our doorstep. In all, there were about a half-dozen women in the executive, and they—we—were a force to be reckoned with.

The women were my mentors and companions. Kelly was the master to whom I was apprenticed. I watched him work, and I learned. He never shot from the hip, he never raised his voice, he returned every phone call, and never put something off because it was unpleasant. He was one of the most politically astute people I've ever known, surveying the lay of the land and correctly predicting the outcome of myriad disputes and controversies among the university's bewilderingly diverse constituencies. There was, though, one group that stumped him: the alumnae of Newcomb College, the women's coordinate college of Tulane. Those women presented him with one of the biggest crises of his career, and they gave me the biggest opportunity of mine.

Newcomb was founded in 1886 on the model of Radcliffe and Barnard, a women's college within a research university that otherwise admitted only men. It was the first such institution in the South, and its alumnae were proud of that history and of the superb education they had received. When the college celebrated its centennial in 1986, alumnae took a renewed interest in their alma mater, and they didn't like what they saw. They believed that the autonomy and special quality of the college had been eroded. It no longer had its own classes or faculty. Its current students didn't seem to understand that they were in a college that was distinct from that attended by male undergraduates. Worst of all, the university had spent all of the money given by Josephine Louise Newcomb to found the college to pay down a deficit in the 1960s, a financial crisis that was in no small part generated by the university's expensive, unimpressive football program. Now the university was contemplating a streamlined, more cost-efficient organizational structure that would do away with the practice of having separate academic deans for

Newcomb College and the College of Arts and Sciences, the undergraduate college for Tulane men. It was a bridge too far for Newcomb alumnae. They began an energetic, highly public protest.

The alumnae pummeled the president and board with angry letters, staged a media campaign, and filed a lawsuit against the university for spending Mrs. Newcomb's endowment. They held candlelight vigils on the college's quadrangle and organized a separate alumnae fundraising operation, diverting money away from Tulane's own development campaign. Kelly met with leaders of the Newcomb alumnae and deployed the low-key, rational political skills that had worked so well for him over the course of his presidency. At the end of every meeting, he thought he'd addressed their concerns and won their support. Then there would be another candlelight vigil.

Kelly called me into his office on the eve of a meeting with a particularly powerful triad of Newcomb alumnae, Betty Carter, the widow of the pioneering Mississippi journalist Hodding Carter; Rosa Keller, heiress to the fortune of the Coca-Cola bottling company in New Orleans; and Lindy Boggs, at the time one of the most powerful and respected members of Congress. "I want you to sit in on this meeting," he told me. "At the end of meetings with alumnae, I think that everything went well. Then there's another vigil or letter to the editor. It doesn't make sense."

The next day, the three women were ushered into Kelly's office, where they took their seats on its chairs and sofas, crossed their ankles, sipped the coffee they were offered, and listened politely to what he had to say. Then they responded, their ankles still crossed, their heads tilted, gently smiling, explaining in the nicest possible way that the rather vague explanations and assurances he was offering would not palliate the alumnae. When he closed the door behind them and said to me, "I think that went well," I realized that he literally couldn't translate what the women had said. The crossed ankles and smiles scrambled the message. "No," I told him, "that didn't go well at all. They are angry, and they left you with a warning that the protests would continue if you can't address the alumnae's concerns more convincingly than you have." He issued no new statements. There was another candlelight vigil a few days later.

Over the next few months, Kelly gave me a new set of responsibilities. I replaced the man with a PhD in English hired to write the annual president's report; more importantly, I drafted an essay on the evolution of Newcomb since its founding. I realized that every woman who graduated from the college attended a different Newcomb. It had changed over time, from a college founded explicitly for white women to one that embraced all women, and from a place that sheltered women from direct competition with men to one that taught them to engage men as equals. It was the first piece of historical writing I'd ever done, though I didn't know that's what it was until much later.

At the same time, I was appointed to be the liaison between the president, board, faculty, and alumni on what had now officially become the "Newcomb crisis," and I staffed the board committee charged with crafting a solution. In the weeks leading up to the marathon board meeting that would wrestle the issue to the ground, I worked with the chair of the board committee to draft a series of resolutions that offered alumnae concrete guarantees about matters related to college finances, administrative structures, and traditions. The board met in executive session to discuss the resolutions for a full day. They tweaked a few things. In the early evening, four male board members came to a room in the library, where the secretary who staffed board meetings and I waited to meet with them to finalize the draft. They spent an hour or so giving us the gist of what they wanted added or deleted, then left to go to dinner at the president's palatial home. None of them asked the secretary and me if we might like something to eat. The two of us worked until midnight without a break. The board members returned from their dinner, well-watered and -fed, signed off on the draft, and left us as the library turned out the lights.

After the resolution of the Newcomb crisis, I was promoted to be vice president and assistant to the president, a position that most places call chief of staff. Three years after that I was made vice president of public affairs. I was thirty-six years old. In 1993, after six years in Tulane's executive administration, I had another of my realizations that I wasn't in the right job. From the outside, it seemed obvious to many that I was doing what I was meant to do. I kept getting promoted, after all. What made me happy at Tulane, though, wasn't the money and power that came with being a vice president. It was being around people engaged in creating and passing on knowledge. Gradually, insistently, my vocation came out of hibernation. When the president asked me to coordinate a massive restructuring of the university, I agreed to undertake a task destined to make me the most unpopular person on campus on one condition: that he allow me to take the voluntary separation package we planned to offer to thin the ranks of administration on terms that would allow me to spend five years earning a PhD in history.

I was as in love with the past as ever, and as I got to know some of the faculty at Tulane, I began to understand that historians, especially those who work on America's past, play a critical role in working toward social justice. The historian Eric Foner once said, "A new future requires a new past."[1] Becoming a historian would, I saw, be a way to reconcile my vocation and my social conscience. It had taken decades for me to figure it out, and it would take another half decade before I could even attempt to find a job. It was a big gamble, but I had to try.

There was no question that it would have to be at Tulane. I was approaching forty. My husband had a good job in New Orleans. I'd never taken a history course in my life, but the department at Tulane might be willing to take me. It turned out that they were, provisionally, and in the fall of 1993 I took my first history classes. It was a lot harder than I thought it would be. I read until my eyes itched. I wrote until my brain clouded over. I cringed over my inarticulate, amateurish contributions to discussion as I left the seminar room. Everybody else seemed so much smarter, so much more suited, so much more certain. But I knew that I was home when the formidable early American historian Sylvia Frey agreed to take me as her advisee midway through my first year. It was going to be hard, but if she thought I could do this, then I could.

Sylvia terrified me into learning how to be a historian. There was no way I was going to disappoint this brilliant, demanding, infinitely generous mentor. She had far better things to do with her time than waste it on someone who wasn't going give it everything she had. So, I pushed through my doubt and exhaustion and began to find my way. Sylvia was there for me at every turn.

It's probably not often that a dissertation topic is inspired by a scowl, but mine was. When I told Sylvia that I was interested in doing something on religion and women in the colonial period, she said: "Good luck. The sources are pretty thin."

"But, Puritan women wrote a lot," I ventured. She scowled: "There's enough out there on Puritan women." Desperation surged through me and drove me to blurt out something that had just popped into my head: "What about the Ursuline nuns in colonial New Orleans? They must have produced sources."

Sylvia tilted her head to one side. "That could be interesting," she conceded. "Do you know French?" "Yes," I answered, thankful that the New Orleans public school system had at least given me that. "Well, go see if there's enough out there for a dissertation."

There was enough there, a whole archive full of manuscript records produced by eighteenth-century women. The first thing that I looked at was the register of an association of laywomen founded under the nuns' aegis in 1730. More than eighty women, socially and racially diverse, joined it. They evangelized the enslaved. There was nothing like them in Puritan New England, or in any of the thirteen British mainland colonies that preoccupied most early American historians. That was both scary and freeing. I wrote my master's thesis on them. At the end of my defense, after telling me that I'd passed, Sylvia said, "The committee members agree that you should revise it into an article and submit it to the *William and Mary Quarterly.*"

Sylvia never thought small, but this was way beyond anything I wanted to attempt. On the other hand, I didn't dare reject the task she'd set me. When the revisions were done, I submitted the manuscript to the *Quarterly,* which was fortuitously putting together a special volume on religion in early America. Jon Butler, a giant in the field who taught at Yale, was guest editor. One afternoon my phone rang. It was Professor Butler. He told me that he liked my article and then mused on a bit. I couldn't tell where the conversation was going, so I ventured, "Does this mean that you want to publish it?" "Oh, yes, we most certainly do!" he answered in his kind, sincere Minnesota voice. "We'll be sending you some suggestions for revisions."

Professor Butler made the revisions sound like nothing much. In fact, the suggestions that I received from the legendary regular editor of the *Quarterly,* Mike McGiffert, were daunting and discouraging. McGiffert, a scholar of Puritanism, insisted that I connect my article on a group of Catholic women who evangelized the enslaved to . . . Puritan women! The scholarly discourse about women and religion in early America had been almost exclusively about Puritans, so, he told me, I had to relate what my women did to what scholars thought about what Puritan women did. Halfway through, I told McGiffert that I just couldn't do it. Neither he nor Jon Butler would let me off the hook, though. Neither would Sylvia, despite the fact that Puritan women had wormed their way into what would be my first publication.

When the page proofs arrived, I got cold feet and nearly pulled the article. It would be out there for the world to see and judge, and I was absolutely sure that everyone would find it a feeble piece of scholarship. It would reveal in no uncertain terms the folly of my thinking I could actually have a career as a historian. By this time, though, I had not only Sylvia, but Jon Butler pulling me along. I let the article go to press.[2]

Meanwhile, there were comps to take. I spent some time studying with other graduate students, a group of female Americanists and a male Latin Americanist. The women were convinced that our examiners were out to fail us, or at least make it as difficult as they possibly could. I didn't think that was the case, but the Latin Americanist did something that revealed that there were, indeed, some men who did not particularly like sharing the profession with women.

The Latin Americanist and I were taking a killer of a course on historical theory the semester before comps. Each week we explored a different approach. There were the structuralists and poststructuralists, the psychohistorians, the proponents of the linguistic turn, the unreconstructed narrativists and political historians, and the acolytes of Foucault, Derrida, Barthes, and Habermas. We had to read a common book that exemplified the approach of the week and choose an additional book that we hadn't read from a list on the syllabus. That was sometimes a challenge for me because I'd been reading widely and wildly since I'd begun graduate school to make up for my lack of historical training. Some weeks, the instructor had to come up with a book for me that hadn't made it to the list.

Over a lunchtime meeting to draw up a bibliography for one section of the comps, the Latin Americanist said to me, "You know, a couple of people in the class think you're a nut cracker." "Excuse me?" I replied. "You know, they're intimidated when you act like you've actually read all of those books."

"I have read all of those books," I said coldly. "And if you think you're going to intimidate me into acting like I haven't to make some of the men in the class more comfortable, you're wrong. Excuse me," I said, rising to leave, "I have better things to do right now than sit here with you."

The comps were predictably awful, but I passed. Grinding out a dissertation was predictably awful, but I did it. They were a piece of cake compared with looking for a job in 1998 at the age of forty-four as an about-to-be newly minted PhD. Nobody seemed very interested in me at the AHA cattle call. I had a couple of interviews in the corral, the big ballroom full of booths, the job fair version of speed dating. Nobody invited me to one of those coveted interviews in a hotel suite. Nobody called me back to invite me to a campus interview. So much for having an article published by the *William and Mary Quarterly* when I was a master's student. I watched younger graduate students without a publication to their names whiz past me to multiple interviews with big-name schools.

A couple of months before graduation, Jon Sensbach, a wonderful historian then at the University of Southern Mississippi in Hattiesburg, wrote to say that he'd accepted a job at the University of Florida. Would I consider applying for the tenure-track job he was vacating? Hattiesburg was a two-hour drive from New Orleans. I could commute. I applied and got the job.

The day after I accepted the offer from Southern Mississippi, the Mellon Professor of American History at the University of Cambridge, Tony Badger, sent me an email saying that I'd been awarded the Mellon Postdoctoral Fellowship there. I'd met Tony a couple of years before, when he and Sylvia collaborated on a series of conferences held alternately in New Orleans and Cambridge. I'd given a paper at one of them, coordinated the New Orleans conference, and had run into him at a few academic meetings since. It was a long shot, but I thought I might as well apply for the postdoc in his department. The kind people at Southern Mississippi told me they'd hold the job for me during the two-year Cambridge fellowship. So off I went, back to England.

Newnham College in Cambridge offered me a fellowship to go with the postdoc. It was at the all-female Newnham that Virginia Wolfe delivered the lectures that would become her famous essay "A Room of One's Own." Newnham is now the only Cambridge college whose faculty and students remain all female. The college offered me a room of my own, literally, in the form of a rent-free apartment, and figuratively, by supplying me with the support and stimulation of a collection of stunningly brilliant women. Other Cambridge colleges celebrate the kings and bishops who passed through their doors. Newnham claims Rosalind Franklin, the "dark lady of DNA," and the poet Sylvia Plath. Before too long, I suspect the name of Onora O'Neill, who won the $1 million Berggruen Prize for Philosophy in 2017 for her work on ethics, will be added to Newnham's pantheon. She was head of Newnham when I was there, a stunning example of an academic making a difference in the world. Newnham colleague Jean Gooder taught Emma Thompson her Shakespeare, Gillian Sutherland presided with grace and astonishing erudition over the college's cadre of budding women historians, and Mary Beard made classics into fuel for stratospheric television ratings on the BBC. Every one of my Newnham colleagues taught me and inspired me. The history department at Cambridge, meanwhile, with its two hundred–plus faculty, was an exciting, if intimidating, idea factory. There, the irrepressible Betty Wood joined Tony Badger to mentor me and make me welcome in the rarified world of Cambridge. The students whom I taught were exponentially more intelligent and cultivated than I was, but I found that the knack for teaching that I'd discovered in social work school transferred pretty well. At the end of my first year in Cambridge, several of my students took firsts in their final exams, and I danced a little jig in the privacy of my office.

Ron managed to find a job in Cambridge raising money for one of the colleges, and we spent a wonderful two years together in England. To my great relief, he loved the country and the university as much as I did—maybe more than I did. Among the fellows at his college was Stephen Hawking, and Ron would come home to report the witticisms that emitted from his electronic voice. My favorite was his response to someone asking whether or not Al Gore would make as good a president as Bill Clinton. Hawking had met both. His response was a pithy: "Clinton is smarter than Gore."

It was time to come home in 2000. After a year at Southern Mississippi, a headhunter who knew me from my days as a vice president at Tulane talked me into being considered for a post as a vice president at Lewis & Clark College in Portland, Oregon. I went up for a couple of interviews, and, once the president arranged for me to have an appointment in the departments of history and religious studies, I agreed, reluctantly, to go back into the administrative ranks. My mother had died, and my father was soon to follow. With a developmentally disabled sister to support, I needed to make money, and this was a way to do it.

It was a big mistake. I hated being back in administrative harness, and I found that I was not suited to teaching at a liberal arts college. There was no research library within a hundred miles. I was too far away from family, friends, and my archives. My colleagues loved the vibe of a liberal arts college and the constant presence of students in their offices. I didn't. I wanted to spend my days in the archives and write. After a couple of years, I went on the job market. Again.

It was ever so slightly easier this time. My scholarship was starting to get noticed. There was another *William and Mary Quarterly* article, coauthored with Virginia Gould, that revealed that the Catholic church of early New Orleans grew and thrived because of the dedication and activism of enslaved and free women of African descent. My first monograph had been provisionally accepted by the Omohundro Institute of Early American History and Culture at William & Mary. If you are an early Americanist and a first-time author, this press is about as good as it gets. So, I got interviews. Campus interviews. At the end of it, I had two job offers. One of them was from Tulane. I was going home.

The offer came in the spring of 2005, and Ron and I moved in midsummer, just in time for Hurricane Katrina. The next two years were miserable. My hometown was destroyed. My disabled sister was flooded out of her subsidized apartment and came to live with Ron and me, straining our marriage and our sanity. At Tulane, we were all teaching overloads and huge classes and didn't get raises for years. I knew that I was doing what I was meant to do, where I was meant to do it, but I was so exhausted and dispirited that I felt myself sinking into despair. The workload and emotional burdens made it difficult to even contemplate going to conferences to maintain my networks and visibility. I felt as though I was slipping into oblivion.

Inexplicably, when I look at my CV, the years immediately following 2005 reveal that I was not slipping into oblivion, at least as far as my public, published self was concerned. In the four years after Katrina struck, two books and five articles appeared. Collectively, this work asserted the importance of women, black and white, to the making of colonial New Orleans. Only time will tell if it, and what I've written since, will make a difference to the arc of social justice. But I've labored now for nearly a quarter century in the archives of New Orleans, France, Spain, and Africa to excavate the lives of women and free and enslaved people of African descent so that they can be written into the history from which they'd been excluded. That's what I was called to do, I realize now. Not just to love the past, but to love these forgotten historical actors into popular consciousness. The nation's slow response in the aftermath of Katrina to the plight of the people descended from those early New Orleanians seemed only to make what I was trying to do more imperative. There was no longer any doubt or restlessness. I'd found my professional home. Historians don't take final vows like nuns, but I knew now that my commitment to my vocation was forever.

During those bleak post-Katrina years, I mostly kept my nose to the grindstone and skipped the professional conferences that had once structured my academic year. The one meeting that I did try to get to each year was the Southern Historical Association (SHA). I'd given my very first academic paper there, and, though I'm only a southern historian if you squint and let your eyes go out of focus, I loved the people I met at the SHA. Especially the women. There was Elizabeth Payne, who had come to speak about the redoubtable Myrtle Lawrence of the Southern Tenant Farmers Union to the first seminar I ever took as graduate student. Elizabeth was beautiful, brilliant, imaginative, warm, and I loved her as soon as I met her, though I felt she occupied an orbit in a galaxy far beyond my own. I think that perhaps it was Elizabeth who told Betsy Jacoway about me. Betsy invited me to breakfast at an SHA meeting—I can't recall exactly when—and I remember being starstruck by her poise and graceful intelligence. When Elizabeth and Betsy founded a small writing group of women historians a few years later, they asked me to join. I had no idea what it would be like, or what in the world I had to offer this group of historians working mostly on the nineteenth- and twentieth-century South, but I wasn't going to pass up the opportunity to be with this pair of women and the others they invited to join them in the experiment.

From the beginning, the group that eventually adopted the name Delta Women Writers was special. They read and gave me advice about the workshop paper that evolved into my second monograph, *The Strange History of the American Quadroon*. It wasn't the book that I'd planned to write, but the Deltas convinced me that it was the book that I needed to write. So I did. As important as the thoughtful, helpful—and sometimes maddening—feedback on the various papers that the Deltas workshopped for me over the years was, the real gift of the group was in its diversity and the deep camaraderie that evolved among the members. There were young scholars just starting their first jobs, writing their first articles, figuring out what their first books would be. There were old hands like Sheila Skemp and Martha Swain who had encyclopedic historiographical chops and lengthy publication lists to match. There were historians from small liberal arts colleges, big research universities, teaching universities located far from the academic centers of gravity of the Northeast, Midwest, and West Coast, independent scholars, and museum professionals. We learned about each other's intellectual communities and about each other's intellectual isolation. Nobody's pond is ever the ideal pond, we discovered. Most important of all, we learned to trust across the lines of race and class and academic hierarchies that would otherwise have separated us.

Some members of the group think of it as a sisterhood. I came of age in the early 1970s at a posh private university ruled by Greek life, a poor girl with a bad wardrobe, always on the outside looking in. I don't like sororities. The Delta Women Writers are family, though, and like all good family, they celebrate their members' victories, salve their defeats, defy their setbacks, affirm each other's worth. Like all families, too, there is the irritation, the conflict, the impatience that is inevitable whenever more than three or four are gathered together. The bonds of affection and trust, though, just seem to grow stronger. So does the work of those who've come together to make sure that women who have fallen in love with history can follow their vocation, even if it means cracking some nuts along the way.

NOTES

1. Eric Foner, *Who Owns History?* (New York: Hill and Wang, 2002), 77.

2. Emily Clark, "'By All the Conduct of Their Lives': A Laywomen's Confraternity in New Orleans, 1730–1744," *William and Mary Quarterly*, 3d ser., 54, no. 4 (October 1997): 769–94.

CREATING MYSELF

PAMELA TYLER

The philosopher and orator Cicero once observed that not to know what happened before one was born meant remaining a child forever. Thus, if you judge me by the old Roman's standard, I was a child only briefly. As an eager youngster, I began learning about the past, through our family's oral tradition of stories told and told again. In hindsight, however, I see that, for years, I was actually more at home in the past than in the present, because I had not created the self that I was meant to be.

But first, the past. In the fashion of many southern families, mine frequently visited graveyards, and our graveyards were scattered all over the county. It was understood that we must keep the family plots in good order, pull weeds, scrub the marble slabs under which departed ancestors slumbered, and leave fresh flowers, not purchased horticulture but blossoms gathered from our own flower beds. The graveyard outings were not so clannish as to be limited to our own kin. Several times a year, a typical Sunday afternoon found me tramping with elders from one cemetery lot to another (in my hometown, Americus, Georgia, or in nearby Plains, or in country churchyards) as my father, mother, or grandmother paused to recall a detail about the dead of someone else's family. I noted the dates on the headstones and waited for the stories to begin. This one had been bad to drink; that one had a heart of gold. This one had died of pneumonia and that one in childbirth. I recall vividly the tale of one who died because he had flung himself in panic from the cab of a speeding truck loaded with logs. When the Model T's notoriously unreliable brakes failed just as it began its descent down a steep hill, the man had feared that the vehicle, gathering speed, would surely overturn when it reached the road's sharp curve at the bottom of the hill, and so he jumped to save his life. The driver, who did not jump, lived to tell the tale; the terrified passenger who jumped died of his injuries. Listening to my elders remember how his widow had coped after his untimely death, I learned about how hard life had been in the year 1931. Gradually, I learned about other years, too. To a child, none of this learning seemed like "history," of course, only my family remembering. The stories were marvels of narrative, never rushing to the end but building, building, with telling details and imagined dialogue. Alas, history in the schoolroom was no such thing. It seemed to be only a dreary line-up of facts to memorize because teachers seldom brought the past to life as my storytelling kin did.

Upon becoming a reader, I found excitement between the covers of books: first, the little blue biographies shelved in my elementary school classrooms, later in a handful of novels which I read repeatedly. I discovered a particular affinity for Amelia Earhart, then was entranced by the heroics of Jo March and Nancy Drew, later by the arcane knowledge and derring-do of Sherlock Holmes and the Count of Monte Cristo, and later still by that treacherous and magnetic heroine Scarlett O'Hara.

Looking back, I see that the individuals who won my admiration displayed courage. My parents, by injunction and by their excellent example, had instilled in me the importance of fair play, courtesy, diligence, and consideration for others, which traits I acquired, I hope to their satisfaction. But courage—ah, courage was the virtue I longed to display. Earning Girl Scout badges, I envisioned myself tying a tourniquet to save a snakebite victim. Through Junior and then Senior Lifesaving, I dreamed of rescuing a drowning swimmer. Volunteering as a candy striper, I saw myself intervening with skill in a medical emergency. But when I once created an episode which called for moral courage, I mustered a flicker but could not sustain it. Mae Julia Griffin, who cooked for our family, was a special friend to me all one summer; I enjoyed hearing her stories about her family as she fried chicken and made blackberry pie for dinner, the large midday meal always served at one o'clock. I wanted Mae to eat with us instead of waiting to have her food in the kitchen after we finished, and when told that that would be inappropriate (because she worked for us and was not family, my parents said), I announced righteously that I would wait and eat my meal with her. But because I also wanted my biscuits hot enough to melt butter, not served stone cold after my folks had eaten, and because I missed my parents' company and conversation at dinnertime, that bit of courage lasted less than a week. My disquietude was soon forgotten, and my stand against injustice was short-lived; like most southern children, I had learned a lesson of racial etiquette. There wasn't even a whimper.

Writing was always a pleasure. I served as editor of our high school newspaper, the *Paw Print*, cranking out some standard reportage, some stuffy editorials, and a few genuinely funny columns. I also enjoyed writing my first research paper, for a high school English class, on the subject of my choice, John Dillinger. I loved the challenge of digging up facts and stitching them together to make a coherent narrative. At my request, the local Carnegie library ordered back issues of *Liberty* and *Time* for me, and I landed in heaven—pages and pages of the real past just as it was, no filter of a history book standing between 1934 and me. I read each issue cover to cover, gaining "deep background" as I tried to understand Dillinger's time. This marked my first experience with primary sources.

College for me represented no drastic change from high school. I attended Georgia Southwestern College, an undistinguished branch of the University of Georgia system then expanding its enrollment exponentially because of the Vietnam War's effect on young men, great numbers of whom sagely discovered a thirst for higher education in the late 1960s. I continued to live at home. My parents had intended that I spend two inexpensive years at Southwestern and then transfer to an out-of-town institution to complete my degree, but when my third year neared, I felt no desire to move. Observing that the classes were not exactly taxing me, I had begun taking course overloads early on. By this time, I was studying history, English, and political science, making dean's list and racking up sufficient credit hours to graduate a year early. I had no particular career goals that I can recall.

As in high school, history at Southwestern was largely a feat of memorization. History instructors assigned a textbook and stuck to it. Most lectured drily and tested for retention of their lectures' content. I could give them what they seemed to want, but it was only in reading the works of authors like Shakespeare, Fitzgerald, and Twain that I found genuine pleasure. Lost in the worlds of Othello, Tom and Daisy Buchanan, and Huck Finn, I began to acquire tools for examining and understanding the human condition. I learned also to appreciate language well used.

In the fall of 1970, sixteen years after the *Brown v. Board of Education* ruling, the public schools of Albany, Georgia, prepared for full desegregation. Armed with a bachelor's degree in history and certified as a teacher of secondary social studies in the State of Georgia, thanks to some of the dullest and most useless education courses ever devised, I uprooted myself and traveled the grand distance of forty miles to become a green teacher in a mostly black world. I took a position teaching U.S. history to seventh-graders at previously segregated Southside Junior High, which had served only an African American population until that year. The development of "segregation academies" and the reality of white flight meant that, of a total of 150 students assigned to me (five classes of 30 students), I taught about 140 African American students and perhaps 10 whites that first year.

While mine was not a "Conrack" experience to compare with Pat Conroy's, the cliché "I learned as much from them as they did from me" is appropriate here. Unlike the several young "Yankee" teachers, wives of military guys stationed at one of the two bases in Albany, I could easily understand the broad dialect of our students; I could even do simultaneous translations for my baffled midwestern colleagues. It was the content of the students' speech that was new to me. In disputes with each other, twelve-year-old boys spoke a swaggering, hypermasculine patter, learned from older adolescents or men in their community ("*Boy? Who you callin' boy? I got chirren older than you!*") They talked of drinking liquor and being "roguish." Fights constantly erupted because someone was "*talkin' 'bout my mama.*" Many had tough lives and few material resources. I learned to expect 100 percent attendance on very cold days (because the schoolhouse was probably warmer than home) but abysmal turnout on days when it rained. I can still remember the selfish relief that would flood over me when I waked to hear a downpour on my roof on a school-day morning; the rain predicted high absenteeism and guaranteed an easier day for me.

My students were playful and curious and mostly responsive to what I was trying to do. But, in addition to teaching confidently about General Washington and the Redcoats, the Industrial Revolution, and the abolition of slavery,

I was expected to impart lessons in *science*. I have vague and unhappy memories of hours spent cutting out letters for a bulletin board featuring vegetables and vitamins, memories of trying to teach the workings of an internal combustion engine, memories of being utterly not up to the task of explaining the mysteries of the universe. After I painstakingly detailed a sketch of the solar system on the chalkboard, in response to my statement that the universe was eternally in motion, a genuinely curious boy had asked, sincerely, "*What it run on? Gas?*" I could not explain coherently what made the planets keep moving.

In my free time, I was reading widely in the popular literature of the day, feeding a taste for biography. I recall devouring T. Harry Williams's *Huey Long* and James MacGregor Burns's *Roosevelt: Soldier of Freedom*, both of them just out that year. During those first months as a challenged schoolteacher, I thirsted for more learning. I registered for the GRE, thinking vaguely that a master's program would offer me the chance to read more good books. Moreover, an MA would boost me into a higher pay bracket. I did not know that one "prepped" for this exam and, beyond clearing a Saturday on my calendar, I did nothing to prepare. Somehow, my scores sufficed to get me into the graduate program at the University of Georgia. In the summer of 1971, I headed off to Athens.

I did two summers at Georgia, feeling envious as I listened to other graduate students discourse at length about our assigned books. Nothing in my educational background had readied me for identifying arguments or understanding historiography. How did they speak so fluently in this new language? I read my pages, wrote my papers, and hung on for dear life. To my surprise, the experience turned out just fine.

I do not believe that I really expected to persevere long enough to obtain an MA. I think I saw summer coursework at the University of Georgia as intellectual nourishment that could tide me over the starvation times of the school year, when I would again be consigned to teaching history and science to seventh-graders (at least until I married, as I assumed I would). When news came that nearby Georgia Southwestern College was instituting an MEd program, I immediately enrolled there. Transferring the credits from Georgia, carrying summer loads, and taking a few night courses while I continued to teach allowed me to earn my degree in 1975. As with my prior experience at Southwestern, I found nothing that particularly challenged or inspired me.

In my eyes, the education degree was only a credential that allowed me to earn more as a teacher—ironically, more than a mere MA in my discipline would have done. In a choice that clearly advertised my priorities, I skipped commencement to play golf.

Meanwhile, I had received a coveted reassignment to a position at Westover, then considered the most academically rigorous of Albany's four public high schools. Teaching U.S. history and government to juniors and seniors turned out to be fun, and I made an important discovery: I was pretty good at this. Classroom management, that art of maintaining good order and keeping students on task, somehow came easily, so for the most part, I avoided the dreaded discipline problems that plagued many teachers. In an effort to enrich the material afforded my students in the available textbooks, I read constantly in a wide variety of sources, and frequently, I read aloud in class—speeches, diary entries, letters, passages from autobiographies and novels. Students responded encouragingly, and robust discussions ensued. Suddenly, these classes seemed alive and meaningful to me.

At Westover, I formed an important friendship with a veteran English teacher whose classroom adjoined mine. Gordon Wright was a gifted soul who possessed a dynamic personality, a wealth of knowledge, and a passion for connecting with students. Good teaching is highly idiosyncratic; one cannot learn to be a good teacher merely by watching a master whose talents may be vastly different from one's own. But seeing Gordon's magnetic interactions with students helped me. Reasoning that I already commanded my students' respect, I moved toward incorporating lighter moments at the start or end of class, leading to interludes of laughter. Hearing one student perform a pitch-perfect imitation of Lily Tomlin's then-popular character Edith Ann, I began calling Edith Ann's name when I called roll. This student then responded in the character of that precocious five-year-old, and we bantered impromptu. After I mentioned my love of old music, radio, and classic movies, a pair of students memorized the well-known Abbott and Costello routine and performed "Who's on First" for their delighted teacher and classmates. Another fellow matched them by nailing a Groucho Marx monologue from *Animal Crackers* as a goofy prologue to class one morning. We laughed a lot.

In addition to teaching 150 students every day, I, in partnership with my friend Gordon, frequently directed plays and staged pageants, oversaw decorating for the all-important homecoming and junior-senior dances, and chaperoned students on trips. These time-consuming activities cemented our standing in the eyes of most students and were immensely valuable to the school, but we were never compensated with so much as one nickel. My basic teaching duties entailed being on campus for a regular forty-hour week, while the grading, prepping, and reading that I put into my teaching ate up more time every week. The extracurriculars were consuming many nights and parts of weekends. Athletic coaches earned 10 percent of their base salary for each interscholastic sport in which they were involved, whether their teams excelled or failed. Our productions grew more popular each year, selling out the auditorium where we staged them, but our excellence was expected to be its own reward.

Finally, I had an epiphany which was this: *You cannot go on doing this when you are forty years old.* The energy, commitment, and time I was putting into my job were simply unsustainable. Did I enjoy it? Emphatically yes. Could I continue to perform it in this way? Emphatically no. Moreover, my take-home pay, even with an MEd and nine years of experience, was paltry. These considerations led me to take the next step.

It was time for graduate school again, only this time with a clear goal: get serious, obtain a PhD and teach in college. Until this point my graduate work had been deeply unserious. Again my naiveté shows itself. I wrote for information about four universities, Duke, Emory, Vanderbilt, and Tulane, chosen solely because they were in the South. I did not study catalogues. I gave no thought to scholars who might teach me or what the focus of my studies might be. When a professor from Georgia Southwestern urged me, with utterly unmerited optimism, to apply to Harvard, Yale, and Princeton, I had scoffed, "*Why do people think the sun rises and sets on the Northeast?*" The bravado was an obvious cover for the insecurity I felt when I thought of going among the Yankees in their ivy-covered sanctuaries. I, who had scarcely left the provincial confines of southwest Georgia (except for summer interludes at camp in the north Georgia mountains and some larking about in Europe), had never interacted with people who were *not like me*. Didn't I know full well that Yankees were different? In the depths of my secret southern heart was the assumption that smart Yankees would be really, really different and that the difference would be all to my disadvantage.

When Tulane University, God bless that institution, came through with a tuition waiver and a living stipend, I moved to New Orleans. I rented an apartment in a once-grand Garden District house, stocked it with a small U-Haul's worth of furnishings, and gradually became acquainted with my neighbors in that crumbling firetrap. Like me, they were unmarried; among them were an attorney, a real estate agent, an engineer, a merchant sailor, and a compulsive elderly hoarder. (I called him "the paper man," because my one glimpse through his open door had revealed newspapers and magazines stacked shoulder high, leaving him only a canyon-like path threading through that combustible mass.) They were not southern; they marveled at my deeply southern pronunciations, which I had not known to be unusual to anyone's ear. (They noted that I was capable of pronouncing an "R" only if it came at the start of a word. Thus I said "Reagan," but also "Cahta.") These generous nonsouthern acquaintances began the work of helping me decode the emphatically nonsouthern city where I had landed.

At this point, reader, I fell in love.

The object of my affections was the city herself. New Orleans completely dazzled me, and I fell hard for her quirky charms. Fun, nonserious dating with a variety of young men introduced me to one appealing aspect after another of the Crescent City. The restaurants, the race track, the bars, the riverboats, the festivals, and the music, oh the music. I ate well, I played hard, I slept little—I devoured New Orleans. Every outing taught me more about the city. I enjoyed engaging with locals to learn their folklore, their stories, their customs, their dialects. The realization that New Orleans was not remotely southern, insofar as I understood the term, came as a shock, but not an unpleasant one. It was too delightful a place and I was having too much fun to resent her challenge to my provincialism. New Orleans was wildly *multicultural*, a term I had never heard at that point, but a reality that nourished a deprived Georgian whose previous world had been solely Anglo Protestant punctuated with African American.

My best graduate school friend later confessed that she had felt certain I would not return after the first year, convinced that my lifestyle meant I would fail my courses. But five mornings each week, fueled on coffee alone, I walked hungrily past Commander's Palace, through the insistent aromas of stocks simmering in preparation for the coming multitude of luncheon and dinner orders, and took the streetcar up to campus. That first semester, I was enrolled in four courses: "U.S. Foreign Policy 1898–1932," "World War II," a seminar on the 1920s, and "The Cultural History of the United States to 1860." Across the board, I loved the readings. I found the lectures to be mostly very good, and in the case of Bill Malone's, brilliant. Malone, a demanding and somewhat forbidding scholar, taught the fascinating cultural history course. He entered the classroom without acknowledging his students, wrote a question or topic on the board, fixed his eyes on the back wall, and began to lecture, never using notes. My limited prior exposure had shown me that "history" meant political, military, and diplomatic developments, so it came as a delicious discovery that "history" might also include serious exploration of the place of religion, architecture, music, and literature in America's past. Malone's encyclopedic knowledge simultaneously impressed and intimidated.

That semester I wrote research papers on the *New York Times*' coverage of the pre-1933 rise of Hitler, on Eugene Talmadge's pregovernor years as Georgia's secretary of agriculture, and on Margaret Fuller's life. The challenge of serious coursework coupled with giddy nightlife came at a price, of course. I spent the week of Thanksgiving in Tulane's nearly deserted infirmary, depleted of energy and laid low by pneumonia, genuinely glad of a routine which consisted only of deep sleep interrupted by pleasant people bringing me trays of food. When at last the first semester ended, what did I have to show for it? A growing knowledge of the city of New Orleans, a frame lighter by ten pounds, and four As. I would not be failing out after all.

The second semester at Tulane presented me with the second-most-important discovery of my life. (More about the *most* important discovery later.) I learned that there was such a thing as "southern history." Wonder of wonders, very perceptive scholars were studying my region and my people, and I too could do that. This came as a complete revelation to me. My initiator was the incomparable John Boles, whose class "The New South" fitted me like a glove. His charming, self-deprecating humor, making gentle fun of himself and his early experiences, made him a bit like an east Texas Woody Allen at times, while his near perfect mastery of historiographic detail awed his students. The class was so good that I recall walking faster just to get there, my anticipation propelling me at a brisker-than-usual pace on those mornings. We read and discussed the usual monograph a week, but there was an extra dimension. John was just beginning his "knowing the South through the self" approach, which involved assigning students to read autobiographies of notable southerners as well the works of scholars. This was in preparation for a "Growing Up Southern" paper. The details are a bit hazy at this remove, but I seem to remember reading at least a dozen books from the list of autobiographies he provided. This was no effort to curry favor with my professor by doing far more than was required. Every book was like eating dessert. Will Percy, Maya Angelou, Willie Morris, Katherine DuPre Lumpkin, Lillian Smith: I read their lives and wanted to meet them for lunch.

In a seminar on the American culture of the 1930s, I dived into back issues of a southern periodical called the *Progressive Farmer,* hoping to emulate Barbara Welter's technique to determine didactic messages its pages gave to rural southern women concerning proper conduct and aspirations. This project married my scholarship with family experience; my own mother and her sisters had frequently leafed through copies of this magazine that came to their farm home every month. My excitement was considerable when, at John Boles's suggestion, I submitted the manuscript to *Southern Studies.* When that journal accepted it, I had my first article.

In due time, I completed coursework, then passed language exams and the dreaded comprehensive exams, but I still had no idea about a dissertation topic. John Boles had latterly left Tulane for his dream job, a post at his alma mater, Rice University, and editorship of the *Journal of Southern History.* Deprived of his guidance, I floundered, reading this and that, taking notes, posing questions. Could I research the history of southern women's colleges? Perhaps a biography of Lillian Smith? Topic #1 seemed too broad, and I learned that someone else (Anne Loveland) was nearing completion on topic #2. Then came another fork in this scholar's winding road.

Ever in need of funds, I taught English as a second language at a local college one summer, and I later worked as assistant to the editor of the *Sugar Journal,* a trade publication. In October 1982, just after I completed comps, Curt Jerde, a grad school friend who headed Tulane's Hogan Jazz Archive, offered me a part-time job, which my finances very much needed, and I began a happy connection with that center. My task, five days each week, from nine till one, involved cataloguing stacks of sheet music, ranging from antebellum parlor music, to late nineteenth-century rags and marches, to songs from the

Tin Pan Alley era, 1900–1930. I noted the composer and the lyricist, if any, their dates of birth and death, the publishing house and date, the artist who created the cover art, the key, and whether there were notations for ukulele, banjo, and/or guitar. I assigned the piece to one or more Library of Congress subject categories. I then input this information into an online database to give scholars remote access to our holdings. Funds from a Rockefeller grant paid me slightly more than minimum wage, on which I lived an impoverished but very happy life.

How lucky I was to have landed at "the archive," an eccentric's paradise. Its holdings included recorded music in various formats, tapes and transcriptions of interviews with jazz musicians, collections of photographs, musicians' papers, vertical files of clippings and articles, jazz posters, and music scores. Working across the littered table from me was sixty-year-old Francis P. Squibb III, a scion of New England, Dartmouth graduate, and jazz historian, who inevitably announced his intention to chat with me by spraying a blast of Listerine into his mouth before scuttling over, crab-like, in his office chair. There was Bruce Raeburn, a fellow grad student, jazz drummer, and aspiring jazz historian (who has just recently retired as head of the Hogan Archive). There was the frail octogenarian Bill Russell, wrapped in a flannel shirt and overcoat even in July, a pioneer jazz historian who spoke Chinese and played violin in the New Orleans Ragtime Orchestra.

Best of all, there was Richard B. Allen, cofounder of the archive and also one of the founders of the New Orleans Jazz Festival. Dick, like me a Georgian seduced by New Orleans, had settled in the city after World War II. Year in and year out, he heard as much live music as possible and befriended those who made it, regularly crossing the color line in order to connect. Beginning in the 1950s, Dick conducted and recorded interviews with jazz musicians, ultimately leaving more than two thousand reels of taped interviews, the largest collection of jazz oral history in existence. He had a fine command of the English language, a love of wordplay, and a sometimes gentle, sometimes bawdy sense of humor. It was my great good fortune that he made me his protégé, taking me to hear music again and again—in backyard sheds, in recording sessions, at parties, in the streets. I accompanied him on some oral history sessions and marveled at his fine technique, his unerring ability to gain the trust of his usually elderly subjects through a little casual conversation, a little ribbing, and above all, a total grasp of their milieu, and thus to get them to open up and *tell.* My work at the archive amounted to a three-year tutorial in New Orleans jazz history, taught by a master.

My experiences at the archive and out and about with Dick were steering me effortlessly toward a deeper understanding of the unique New Orleans culture. Our music came from the people, who lived in distinct neighborhoods that featured landmarks. I came to know this Italian bakery and that parish church, this fire hall and that corner po-boy joint. Interviewees cited long-gone venues, dance halls like Luthjen's or the Eagle Saloon. They often referenced events and places by saying, "when Maestri was mayor" or "out by the New Basin canal." Without intending to do so, I was learning early twentieth-century New Orleans and finding it fascinating.

After a year or so of this, a tiny green shoot of an idea formed in my mind: I should choose a New Orleans topic, rooted in the twentieth century, for dissertation work. Ever since reading *The Southern Lady,* Anne Firor Scott's pioneering examination of southern white women's lives, I had hoped to identify some aspect of southern women's experience that I might research. When I read Numan Bartley's *The Rise of Massive Resistance,* I had wondered how southern white women handled the news that their men intended to close the public schools rather than see them desegregated, and I wondered what had happened in New Orleans. When I mentioned my thinking to Dick, he offered to introduce me to his friend Cynthia Sanborn Ware, a white woman who had been instrumental in the desegregation of the Audubon Park public pool in New Orleans. She knew other white women who had worked to keep the New Orleans public schools open in 1959 and 1960. A little reading and a few interviews showed me that liberal and moderate women in the schools crisis traced their activism back to their previous participation in an earlier association, the IWO (Independent Women's Organization), and that members of that group credited their awakening to experiences with the 1940s League of Women Voters and in political campaigns against the Long machine in the 1930s. I was discovering a chain of postsuffrage women who had mentored each other across generations, inventing a public role for themselves and using single-sex organizations to advance their activism.

When I left the jazz archive each day, I spent the next four hours reading microfilm of New Orleans newspapers, of which the city had once had three. No Lexis-Nexus, Google, or index of any kind, of course. I simply sat and read the papers, searching out news of the city's political climate and of women's political activities. I read promiscuously, of Huey Long's regime and women's organizations, of course, but also of Sugar Bowl football games, debutante parties, strikes, house fires, air shows, absorbing the city as it was in the 1930s, then the 1940s, finally the 1950s. Some women's organizations had preserved their papers, hurrah! and in those papers I found other leads to follow, tracing women's growing civic engagement. Finally I felt momentum toward my long-held goal.

Economic reality forced me to admit that I needed to earn more than the pleasant hours at the Jazz Archive provided. In 1985 I took a position in Tulane's Office of University Relations, serving as "coordinator of special events." This move doubled my income by giving me the task of coordinating logistics for various visiting dignitaries who periodically graced Tulane. This meant managing a welter of details, each one insignificant enough when considered dispassionately, but the visiting dignitaries never considered any details pertaining to themselves in a dispassionate light. Did Arthur Schlesinger forget to pack toothpaste? Never mind, I will buy it. Does a certain prime minister's wife want to go shopping for lingerie? I can arrange that. Does brilliant English director Jonathan Miller want a spree of cocktails and jazz after his lecture? I will accompany him. And does he want the band to play "Royal Garden Blues"? I'm on it. Does a dignitary's wife turn out to be morbidly obese and nonambulatory, requiring installation of a special ramp to accommodate her wheelchair at the university president's house? My job. Coordinating special events also meant working with graphic artists for effective posters to draw a good audience, meeting with technicians to ensure that sound and lighting would be appropriate, and making special arrangements with campus police.

In the run-up to the 1988 Democratic national convention, Tulane hosted a televised debate among the seven contenders for the party's nomination, whom the press derisively labeled "the seven dwarfs." Seven campaigns, seven entourages, seven men dreaming of being president. Dealing with those seven egos was like herding cats. No matter what instructions I extended, it seemed no one conformed. Jesse Jackson arrived alarmingly late, just at airtime. Paul Simon, refusing our makeup artist's ministrations, excused himself a moment and then popped up with a garish scar of scarlet smeared across his lips. "It's my wife's lipstick," he confided proudly to me, adding needlessly, "I did it myself." Thankfully the event went off reasonably well, and the traveling circus moved on.

I recall arranging a conference for the forty-seven presidents of the AAU (American Association of Universities). The grand finale was dinner at Antoine's, the oldest of the city's *grande dame* restaurants. I decided to hold the dinner in five separate small dining rooms on the main floor. It was my intention to assign the diners to the Rex Room, the 1840 Room, and so forth, according to colors. I had festooned the arches above each dining room doorway with clusters of Mardi Gras beads, one color to each room. The visitors enjoyed cocktails (ahem . . . many cocktails) as they mingled before dinner. Then, according to my plan, Tulane president Eamon Kelly called for quiet and explained that each president accompanied by a spouse should step forward and draw a strand of Mardi Gras beads from the silver bowl he held. Presidents dining solo should take a Mardi Gras doubloon. Thus, a diner who drew purple beads would go with his wife to the purple-blazoned Proteus Room, and so on. Appropriately colored doubloons directed singletons to their spots. The scheme, designed to send the proper number of diners to the differently sized dining rooms, seemed simplicity itself, based on my careful counting. But once these distinguished presidents of the nation's most influential universities had taken their beads and doubloons, a confusion rivaling fire drill in kindergarten ensued. Harvard, Chicago, Michigan, one and all, they needed help. "*No, sir, you have red beads. You don't belong here in the green room. See the beads above the door? You want to go next door, to the red beads. That's right. Yes, sir.*" The good news was that all seemed delighted with the surprisingly taxing exercise of matching colors to find their dinner and took the scramble in good humor.

I enjoyed my work. The potential for disaster added a *frisson* of sheer terror to each occasion, a phenomenon I likened to working without a net, but I was never bored. Because many of the special events I coordinated at Tulane were designed to appeal to affluent individuals who were or might become donors, I met many local movers and shakers. True to human nature, some were warm and accommodating, others self-important and difficult. I recall a meeting with a prominent civic activist, much loved for his commitment to New Orleans, working to arrange a program in which he was deeply interested. This was in 1985, when AIDS was still a new and misunderstood phenomenon. Evidently intending it as a sort of icebreaker, he told a joke about this subject. There were three senior Tulane employees present, all of whom outranked me and all of whom laughed at his joke. I looked at the important man with an even gaze but did not smile. We proceeded with the business at hand and made plans for his program. When we broke up, he chose to walk out with me, and, out of earshot of the others, he apologized for his tasteless humor; he told me that he would never repeat that joke. My quiet refusal to laugh at cruelty had helped him to know how wrong he was. I was an insignificant cog in the big Tulane machine, but I felt that I had had an important impact that day.

The job was amazingly time-consuming, and even when I was not at work, I thought more about upcoming events than about my own research. I was making slow progress toward writing a dissertation. At last, I took a leave and committed to diligence. The necessity of earning drove me back to work, but another leave the next year allowed me to produce a full draft at last. My inclination was to continue polishing these pages, adding newly gleaned details as I obtained them, but a fortuitous conversation with Tulane's president dissuaded me. As I confided my plans to continue revising, Dr. Kelly sagely said: "The best dissertation is a finished dissertation. Go ahead and defend it. You can revise when you work with your publisher."

I had not thought of publishing. I was only hoping that those pages would be deemed adequate by my committee, and that, at age forty, after a successful defense, I would finally possess a PhD, which would let me go and teach in some small college. The defense turned out to be a sunny session full of compliments. There was a question about how I would classify the work—women's history, southern history, urban history? All three, I said. The committee members shook my hand and concluded with advice about which university presses I should approach. I was simply stunned.

I had had the pleasure of interviewing many local women as I finished my project. In our conversations they turned their thoughts to events of thirty, forty, and fifty years before, recalling for me their efforts to shape the city's future by their use of the ballot. From them, I gained a really sound understanding of New Orleans politics and heard a quantity of unforgettable anecdotes (some of which they enjoined me not to repeat, alas). They were impressive women, in some ways ahead of their time, women whose unacknowledged activism formed a link between the suffragists' generation and the rebirth of feminism in the 1960s. The book that resulted from my dissertation, *Silk Stockings and Ballot Boxes: New Orleans Women and Politics, 1920–1963*, displayed its share of shortcomings. I focused chiefly on women from the city's comfortable classes. I wrote narrative history with no thought of theory. However, I take genuine pride in having illuminated the activities, personalities, and contributions of many unsung, wonderful women. Knowledge of their deeds might have died with them had we not had our interviews, had I not dealt with all those Hollinger boxes and microfilm reels, and had not my book been published.

But to speak of the publication of my book is to put the cart before the horse. First came the process of applying for positions. A plethora of applications sent out netted me two interviews. About the first, with UNC–Chapel Hill, the less said, the better. The reality of sitting across from Jacquelyn Dowd Hall, whose *Revolt Against Chivalry* I admired and whose *Like a Family* I revered, rendered me an absolute moron. In response to Jackie's questions, I babbled as if I had been bitten by a radioactive spider. But in the other interview, I must have acquitted myself reasonably well, because it led to an on-campus visit and a job offer, which I accepted. Thank you, North Carolina State University (NCSU).

I loved NCSU. I taught my share of budding textile engineers who had enrolled for their required helping of the humanities, but I also taught history majors who were the equal of any students anywhere. In small classrooms, where technology consisted chiefly of chalk, they discussed with insight and passion; they read and questioned. Teaching at NCSU really put me on my mettle, and being selected for that university's Academy of Outstanding Teachers in 2000 (one of only seventeen professors campus-wide) was a signal honor. Though I had never had a women's history course (indeed had never even had a woman professor), NCSU had hired me to teach courses in U.S. women's history. This presented a challenge, but I was eager, willing to read and prepare diligently. Fortunately for me, I had the great good fortune to have landed in Raleigh, situated in close proximity to Duke and Chapel Hill, where women's history was a thriving subdiscipline. Women history faculty and their graduate students at those institutions generously invited me to join the Feminist Women in History group, which met monthly to hear one of the group present her current research. What a wonderful opportunity it was for me to be educated by the best of the best and to hear their ideas long before they appeared in print. They provided me a superb postgraduate seminar in women's history.

Although Duke's Anne Firor Scott had taken *emerita* status by this time, she very occasionally attended these invigorating sessions, giving me exposure to her brilliance in the relaxed setting of someone's living room. On the evening when I was slated to discuss my research on Eleanor Roosevelt, Anne turned up, and my nervousness increased accordingly. My book on New Orleans women and politics had then been out for a few months. She took me aside in the privacy of the kitchen to tell me that she had read it; not only that, she liked it. Moreover, she urged me to tackle the postsuffrage activities of North Carolina women, spanning 1920 through the rebirth of feminism for Tar Heel women just as I had for the women of New Orleans. She praised my narrative approach for readability and accessibility and promised to share her voluminous files with me if I would make this endeavor my next project. "You are the right person to do this," she said. I stood speechless. Although I never began that effort, the astounding fact of being validated by the person I most admired in our profession provided a never-to-be-equaled prop to my self-esteem. This wise, warm woman has meant much to many, and I am proud to number myself among them.

It was during my graduate school years that I made the most important discovery of my life. In my twenties, I had twice planned my wedding (first to a fellow teacher, later to a young lawyer), but I had broken both engagements. I had never experienced the all-consuming "in love" state depicted in fiction and played out among my friends. I tried to convince myself that I had simply not yet found the right guy. As for the stuff of song lyrics, "burning love," "my heart's on fire," I concluded I wasn't the combustible type. The reality—that I would find that experience only in a same-sex relationship—was too frightening for me to face. Homosexuality in my provincial corner of the world meant deviance, ostracism, a friendless and outcast status, according to what people said, according to popular culture. The lesbian dies at the end of the movie. I had never known an "out" gay person in Georgia and thought they must be a twisted and miserable lot. I believed this nonsense just as gullibly as I had once believed that a stealthy fairy would fly into my room at night to buy my lost teeth. But thankfully I outgrew the mythology about gays just as I outgrew the tooth fairy. In New Orleans, I met gay men and women who were happy, smart, productive, well-adjusted people; they also claimed their gayness with no equivocation. Seeing affirmation daily that one could be gay *and* normal was the most important discovery of my life, and for more than thirty years, I have been "out" to my friends, neighbors, and colleagues. A major development, indeed.

This aspect of my identity accounts for a drastic change in my professional life. My partner, Leslie Parr, and I endured a commuter relationship, she a professor at Loyola University in New Orleans and I at NCSU in Raleigh. Because we deemed weekends in her New Orleans superior to the same time spent in my city of Raleigh, I did most of the flying, and, so long as a nonstop flight was possible, the situation was acceptable. I was well satisfied with my job at North Carolina State University, where colleagues were congenial, students were capable, departmental support in the form of travel money and time off for research was provided, and my little house was within walking distance of campus. But alas, Midway Air canceled its nonstop between New Orleans and Raleigh-Durham Airport, requiring me to make a connection in Atlanta. On more than one occasion, I missed that connecting flight because my flight from Raleigh was late, which meant wasting a night in Atlanta and arriving in New Orleans the next day, cutting our weekend a full day short. *Not* acceptable.

In 2004, I began to look for jobs in south Louisiana or south Mississippi. A few years earlier, *Silk Stockings* had won the Louisiana Historical Association's L. Kemper Williams Prize for the year's best book, and I had proceeded to rest on my laurels. I drifted along in the shallows of our profession, enjoying my teaching, reviewing books, presenting at a conference here and there, contented with my tenure and not driving hard toward the next project. I had a couple of book chapters in the pipeline but no second book in print, no second manuscript in progress, not even a clearly defined second project. My idea to research Eleanor Roosevelt's complex and ambivalent relationship with the South had taken me to Hyde Park's Roosevelt Presidential Library for three research trips, but each time I delved into ER's letters, I felt I understood her less. The uncertainty that I would ever "know" the peripatetic First Lady's true feelings about the South and southerners made me question my choice of topic. Now, in 2004, I devoutly wished that I had been more disciplined and productive, more tenacious in pursuit of the opaque Eleanor. I wanted to compete successfully in the drastically limited job market for associate professors who hoped to make a lateral move, but I lacked the all-important second book.

Quite out of the blue, Tulane's Randy Sparks called to ask if I would organize a weekend conference on his campus, focusing on the South's experience with World War II. He was then heading the Deep South Regional Humanities Center, one of several regional centers created by the National Endowment for the Humanities (NEH), and knew that I had done some programming at Tulane. I was happy to put the event together, as it allowed me to spend more time where I wanted to be. Out of that weekend grew an offer for me to serve as associate director of the center. Permission came from NCSU for me to take a year of unpaid leave, and I happily made the move to New Orleans in 2004. When Randy stepped down in 2005, Tulane made me acting director with the understanding that there would be a search to fill the post permanently, a search in which I intended to finish first.

Mother Nature had other plans. I left the office on Friday afternoon, August 26, 2005, chatting with the Humanities Center staff as we urged each other to take necessary and familiar precautions. We all knew that, although a storm had crossed Florida and entered the Gulf of Mexico, its predicted path took it to the Florida Panhandle, but we also knew to be vigilant. By Saturday morning, Hurricane Katrina had defied predictions and was heading directly for New Orleans, gaining strength from the superheated waters of the Gulf and roaring closer and closer. The National Weather Service images shown on TV left no doubt that this was a massive storm. Leslie and I packed quickly and took to the gridlocked interstate, jammed with refugees like us, trying to escape a cyclone by going fifteen miles per hour, when we moved at all. Three hours later, we were only forty miles from home. But once we had finally left the metro area of New Orleans fully behind, the drive became less congested. The goal was Dallas, where Leslie's family would welcome us for two or three days until the storm blew through. Little did we know that more than three months would pass before we would see New Orleans again.

There is no need for a full recounting of Katrina's impact. I have written about it elsewhere and find that it is still painful to look back on the details. Our home was left intact, but my employment situation was in tatters. Tulane, much affected by the floods, coped by canceling some programs and eliminating whole departments. I learned that the Deep South Regional Humanities Center had died on the budgetary chopping block, and with it my job. Though the path was still open for me to return to my tenured post at North Carolina State University, our intense experiences during the recovery period in New Orleans had cemented us as a couple as never before. But unless I found another academic situation in the vicinity, I would once again be one-half of a commuter relationship featuring Leslie at Loyola University and me back in Carolina.

At this juncture, a friend on the faculty of the University of Southern Mississippi urged me to apply for an open position there. They sought to hire an associate or full professor to teach U.S. women's and southern history. I had no desire to live in Hattiesburg, but the map revealed that it was only 110 miles from New Orleans. I applied, they offered, and I accepted. I bought a house there, and once again, Leslie and I had our weekends.

The moral of this episode is: be careful what you wish for. The step down from North Carolina State University, a Research-1 university with a college-ready student body, to the University of Southern Mississippi (USM) was a jolt. My USM students were a pleasant lot, but for the most part not of the caliber of their counterparts at NCSU, a significant difference, yes, but certainly not an insurmountable one. Of much greater importance was the difference in departmental cultures and professional standards. My department at NCSU had been harmonious and professional. Our faculty meetings were conducted with attention to Robert's Rules of Order, and there were clearly defined policies for every eventuality. Matters of personnel, budget, scheduling, and policy were transparent and scrupulously fair. I always felt valued and respected for my contributions. Sadly, my department at USM proved to be nothing like that. Instead, favoritism and factions defined life there, and I soon regretted the move I had made.

I was not alone in my disillusionment. One colleague in the USM history department quit his tenure-track job after only one year. Even though he did not have another position and had no idea how he would earn his living, he refused to continue in what he called "that dysfunctional environment." Another history colleague, also tenure-track, departed with the observation that she would rather flip burgers than stay where she was. However, I was tenured and a full generation older than they; leaving did not seem like a viable option. Though deeply disenchanted with the university, I met every responsibility there, carried a heavy student load, and, beyond the campus, accepted speaking invitations from community groups and gave service to my profession. But, as a counterweight to the toxic situation at USM, I invested myself in New Orleans more than ever. Weekends were a time for recharging my depleted self, getting ready to return to underprepared students and a depressed tyrant of a department chair who made no pretense at impartiality in her decision-making. Weekends brought plays and movies, music and restaurants, time with friends, cooking at home, the stuff of life that really counts.

In addition to the personal benefits, there was a professional silver lining to spending more time in New Orleans; it allowed me to research and write about various aspects of the city that I loved. I published accounts of the valuable work being done by creative women's organizations to aid the painfully slow post-Katrina recovery. I wrote about the early history of Sophie Newcomb College and contributed entries on local women to a new Louisiana encyclopedia. Then, fortuitously, the Newcomb College Institute at Tulane University made me their Dora Bonquois Ellis Visiting Historian and gave me the entire year of 2012 free from the University of Southern Mississippi, an entire year to spend in New Orleans, conducting research. Thanks to the Board of Managers of a local institution, the Poydras Home, I had a terrific topic. These women (the Poydras board was, and had always been, in the hands of women only) had approached me about researching the history of their institution, which would celebrate its bicentennial in 2017. The Poydras Home, in continuous operation for two hundred years, had existed in its first incarnation as a home for orphaned and/or indigent girls, and since 1959, served the elderly as the city's premier continuing-care retirement center. Its managers had faithfully preserved relevant documents across the decades; a preliminary trip to the manuscripts division of Tulane's Howard-Tilton Library, which housed the papers, revealed that I would be drowning in rich primary sources.

But writing this book also meant I was embarking on an exploration of social services, city government, and women's activities in the nineteenth century, all *terra incognita* for me. At times, I was almost overwhelmed by my foolhardiness in taking on a topic so far from my comfort zone and area of expertise, which was the political activities of twentieth-century women. I read madly to assimilate new knowledge, and other scholars, patient and generous, helped me time after time. The result was my second book, *New Orleans Women and the Poydras Home: More Durable Than Marble,* which LSU Press would publish in early 2016.

The happy New Orleans interlude came to an end, and I returned to the University of Southern Mississippi, back to a teaching load featuring, in addition to small sections of upper-division courses on topics such as the New South and U.S women's history, auditorium sections of "world civilization" for two hundred underprepared, mostly first-year students, a significant percentage of whom struggled with literacy. Heavy stress on retention, no matter what compromises had to be made, pressure to adopt "clickers" for students (to keep them "engaged," so the justification went): this constituted the new normal in the place where I found myself employed. Then I learned in 2015 that my university had denied my request for a sabbatical for spring 2016, and I felt that a Rubicon had been crossed. In ten years of employment at USM, this was my first such request. I was eligible for the leave and had a well-developed prospectus for a history of southern women since the Civil War, then under contract with a major press, around which to focus the sabbatical's months. Leslie and I talked endlessly about the right response. Should I resign? Should I continue? Money was not the major issue. Paramount for me was not retiring without promotion to the rank of full professor, a status that I desired and deserved. Publication of my Poydras book, the all-important second book, not slated until April 2016, would be the necessary final addition to my *curriculum vitae,* making me eligible. Thus, until publication, I would need to persevere where I no longer wanted to be, but I was determined to stay long enough to extract promotion, that meaningful badge of status, from the department. In fact, my promotion to full professor worked its way through the appropriate committees and did come in 2017.

When I attended my fiftieth high school reunion that same year, I saw classmates who looked good and seemed happy. The secret, they said, was retirement. Back in Hattiesburg, the departmental bully had finally moved on, the notorious department racist and misogynist had retired, and our department had made some good hires in the last few years. I was finally a full professor, one of only five in the department. But I had long since lost any desire to continue at USM. A session with my TIAA-CREF agent revealed that a financially secure retirement would be a reality, and so, farewell.

There have been so many bright spots in my checkered career and so many wonderful individuals who guided and helped me when I needed help. I have mentioned many in these pages, but first among all ranks Clarence Mohr, the most generous mentor I have ever known. His arrival at Tulane after I had completed coursework meant that I never sat in his classes, but he made himself an integral part of my dissertation advisory team and shared his ideas to a remarkable extent. To say that he gave my manuscript a "close reading" is putting it mildly; he interrogated every line and peppered pages with suggestions and queries. The final product owes so much to his wise and generous input. As time passed, he shifted from mentor to friend, and we talked regularly, at conferences and on the phone, about my work, his work, and the state of the world in general. I sought his advice about every professional decision and his input on every piece written for publication. I relished especially our New Orleans hours spent in conversation on the porch at The Columns, shaded by live oaks as streetcars rattled past. There Clarence relaxed with a drink and allowed his rapier wit and unparalleled intelligence to shine. His far-too-early death in August 2017 leaves a hole in my life.

The Delta Women Writers, a group mentioned in these pages by other contributors, offered rigorous critiques of my projects, always leavened by warmth and good humor. Meeting with these delightful women scholars twice each year for a weekend of scholarly inquiry and good fun helped me to keep going when I at times felt so wearied with my situation in Hattiesburg.

Realistic self-appraisal is a difficult endeavor. One's skills and accomplishments tend to loom large in retrospect, while one's limitations and shortcomings are suddenly small, like objects seen in the rearview mirror. Truth compels me to say that I have been neither an ambitious nor a tremendously productive professional historian, nor can anything in my publications be called truly pathbreaking. I honestly do not mind. I have had a solid career. I have written some pages that will last, because they will be consulted long after I am gone. My work ensures that certain women will not be forgotten;

they and their contributions have received their due in print. I have taught legions of students, and, on many, my influence is lasting. "Delightful" is an accurate description for many classes I remember.

Had I worked harder, focused more single-mindedly, and applied myself more fully, I feel sure that I could have climbed higher, but reflection shows me that, time and again, I chose the personal over the professional. I needed a full decade to earn a PhD. That could have been accomplished in less time, but I chose instead to savor New Orleans, every Sazerac, every oyster, and all that jazz, literally. New Orleans was the milieu in which I created the self I was meant to be. After having spent the first half of my life denying myself the pleasure of a meaningful relationship with a loving partner, I later quite literally rearranged my life to sustain and nurture such a relationship. Since this rearrangement meant leaving an enviable situation at a respected university, I paid a professional price, but I gained infinitely more than I lost.

As I write these lines, it is autumn. On college campuses, students are obsessing about gridiron outcomes, about "rush" and "bids," possibly even about grades. For the first fall in three decades, I have no schedule to keep, no papers to grade, no discussions to plan. However, I will continue to watch developments in higher education with interest and more than a little unease, observing as universities struggle to do more with less, as some succumb to the siren song of "classroom technologies" and "distance learning," as history departments labor to teach a discipline predicated upon close reading of sources to students ever less willing or even able to do sustained reading of anything. I wonder about the future of tenure. I worry about younger colleagues who may have difficult years ahead in our profession.

History is no longer my profession, but it will remain my passion. Although retired, I will always be a historian. Just this summer (2018), I had the pleasure of teaching a seminar on the history of the South to thirty-five sharp and eager visiting teachers, under the auspices of the Gilder Lehrman Institute, and currently I am researching the life of congresswoman Lindy Boggs. Whether I am reading newly published scholarship, squinting at unfamiliar handwriting in the quiet of an archive, listening as colleagues present their ideas, or trying to string together some historical writing of my own, learning history fills a desire which was born in me a long, long time ago.

Detours and delays have marked my professional journey, but also perseverance and resilience, learning, and growth year in and year out, no matter what came. Come to think of it, a straight path would have been stultifyingly boring, and that was never the case. Best of all, I now live an honest life, as one-half of a happy couple. And we live that life in New Orleans, our battered and resilient city, a city of such variety, such zest, such flavor.

George Bernard Shaw reportedly said: "Life isn't about finding yourself. Life is about creating yourself."

Mission ongoing, mostly accomplished.

ONCE A TEACHER, ALWAYS A TEACHER

MARTHA SWAIN

When my mother was seventeen, she had had two years of college and was teaching in a one-room school.[1] She finished her degree in the summers and graduated from Cape Normal School (now called Southeast Missouri University). Later she was a principal and teacher in Hayti, Missouri, when she met my father, a 1913 graduate of Mississippi Agricultural and Mechanical College, who was doing work on Mississippi River flood control. When my twin sister, Margaret, and I were born, Mama's first outing was to Shiloh Battlefield. She trained my daddy to slow down and then brake for all the historical markers on the then-two-lane roads. I never had another chance in life but to be a history teacher!

From earliest childhood, I wanted to teach. I started school when I was six in 1935, and I noticed that the teacher had pictures on the corkboard around the wall. There was *The Blue Boy, The Age of Innocence, The Gleaners*, and that fat-faced little Tudor child—I think it was Henry VIII. I decided then that I was going to have pictures on my corkboard around the wall when I was a grown teacher. I started cutting out pictures for my corkboard, and I kept cutting them out for several years, until I finally stopped and threw them out.

We moved to Tupelo, Mississippi, in 1936, when my big sister, Mary Elizabeth or Mimi, started college at Mississippi State College for Women (MSCW). Margaret and I were in second grade. Mimi, too, meant to be a history teacher like our mother. I looked at all her history books, even before I could read, because the pictures intrigued me. For instance, there was one of a tall man in a big hat standing under a tree holding up a paper before a group of Indians sitting on the ground. In others, Mama explained to me what was going on. I could not wait for the fifth grade, when we had our first history book. We had to go downtown to buy our textbooks. We didn't have free textbooks then; you had to buy them so the drugstore would have a commission. I would go down ahead of time and find out what my books were going to be that year. I was a very nerdy child.

I had many fine teachers in elementary school who inspired me and made me want to be like them. My family moved to New Albany, Mississippi, halfway through my third-grade year and stayed through half of my sixth. Margaret and I had the second half of the sixth grade and seventh grade in Holly Springs. (Daddy was a civil engineer; he'd do a project with the highway department, and when one project was finished, he would move on to another one when he was transferred.) In Holly Springs, our kitchen at home had a linoleum floor, and I pretended that there was a student in each square; I would ask questions about something I had learned in class that day.

I knew from the time that Mimi went to college at MSCW that someday Margaret and I would follow in her footsteps and go to the "W." It was just a given that all of us would go to college. The summer between my sixth and seventh grades, Mimi had a fellowship at Indiana University to study government; she started graduate school on a full scholarship, working toward a master's degree in government. The same summer, Senator Pat Harrison died, and when I asked Mimi what she would do in graduate school, she explained that she would take courses and then be writing a thesis, or a long research paper. During that time, the newspapers were full of Pat Harrison's death, and I decided I would write my thesis on him some day.

We had just moved from New Albany, where Hubert Stephens lived. He had been a U.S. senator, and Wall Doxey, a seventh-term congressman from Holly Springs, was going to run for Pat Harrison's seat, but first Jim Eastland served in the Senate for ninety days. I was just awash in the U.S. senators from Mississippi. Twelve years later I wrote my master's thesis, "The Senate Career of Pat Harrison of Mississippi, 1911–1919," and I wrote my doctoral dissertation on him a few years later. I suppose you can say that I determined my dissertation subject before I entered the seventh grade.

When I was in eighth grade we moved to Starkville from Holly Springs. I liked moving around. I had a proprietary interest in all those cities, and I still do. I still read the Tupelo paper for all the news. We were in Starkville eight years, where I went to high school. My family lived across the street from the campus of Mississippi State College (now University). My earlier dream had been to go to the "W," but I was very pleased instead to go to Mississippi State. Margaret and I lived at home, and we went through and graduated in three years. We took classes year-round, 18 hours each regular semester, and 12 hours in the summers. In those days you had to take 144 hours to graduate; of those 144, I took 78 in social studies. When I got my teacher's certification, I was certified in history, government, economics, geography, and sociology.

I loved my time at Mississippi State, particularly because of Dr. Glover Moore and Dr. John K. Bettersworth, two published historians.[2] As an undergraduate I typed Dr. Moore's manuscript on the Missouri Compromise, which would be published by the University of Kentucky Press, and even as a freshman I graded papers for Dr. Bettersworth, who taught courses on the New South. Dr. Bettersworth had just started writing the history of the university, the first history, and I typed some of that. He also was writing with Charlotte Capers of the Mississippi Department of Archives and History about historical markers, which I also helped type. Dr. Bettersworth had a keen sense of humor, so he was fun. I typed all his exchanges with Ms. Capers while I was there.

I worked in the History Department office from the time I was a second-semester freshman, and I would check on all kinds of things for the department members in the card catalogue in the library. As a consequence, I really knew a lot of bibliography, which came in handy when I got to graduate school. I heard all the discussions with graduate students, I typed from old newspapers for Dr. Bettersworth's history of the school, and just did a number of other helpful things.

I knew from the start that I would go to graduate school, but Dr. Moore and Dr. Bettersworth said that I must teach two years before I could go. They knew I lived at home, and I think they realized that I was really socially retarded. I graduated from Mississippi State in 1950 among many veterans who wanted to be coaches and therefore majored in social studies.

When I finished my undergraduate degree at Mississippi State, I was twenty-one years old, and I was lucky to get a job at Vardaman High School. It was really a primitive school building, and I remember making a fire in a big stove when I went to school every morning. The first year I taught history, twelfth-grade government, eighth-grade American history, tenth-grade world history, and even seventh-grade science, and I kept two study halls; of course, we did not have any break during the day. I chaperoned the cheerleaders on all football trips and even ran the electric clock for the basketball games. It was hard work, but I actually enjoyed it. I am still in touch with one eighth-grader who is eighty-one years old, and she also taught history in high school. I was twenty-one, and the eighth-graders were thirteen, so I had some real discipline problems!

At the end of that first year, the new coach coming in had majored in social studies, so he took all my classes. They moved me to teaching sixth grade, which I could do under my teaching certificate, for some reason. This was fine with me, except for arithmetic reading problems—those two trains coming at each other—I never really got that. I still have the Valentines that the eighth- and sixth-graders sent me; I just can't throw them out.

Then it was time to go to graduate school. In the spring of that year I went back down to Starkville to get my old professors' advice. They sat me in a straight-back chair, and five of them lined up and told me there were five strong history graduate schools in the South: Texas, Vanderbilt, Duke, North Carolina, and Virginia. Of course, those were the schools that they represented. I always had hopes of going to Vanderbilt because it was small and close to home. My professors encouraged me to believe I could secure scholarship money to pay my way, and my parents were delighted because they had always wanted to send Mimi there, but they didn't have the money to do that.

I got a letter from the department chairman, Dr. William Binkley, at Vanderbilt. The acceptance letter said, "I can assure you that your recommendations from Drs. Moore and Bettersworth will carry weight in this department." I ended up with a full scholarship, and I got my master's degree working with Dr. Dewey W. Grantham, the author of numerous fine publications in southern political history.[3] Vanderbilt gave me full tuition plus an additional one thousand dollars; that was enough, because living in the Peabody dormitory, where the university's graduate women lived, cost me all of forty dollars a quarter. Never mind that the Peabody boys called the dorm that we were in "Menopause Manor."

Dr. Grantham was teaching his first year at Vanderbilt, and I may have been his first graduate student. I was twenty-two, and Dr. Grantham was only nine years older than I, but of course that was a tremendous gulf then. I took recent American history for three quarters with Dr. Grantham. I also took southern history all three quarters. I took historiography from the chairman of the department, all three quarters. I also took constitutional law, which really is a history course, and one quarter of administrative law (that made my minor government). So that was it. That year was tremendously strenuous, because I knew I had to go teach to make a living. And so, in twelve months, from September through August, I took courses and researched and wrote the thesis on Pat Harrison's years in the House. I *had* to do it, because I had a job at Natchez High School.

After finishing my master's, I taught at Natchez High, and I taught there from 1953 to 1956. It was a very good high school. I taught world history, American history, civics, and government. The principal at Natchez High was Miss Margaret Martin. She was about fifty and a Latin teacher. Now, for some reason, Latin teachers are real disciplinarians, and Natchez High was very smooth. She wouldn't let the band play "Dixie" in the auditorium, because the kids would just go wild. And then one day, the army band came, and they closed with "Dixie," and it took the rest of the day for us to get the kids settled down.

I liked Natchez High, but I didn't like Natchez really. Natchez was where the Old South still lived, and it was a hard town to break into. But I had a good time anyway, because there was a group of girls who had attended Mississippi State College for Women. They also taught at Natchez High, and we ran around and played bridge a lot.

In May 1956 I went to visit a teacher friend over at Pensacola High School, and she encouraged me to apply to teach there. The idea appealed to me, and of course the salary was a little bit better. Since it was a weekend I couldn't imagine how to set up an interview. My friend said I should just go to the principal's house. He was out mowing the yard and trimming his roses, but he did stop and talk to me. He liked the idea that he would have a teacher from Vanderbilt, so he hired me on the spot.

I moved to Pensacola High School, and I really loved it. I was there twelve years, and that may have been the happiest time of my life. Eventually I taught the three top classes in American history. We didn't have Advanced Placement, but we had grouping. Sometimes I taught "Problems in American Democracy" (American government), sometimes economics, and occasionally contemporary world affairs, but the American history courses were the ones I really loved. Also in Pensacola, we had so many resources available, including Edward R. Murrow's *I Can Hear It Now* broadcasts and Walter Cronkite's films *You Are There.*

I also subscribed to the *New York Times* monthly film strips, with a very helpful guide included. I had access to the *Washington Post,* and I used those superb Herblock cartoons. I also could borrow films from Indiana and Florida State. And I got very good films, such as *The March of Time* from the 1920s. I ordered a book of little short plays, about thirty minutes long, and I had the students do those. I would tell the students to ham it up, and to make paper hats and cardboard swords. That was a lot of fun. The students had to read a book each six weeks to report on, and I assigned good books. I remember when I taught the 1920s, we discarded the textbook, and I used Frederick Lewis Allen's *Only Yesterday.* Of course, they read *Animal Farm* and *1984,* which were staples then. The American government classes read *All the King's Men,* and the history classes read *The American Presidency* by Clinton Rossiter. The economics class read *The Great Crash* by John Kenneth Galbraith.

Near the end of my first year we had a 1920s-themed party. There was a place downtown that had a jazz trio. We took up money and hired that combo for sixty dollars. They played for three hours. None of us could really do the Charleston, but we did the Bunny Hop, and we had popcorn and peanuts and Cokes. Of course, that was all we could have, but it was just a world of fun.

I used *Time* and *Newsweek* for current events. They could get student subscriptions for nine months for $1.50. Both magazines sent wonderful teaching aids including a map of the month. And *Time* sent me a full set of "Man of the Year" covers, so that finally I had something for my corkboards! The biggest thrill that I had was my bookcase in the back of the room. It was one of those cases that would close like a book and lock for security when I was out of the room. I'd go out to Good News Distributors and fill my basket with books, mostly historical fiction and nonfiction. I must have sold hundreds of books; mostly my students bought them, but I would open it up at noon for other classes to come in and buy. I bought the books on consignment and sold the books at a 20 percent discount of what the Good News offered, so a thirty-five-cent book cost twenty-eight cents, a sixty-cent book would cost forty-eight cents, etc. I think the most expensive books were listed for seventy-five cents, so I would sell them for sixty cents. I truly believe in putting books in the hands of students.

In 1961, I was invited to give a paper at the National Council for Social Studies (NCSS) teachers meeting in Chicago. I joined the NCSS and went to the annual meetings, over Thanksgiving, for nearly fifteen years, even after I left Pensacola and went back to school for my PhD. I really enjoyed the meetings and gained a lot of techniques that I used in the classroom. I was even on the board of editors of *Social Education*, which is the journal for the NCSS, for three years. I got involved in the Florida Council for Social Studies (FCSS) and went to its meetings every year that I was in Pensacola. I was also president of the FCSS for one year.

In 1963, I had a student teacher from Florida State, and she was *good*. Many years ago, she got a PhD from Georgia State University, and she taught at Florida Atlantic University. I still am in touch with her. The student-teacher supervisor, Ed Fernald, came over to see her from Florida State. She was so good she didn't need supervision, and I wondered why he spent all the time with me down in the conference room in the library, asking me lots of questions. Pretty soon I got a letter from the chairman at Florida State's Social Studies Education Department, Dr. J. R. Skretting, saying he wanted me to come over there and teach a course. Ed was going to be away a year, and Dr. Skretting handed me Ed's syllabus and said I could follow it. So, I didn't have to plan much because I had the syllabus and my own teaching experiences. I saw student teachers along the way, and I taught in the mornings down at Florida High, which was really the demonstration school connected with Florida State; but I didn't do much teaching because most of the time I stood in the back of the room watching a student teacher.

That was my first experience with college teaching. The students were mostly juniors, and it was a general course in social studies. I taught two sections in the afternoon. They gave me the title of assistant professor, which shocked me.

At that point I started thinking about going back to graduate school, but I was so laden with committee assignments that I couldn't see how to extricate myself. I was on the State Social Studies Textbook Committee for three years (I was chairman the final year). I was invited to join the Teacher Education Advisor Council, and I did that three years. I was on some SACS (Southern Association of Colleges and Schools) committees to evaluate high schools' social studies programs. I was on the state Curriculum Committee for three years. These all met in either Tallahassee or Orlando, and I also went to St. Petersburg to look at the work of teachers' aides (which was ironic as I didn't even have one). The only thing I wrote in those years was *A Busy Teacher's Guide to Teachers' Aides.* I was also active in the National Council for Social Studies Teachers and was a member of the advisory board, and also the advisory board of the NCSS journal, *Social Education.* I loved Pensacola High, and I liked my students a lot, but I was tired. I longed to read more books and try writing, but I didn't have any time for reading and writing with that schedule. During that time, I worked every weekend.

Probably the biggest reason I went back to graduate school was because of the experiences I had teaching at Stetson University's summer programs. The first program was for bright sixteen-year-olds, who took an English course, a math course, and a history course and got high school credit for those three courses; then they were eligible to go to college. This was 1959 and 1960, when the trend was to encourage bright students to finish high school early and go on to college. Every summer they had outstanding lecturers; I remember David Potter, whose book *People of Plenty* was all the rage at that time.[4]

After a couple of years, the Stetson administrators transferred me over to the History Institutes for Teachers sponsored by the Ford Foundation. Their idea was that college teachers basically would not know how to teach high school teachers, and they needed a high school teacher to be a liaison. I team-taught with a Stetson history professor those six years, four of which were under the Ford grant. I taught with Dr. Gilbert Lycan, Dr. John Johns, or Dr. Evans Johnson. Each one of the college professors encouraged me to go back to graduate school. I remember Evans Johnson was particularly supportive; he had gotten his PhD at UNC. In the summer of 1965, I joined the faculty of Rutgers University in the same capacity for a History Teacher's Institute. The experiences at Stetson and Rutgers, especially at Rutgers, and the visiting professors really led me to go back to graduate school. I was *so tired* of having to give up my weekends to grade papers, read all those magazines, and prepare lessons, and I knew it was time to make a change despite the fact that I dearly enjoyed teaching high school and working with the other teachers.

In the spring of 1966, my mother died, and the only thing I did that summer was go to Amherst College for two weeks of Discovery Learning in American History. In 1967, my father died after a stroke and being in the hospital for five months. In October, I went on leave from Pensacola High School and stayed in Starkville until after he died. Then I went back to PHS and substituted every day; it was April, and I did not want to take my classes back from the substitute teacher they had worked with when I was with my father. But, when I walked in a classroom as a substitute, the students would say, "Oh, shucks, she's a real teacher." After my father's death, the starch was pretty well drained from me. I taught two more years at PHS. When I told my seniors that I was going to graduate school for a doctorate, but I was apprehensive because it had been sixteen years since I had taken an exam, one of the seniors said, "Aw, Miss Swain, you can hack it!"

So, I went back to graduate school in the fall of 1969, at the age of forty. Pat Harrison was still untouched as a dissertation project. One person had registered him with AHA as a dissertation topic, but when he found out that the papers were so scattered, he changed his topic. The biggest determinant in my returning to Vanderbilt was that Dr. Dewey Grantham was still there, and he agreed to be my dissertation advisor. I went back to work on Pat Harrison.

During graduate school, I got a job supervising the MAT (master of arts in teaching) interns. I would go out to visit them. They were teaching full-time, regular school years, just on temporary certificates. And everywhere I went, I would get to see papers of Harrison's colleagues that I needed to research. I saw the Tom Heflin Papers at the University of Alabama, the James Byrnes Papers at Clemson, the Josiah William Bailey Papers at Duke, and others, and I always trolled the sources while I was on my trips to see the interns.

In 1971, Dr. Grantham recommended me to the Educational Testing Service, and I began grading papers for them. I did that for sixteen years off and on, even in retirement. This was a great advantage for me when I was doing my research because the grading sessions were always up East, and I could travel to Hyde Park to see the Roosevelt Papers and also to the National Archives. On these trips I always tried to see senators who had known Pat Harrison. I saw Burton K. Wheeler in Washington, Lister Hill in Alabama, and A. B. ("Happy") Chandler in Kentucky. I also had excellent interviews with James Farley in New York City and the journalist Turner Catledge, who had both known Pat Harrison very well. I finished my degree at age forty-five, because I got to complete research for my dissertation ("Pat Harrison and the New Deal") while I was at Vanderbilt. And so I was forty-five years old when I began college teaching.

Dr. Grantham wrote letters to various schools where there were Vanderbilt PhDs, and Texas Woman's University (TWU) had two. One was A. Elizabeth Taylor, who had gotten her degree in 1943 and wrote on woman's suffrage. The other was Wilmon Droze, who had also gotten his degree under Dewey Grantham. The TWU department chairman, Dr. Kent Yarborough, called me and offered me a job. I had no interview at all, so I suppose I was a "mail-order bride." Incidentally, Dr. Grantham also received a letter from East Carolina University stating that they wanted a woman historian to meet Equal Employment Opportunity Commission (EEOC) standards; Grantham knew before I told him that I would not accept a job that wanted a woman only so they could meet their quota.

I went to Texas Woman's University in 1974. Since it was a state university, every graduate had to have six hours of American history and six of American government. Therefore, each semester I taught there, I taught six hours of freshman American history. After the first year, I taught mostly "U.S. History, 1877 to the Present" because my graduate training had really been in modern U.S. history.

As professors, we had to teach twelve hours every semester. TWU was open admissions, and the freshman class of students were often nontraditional or first-generation college students. Many of the students were over forty years of age (the average age of the student body was twenty-six). My high school teaching definitely helped me, because I really could relate to people. I also taught some upper-level classes, including "The European Immigrant in American History" and "The U.S. since 1900." I also occasionally taught graduate classes, including a course on the South in American history, and historiography. While at TWU, I also went out to observe student teachers, in addition to the twelve hours of teaching. We also were required to keep office hours for eight hours a week. As far as the undergraduate program in history went, TWU was primarily a teaching university.

I did nothing the first two years but prepare lectures, and I also indulged in reading all the Agatha Christie novels that I had laid aside for so many years. Then I started cutting my 550-page dissertation down for publication. When I gave my first paper based on the dissertation, I saw a man waving a piece of paper at me in the crowd. He came up to talk to me about the paper. He was Barney McKee, the head of the University Press of Mississippi. He then agreed to have it read by the SHA executive director, who was then William E. Holmes. I knew it was too long, and Holmes said so, but he encouraged me to write the book. It finally came out, in 1978, as *Pat Harrison: The New Deal Years.*[5]

After three years, Dr. Yarborough retired as chairman, and the "search" was on. I did not want to be chairman, but at Christmas, Dr. Droze, the provost, called me at home in New Albany, Mississippi. He asked if I had gotten "my goods on the table." I said no, and he told me to get them there as soon as I was back in Texas, and I was named chairman. I did not like that and told them I would take it for only three years. Turning in book orders to the library and bookstore scheduling were problems, and so were many of the other mind-numbing details of running a department.

We did have guest speakers come. Mary Frederickson talked on summer schools for women. Catherine Clinton talked about white women on the plantations, and Sarah Alpern came over from Texas A&M. I went to a conference at Indiana University about integrating women into the history survey courses. The Organization of American Historians was planning a series of conferences on the subject, and TWU was lucky to be selected. Elizabeth Fox-Genovese keynoted the conference, and she was great. We also had Virginia Foster Durr down to talk to my classes. She asked the girls if they had voted in the last election, and very few raised their hands. Durr really lit into them and made quite an impression.

During Summer-1 terms, I went several times to the Roosevelt Library to work on Ellen Woodward and to the Hoover Library to work on Lou Hoover and the antecedents to women's work in the Depression. I also received a grant to go to the Truman Library to work on Joe Short, who was a native of Vicksburg and Truman's second press secretary. I only had the first term of summer to do my research during all the years at TWU.

One year I had a National Endowment for the Humanities travel grant to go to the University of Minnesota to work on Loula Dunn, who was the first child welfare director of the first Children's Division of State Welfare departments. She rose to be the head of the Public Welfare Administration, with offices in Chicago. Wilbur Cohen told me that she and Frances Perkins were the most important women in bringing about Medicare. I gave a paper on Dunn at a conference in Alabama. I also received research grants for this and other projects from the American Philosophical Society and the Smithsonian Institution.

My next major book research project was on Ellen Woodward, again a Mississippi native. I had found Ellen in graduate school because I specialized in the New Deal era. I had read correspondence between Ellen and Pat Harrison. Ellen Woodward was one of the New Deal women Franklin Roosevelt appointed. She was next to Frances Perkins in importance among New Deal women. Woodward was named head of the Federal Emergency Relief Administration, and later, the Works Progress Administration programs for women. In 1938, she became a member of the Social Security Board, and she ended her career in 1954 as a director of one of the agencies in the new Department of Health, Education, and Welfare.

During the summers of AP reading, when I traveled up east, I went to the National Archives. I visited them several times over the years. Finally, the book on Ellen came out in April 1995, and I retired that same year. I had had a couple of semesters when I was free to write, but I still had had responsibilities for the Department of History at TWU. I took off one semester without pay to be able to finish the book, *Ellen S. Woodward: New Deal Advocate for Women.*[6]

TWU was a teaching university. Elizabeth Taylor and I were the only faculty members who were serious about writing. We were both given the Cornaro Award. (Elena Cornaro was Italian and the first female to receive a PhD, in 1678.) We didn't have to deal with jealousy within our department because most of our colleagues simply did not subject themselves to the academic demands we set for ourselves.

Through my years at TWU, and beyond, I truly enjoyed the Southern Historical Association. I served as chairman of the Fletcher Green and Charles Sydnor Committees, and I sat on the Nominating Committee and the C. Vann Woodward Prize Committee. I served a term on the Executive Committee and a term as a member of the board of editors for the *Journal of Southern History*. I was a member of the review board for the *Journal of Mississippi History*, and one year I was a member of the Organization of American Historians (OAH) Program Committee. I was also a member of the Presbyterian Makemie Prize Committee. In retirement, I was president of the Mississippi Historical Society. I was also a panelist for the American Fellowships Selection Committee for the American Historical Association, and I served three years on the American Fellowships Committee for University Women. Eudora Welty once said she was invited to speak so much because she showed up on time and was never drunk. I think I was active professionally because I always got the work turned in on time—nothing else can explain it.

My professional activities and committees were extremely important to my sense of self as a professional, as well as being a lot of fun. I was one of the early participants in the Southern Association for Women Historians (SAWH). In 1969, my first year of graduate school, it just met in a small room, and, really, it was just a woman's caucus.

I was the first SAWH president who had a speaker come in to give an address. I invited Elizabeth Jacoway to be our first speaker, and for her speech, George Tindall and the UNC group came, and some other men attended as well. It was the first time that men came, and I thought it was a breakthrough. Today as many people attend the SAWH meeting as attend the SHA's president's address. Clearly, it was an idea whose time had come.

More and more over those years, I found myself thinking about southern women's history, and women's history in general. It was very exciting to me to be a part of a new departure in my field, as women's history took off and just exploded. The new popularity definitely encouraged me in my writing and in my teaching. Now, however, when I read book reviews I find less and less on women's history. It's been researched so heavily that scholars have turned to other subjects. At least they have turned women's history into the larger subject of gender history.

I retired in 1995 and went home to Starkville, Mississippi, and Margaret and I bought a house there. Margaret had retired after twenty-five years at Mississippi State University, where she was a social work professor and chaired the program in her last years there. Margaret had received her master's of social work at the University of Oklahoma. When I returned to

Starkville, the Mississippi State University History Department chairman, Dr. Charles Lowery, offered me a job, and I taught off and on until I was seventy-five years old. In 2003, Dr. Richard Damms asked me to teach a course in the master's program for high school teachers. I choose to teach modern U.S. history using the transparencies and other methods materials that I had used in high school in Pensacola. I began to have eye trouble and eye operations, and I would miss some semesters teaching. At Mississippi State I taught the second half of the American history survey, as well as "U.S. in the Modern Period, 1917–1945." I also developed a course titled "Southern Women's History from the Revolution to the Present," and I taught post-1945 United States history.

While I was at TWU, I thought there should be a book on Mississippi women, but I was so busy in those years that I just couldn't get into it. When I returned to Mississippi, I contacted Jan Hawks at Ole Miss with the idea of doing the book. Eventually she and I invited Elizabeth Payne (also at the University of Mississippi) to join us, and we just went for it. Sadly, Jan died, and so Elizabeth and I invited Marjorie Spruill, who was at the University of Southern Mississippi in Hattiesburg, to join us. Marjorie had moved to the University of South Carolina by the time we really got under way. That was in about 1996. One morning at the SHA, when Elizabeth and I had breakfast with Nancy Grayson, of the University of Georgia Press, we brought this idea up, and she just really jumped on it.

Our book, *Mississippi Women: Their Histories, Their Lives,* was the first volume in that University of Georgia series about the lives and experiences of southern women.[7] And since then the project has spread to every other southern state, including Oklahoma, and some of them have gone into as many as three volumes. We got out a second book for Mississippi women; the first had biographies, and the second was topical.[8] Of course, it's not known that we started this series, and it has gone on so long that our role in beginning the series has been almost forgotten.

I had been thinking for years about doing a book on Lucy Somerville Howorth, one of the so-called New Deal women. Dorothy Shawhan, my friend who was a professor of language and literature at Delta State, was also interested in the project. She had interviewed Howorth and had also spent about three weeks at the Schlesinger Library, where the Somerville-Howorth

Papers are housed. Dorothy got a world of material. She drafted three chapters of Lucy's early history, which she had gotten in-depth at Schlesinger. And I wrote the last six chapters. Anne Scott wrote a long introduction describing her friendship with Lucy Howorth, and Louisiana State University Press published the book in 2006.[9] Lucy Howorth did not have a New Deal job per se, but her importance lies in her work with business and professional women, the American Association of University Women, and numerous feminist organizations. Bertram Wyatt-Brown, who was editor of the series on southerners at LSU, really liked the manuscript we submitted and decided to publish it.

Since retiring, I have written about three-fourths of a biography of Wall Doxey, which I had hoped to have published by the University Press of Mississippi. Doxey represented Mississippi through seven terms in Congress and one year in the Senate. He was succeeded by Senator Jim Eastland. But my eyes went bad, and I had to give it up.

One of the great joys in my retirement has been the Delta Women Writers. We read papers that other members of the group write and critique them before they are published. That is a great help. I have written on Ross Collins, who in the depths of the Great Depression succeeded in having Congress purchase an incunabulum, including a rare velum Bible. I also wrote for the Deltas on T. Webber Wilson, who became a federal judge in the Virgin Islands and wrangled with Harold Ickes during the New Deal, and Mississippi senator Hubert Stephens (1922–34). It seems that my writing career has been devoted to giving historical visibility to Mississippians.

When I look back on my career, I tend to look on the thirteen years in Florida with the greatest joy. I think it was because of the complete rapport I had with all the kids. Besides, I had them for fifty minutes a day, five days a week for eighteen weeks. At Texas Woman's University, I had the students for seventy-five minutes twice a week for fifteen weeks (you do the arithmetic and see how different high school teaching was from college). I think I taught a lot more history at Pensacola High School than I did at Texas Woman's University. Also, at TWU it was difficult to teach and write at the same. Finding the time to write was a constant struggle. But I enjoyed teaching at TWU very much, and looking back on it now, I'm proud that I did figure out how to write and teach at the same time. Even though it took me twenty-one years to get the first two books out, I am proud of that. But then, I was single, and I had that Vanderbilt training. Also, at TWU, I had some very good students in the survey, upper-level, and graduate classes. I sent doctoral students to Rice (Ginger Frost) and the University of Mississippi (Patty Taylor).

In recent years, Dr. Alan Marcus, the chair at Mississippi State University, has been very kind to include me in departmental activities. Professors Mary Kathryn Barbier and Anne Marshall are good friends and keep me up on department news. They all act like I am still a member of the department.

It is hard for me to believe that it has been fifty years since I left Pensacola High School and twenty-four since I retired from Texas Woman's University. I have enjoyed all of it. In closing, I wish to pay homage to my parents, Jim Henry and Berna Wellborn Swain, for their high standards and their wonderful examples. Without their encouragement and support, I would have had a very different kind of life.

NOTES

1. Because of Martha Swain's limited vision, which makes writing very difficult, this essay has been drawn from a long interview conducted by her colleague, professor Anne Marshall.

2. Dr. Glover Moore published *Missouri Controversy, 1819–21* in 1982 through the University Press of Kentucky. Dr. John Bettersworth wrote or edited ten books, including a textbook, *Mississippi: A History* (1959); *Mississippi in the Confederacy* (1961); and *Your Mississippi* (1975), as well as other publications.

3. Dr. Dewey Grantham wrote, among other works, *Hoke Smith and the Politics of the New South* (1958); *The Democratic South* (1965); *The United States since 1945: The Ordeal of Power* (1975); *The Regional Imagination: The South and Recent American History* (1979); *Southern Progressivism: The Reconciliation of Progress and Tradition* (1983); *Recent America: The United States since 1945* (1987); and *The Life and Death of the Solid South: A Political History* (1988).

4. David Potter, *People of Plenty: Economic Abundance and the American Character* (Chicago: University of Chicago Press, 1954).

5. Martha Swain, *Pat Harrison: The New Deal Years* (Jackson: University Press of Mississippi, 1978).

6. Martha Swain, *Ellen S. Woodward: New Deal Advocate for Women* (Jackson: University Press of Mississippi, 1995).

7. Martha Swain, Elizabeth Anne Payne, and Marjorie Spruill, eds., *Mississippi Women: Their Histories, Their Lives*, vol. 1 (Athens: University of Georgia Press, 2003).

8. Martha Swain, Elizabeth Anne Payne, and Marjorie Spruill, eds., *Mississippi Women: Their Histories, Their Lives*, vol. 2 (Athens: University of Georgia Press, 2010).

9. Martha Swain and Dorothy Shawhan, *Lucy Somerville Howorth: New Deal Lawyer, Politician and Feminist from the South* (Baton Rouge: Louisiana State University Press, 2006).

TURNING POINTS

SYLVIA FREY

What makes us who we are? Is it, as Susan Faludi asks, what you choose or what you cannot escape?[1] A little bit of both. The source of my identity as a person and as a historian are the "fateful forces" we cannot escape: genetics and family, culture and history and personal choice. I was born and raised in a small, not-so-southern town in an area called Prairie Faquetaique, in the heart of Louisiana's Acadiana. Founded by a pioneer lawman, the town was named after his second wife, Eunice, whose statue now occupies a prominent place in the city's main street.

Born into a cultural milieu that was a fusion of French Acadian and German ancestry, I am a descendant of people displaced by the political upheavals of their times. Homer Daigle, my paternal great-grandfather, and my maternal great-grandfather, Duprive Miller, were among the first settlers in Acadiana. Both families originally hailed from Germany but were descendants of the earlier waves of immigrants fleeing ethnic cleansing in Nova Scotia. Their obituaries recognize both as prominent pioneering rice farmers.

My paternal grandfather, Johann Frey, was a veteran of the Franco-Prussian War who had fought on the side of France. Although short-lived in comparison to most wars (1870–71), the war was bloody and chaotic, inspiring Rimbaud's haunting poem "Le dormeur du val." The Treaty of Frankfort left most of Alsace in German control and sent thousands of Alsatians fleeing to revolutionary Paris; my paternal great-grandfather and four of his brothers fled from his farm in Dettweller, Alsace, to Louisiana. Shortly after arriving in New Orleans, the twenty-six-year-old Johann married Marie Schneider, from

Altoberndorf, Germany, and the young couple moved to southwest Louisiana. In a pattern common to emigrants from French peripheries, once in Louisiana Johann reclaimed ownership of his German identity.

I grew up in the shadow of that ancestry in a German cultural and language-speaking environment surrounded by French-speaking Acadian descendants who clung not only to their ancestral language but to the peculiar rituals that still recall medieval rural village social customs—the *courrir de mardi gras* and the *charivari* or shivaree. That peculiar cultural mix explains why I describe Eunice as a "not-so-southern town." To be sure, the town had the usual mix of southern characters but with a different accent: n'onc Alec—who, oblivious to the traffic on the asphalt streets, continued to ride his black stallion across town until he died; Tante Bat—who, rumor had it, had a background as colorful as the vivid orange rouge that stained her cheeks; or Ms. V—wife of a local banker who reportedly favored watering her lawn in the nude before dawn.

Although German Americans made up a significant part of the local population, the cultural and linguistic landscape was increasingly dominated by "Cajun" culture. The anti-German sentiment unleashed by World War I left many German families faced with the choice of shedding cultural vestiges, including language, or clinging to that heritage even in the face of discrimination. Despite laws prohibiting use of the German language and all public expressions of cultural heritage, my paternal ancestors chose to self-identify as Germans, with language as a particular mark of their "Germanness." I experienced that transition from French to German as a child when, on Sundays, our family made the obligatory trek to my grandparents' farm. There I lived in an Old World patriarchy ruled over by my tall, blond, blue-eyed grandfather, Joseph, and his meek wife, Lucette.

Those Sundays spent with dozens of cousins, sliding down haystacks, gorging on fruit from the orchard, were idyllic. Not so for my proud, independent mother, Helen, who privately railed against my grandfather's insistence that the adults speak only German, in total disregard of the French-speaking women who had married into the family. But the worst indignity was the Sunday meal served by women, first to men, then children, leaving, as my mother put it, women to eat the crumbs. In the meantime, my immediate family was writing a dichotomous narrative. Perhaps as a way of resisting linguistic patriarchy, or dodging the label of "Kraut" that became current during World War II, and the legal stigma of a "Cajun" heritage following World War II, or more likely as a bid for assimilation—my parents spoke only English at home. Exposed to two different cultural backgrounds, I was never fully immersed in either, thus losing my multilingual heritage. My closest friends, with family names like LaHaye, Sonnier, Foret, Frugé, assigned me a German or Alsatian identity, which I happily embraced as a badge of difference—an incipient claim to an independent identity.

It was only later in life that I recognized how completely I embody that history. The displacement of my ancestors by war and ethnic cleansing communicated to me a sense of rootlessness that followed me into adulthood. A descendant of displaced or diasporic populations, I was unconsciously drawn to diasporic studies. Genetics predisposed me to perceive different facets of oppression simultaneously and set me on an odyssey of my own that came to inform the issues that consume my writing—class, race, and gender.

I came of age in the 1950s, that horrible age of conformity still defined for me by poodle skirts, backward-buttoned cardigans, bobby sox, and ballerina slippers. In the Catholic school my siblings and I attended, history was a recitation of dates, twenty a day. In rural southwest Louisiana, the memory of the Civil War had little resonance or meaning in my life. I grew up happily ignorant of the Lost Cause myth. In fact, I only recently learned that both my maternal ancestors, Deprive Miller and Homer Daigle, fought in the Civil War on the side of the Confederate States of America, a part of my heritage I prefer not to acknowledge.

No "Lost Cause" but plenty of Jim Crow. The town's racial patterns were distinctly southern. Residential apartheid—with whites living in long lines radiating from the town center, blacks rigidly segregated in two neighborhoods on the east end of town, Happy Hill and Hungry Hill. Black townspeople drank at separate fountains, purchased their hamburgers at a separate window of the local Frost Top, secured their movie theater tickets at a separate window, and sat unseen upstairs in the balcony. I never saw my black peers enter or leave the Liberty Theatre, but I shared the peculiar intimacy that grows out of a paternalistic relationship with the black mostly women who worked for my parents and who, for better and for worse, were cared for by them and in turned cared for them in the final stages of both of my parents' lives.

Although I was still claimed by the past, I was increasingly detached from my home culture. My fantasies of independence were inspired by Nancy Drew, an unconventional investigative reporter who rode around in a blue convertible solving murder mysteries, and Toby Tyler, the orphan boy who ran away from his foster home to join the circus. They promised an escape from the constraints of womanly conventions that I was beginning to recognize. My parents, who held to a labor, ethnic, Catholic culture that in the context of the times resembled liberal ideals of tolerance and rejection of privilege, nevertheless decided, on the advice of our parish priest, to send me off to the "safe" environment of a small, private women's college, which turned out to be the most transformative experience of my life.

In 1953, I left my small hometown world for the even smaller world of a private women's college, in the tiny village of Grand Coteau. Founded in France in the tumultuous years following the French Revolution, the semi-cloistered Religieuses du Sacré Coeur de Jésus brought their revolutionary ideals of equality to rural Louisiana, where they established the Academy of the Sacred Heart, the first school for girls west of the Mississippi River, followed later by the College of the Sacred Heart. This little school was simultaneously conservative and radical. It educated the daughters of generations of French Creole families and provided a safe environment for girls of wealthy Cuban and Mexican families to learn English. Summers in the Yucatán with my roommate, Moza, opened up my worldview to "foreign" cultures and created a lasting appreciation for the beauty of difference.

I did not choose history so much as history chose me, by making me witness to two historic moments. In 1953, at the height of the "Red Scare" and at the urging of wealthy northern Catholics, the nuns hired recent convert Elizabeth Bentley to teach French—an unwise decision, but one that reflected their belief in personal redemption and their welcoming of the weak and demoralized. The notorious "Red Spy Queen" had been the lover of and member of the spy network led by Jacob Golos, the liaison between the Communist Party in the United States and Soviet intelligence, who arranged the assassination of Leon Trotsky. After Golos's death in her apartment, Bentley took over his network and was a spy for Soviet intelligence until she defected in 1945. Her testimony in 1948 before the House Un-American Activities Committee provided essential testimony in the Julius and Ethel Rosenberg case and "started a chain reaction that would transform American politics and culture."[2] Ironically, the Rosenbergs were executed on June 19, the year Bentley joined the college faculty. In 1952, she converted to Catholicism and became an informer for the United States.

It was in Bentley's class that I first experienced the drama of history. Haunted by guilt over her betrayal of friends and fearful for her life at the hands of KGB agents, Bentley suffered nightmares and drank heavily. On one occasion she held our class spellbound with stories of late-night phone calls and heavy breathing. Her fears were exacerbated when she was called back to testify before the House Un-American Activities Committee. Seeking company out of fear or loneliness, she invited a few of us to her apartment to watch Mardi Gras parades on television. We were there when FBI agents arrived to provide the lifelong protection guaranteed her as an informer. We were there when the reporters and banks of television cameras arrived to launch what one biographer calls "the most controversial phase of her witnessing career."[3] The notoriety that her testimony drew was the final straw even for the nuns. She was dismissed from her job and returned to the North, where she died of stomach cancer in 1963.

The moral passion that led the nuns to hire Elizabeth Bentley inspired another fateful decision the same year and sealed the fate of a slowly dying institution. A year before the *Brown v. Board of Education* decision, the little college added another ingredient to the quiet melting pot in the heart of the Acadian prairie by announcing its decision to integrate, thereby giving practical meaning to Gerda Lerner's characterization of religious women as "the most radical women in America." For the first time, I experienced belief in equality as more than an abstraction. It changed forever my worldview. Like most southern women of my generation, I had been raised in close proximity to black women with whom I had emotional bonds of connection, but our physical worlds and spiritual lives sharply divided behind an impenetrable color line.

In the intimate world of a small women's college, the vast distance between black and white evaporated. No howling mobs greeted the two women—one mature, composed, outgoing, secure in her own sense of self, the other young, reserved, diffident, still finding her identity. Guided by the examples set by the nuns, they and we became bound into a color-blind community. I emerged from that experience with a new and different consciousness that coalesced around the principle of social justice. How to translate that new ideal into action was a challenge for me in the context of the conforming, repressive Cold War 1950s. Following graduation, I drifted aimlessly, uncertain what direction my life should take. I did a stint as a classroom teacher, first at Eunice High School in my hometown, then at Alcee Fortier High School in New Orleans. The experience left me with deep admiration for the critical, underappreciated work of the classroom teacher but a sense of personal dissatisfaction.

Fresh out of a rich and fulfilling, if sheltered, experience in a multicultural environment, I was not prepared for the overt racism that confronted me in the classroom, and all too often on the streets of my hometown. Pushback against the incipient civil right movement and laws mandating desegregation expressed itself in toxic language. The N-word is generally recognized today as a unique form of hate speech so egregious that it stands apart from all other forms of hate speech. It was and unfortunately still is all too often a part of common speech. As a beginning teacher grappling with how to respond, I found no playbook: no school guidelines, no social pressure against bigoted behavior much less bigoted language, and laws that tilted in favor of free speech. The history I found in textbooks interpreted the Civil War as a conflict over states' rights and totally ignored the viciousness and horrors of slavery. Lacking the tools to connect the dots between past and present to confront racism directly in the school, I had no recourse but to use my authority as a teacher to ban such language from the classroom.

Following the breakup of a long and emotionally abusive romantic relationship, I set out in search of a new life or career path that would allow me to contribute to a more human and inclusive historical narrative. At Fortier Senior High School in New Orleans I met with less overt racism, but teaching the same course five hours a day quickly exhausted my interest in classroom teaching. With no definite long game in mind, I took a couple of history courses at Tulane University during the summer of 1966. Whether history chose me again or through plain good luck, I cannot say, but at the end of the summer the department chair offered me a fellowship to work toward a PhD. I completed my degree in 1969 and was offered a three-year terminal appointment Tulane kept for a graduate student. Two years later I was offered a tenure-track appointment. Returning to one's home institution can be a mixed blessing. I was one of the fortunate few who were able to find the job I was trained for. I completed my degree in 1969 at the beginning of a fifteen-year crisis in the history job market. A surplus of PhDs and few academic appointments created thousands of academic vagabonds forced to accept part-time positions or seek employment in fields outside of academia.

I had entered Tulane University's history graduate program at the height of the epochal events of the 1960s and at a moment of a monumental shift in the writing of history from "consensus" history to a new social history "from the bottom up." I had always been drawn to stories about loss and reinvention, but I found a depressing failure of historians to incorporate the stories of working-class people and racial and ethnic groups—until I read Jesse Lemisch's "Jack Tar in the Streets: Merchant Seamen in the Politics of Revolutionary America."[4] In Lemisch's attempt to restore to society's memory the history of ordinary seamen, I found a part of the past that resonated with me. It was the inspiration for my doctoral dissertation and my first book on common English soldiers in the American Revolution and a cornerstone of my scholarly career.

Following Lemisch's example, I set myself the goals of discovering the human aspect of soldiering and transforming the image of the common solider as the "dregs" of society into a player who suffered and succeeded and sometimes did impossible things. As a neophyte historian, it was not immediately obvious to me that finding the historical voices of the voiceless would take years of research in archives that crossed borders—historical, intellectual, cultural, and geographic. However compelling the subject, the written records were sparse, mostly unyielding, and widely scattered in British archives. To make matters worse, I was a social historian of American history wading for the first time into the uncharted waters of British military records.

Fortunately for my future as an academic historian, the "publish or perish" pressure was not as intense then as it is today. The three-three course load at Tulane was still substantially less than the five courses a day I had taught as a high school teacher, and it was less than the average course load of colleagues teaching today in many state institutions. Even so, I spent most of my workweek in teaching, which included class preparation, grading papers, creating syllabi, and keeping office hours. What was left of the week I spent in university committee work or community service—the academic equivalent of the pro-bono work of lawyers, which for the most part goes unrecognized by tenure and promotions committees. Until I earned a one-semester paid sabbatical after six years of teaching, my research stayed on hold until the summer break, when I made an annual trek to the UK until I had exhausted all avenues of research.

In a pattern that repeated itself throughout my career as a fledgling scholar, along the way I received support from several of the most prominent scholars working in the field of early British-American colonial history. The fact that they were men reflected the lopsided demographics of the field. Each in his own way fostered my career and taught me valuable lessons about the importance of collegiality. The eminent historian John Shy loaned me his copy of a rare book of regimental records that allowed me to develop a profile of common English soldiers—including their size, geographic origins, and occupations—from which I was able to extrapolate something of the conditions that brought them into military service, and in the process, to challenge the idea that soldiers were the "dregs of society." A major problem for female historians then and now was a lack of representation on panels—for young scholars an essential step in getting exposure and an edge in the job market. John Murrin offered me a rare opportunity to serve as commentator on an all-male panel at Princeton. Jack Greene invited me to participate in four of his Liberty Fund Conferences, an exhilarating experience that brought me into contact with groups of scholars from various disciplines and introduced me to the joy of intellectual exchange. Ira Gruber invited me to spend a year at Rice on a visiting appointment, an all-too-rare opportunity to refresh and experience life away from my home university.

Years of sifting through the voluminous British Colonial Office Papers in search of the elusive common soldier defined for me my professional identity as an Anglo-American social historian—and led me to an even more elusive subject whose voice was almost totally silent in history—the enslaved. Benjamin Quarles's brilliant insight that the loyalty of enslaved people during the American Revolutionary War was "not to a place nor to a people but to a principle, the principle of liberty," was a source of inspiration for me.[5] Quarles's classic *The Negro in the American Revolution* was published in 1961 in a virtual historiographical void on the subject. My own *Water from the Rock:*

Black Resistance in a Revolutionary Age published thirty years later was not so much an attempt to revise Quarles—he got it right—as to expand and enrich his narrative and explore avenues that were, at the time, closed to him.[6]

This time I encountered a different set of problems with the sources. The Colonial Office Papers took me on a tour around the British Empire beyond the thirteen North American colonies and drew me inside a fragmented world of disorder, defiance, and violence among competing forces. Although the papers offered greater detail and new information, the great majority came from fundamentally biased sources—white, almost always men—and reflected the views of national military officers, tribal militia leaders, and aggrieved planters. My task was to find ways to coax out the voices of the enslaved. Over time, and with varying degrees of success, I learned to read behind the bias, the swagger, the fear, the conceit, and less often the shame of white men to find the collective dreams of enslaved men and women for freedom, in whatever form, however achieved, through flight, passive resistance, cultural independence, or violence.

A year at the Smithsonian Institution in 1988–89 as Senior Postdoctoral Fellow, with appointments in the Museum of American History, the Museum of Natural History, and the National Museum of African Art gave me access to museum libraries and curatorial staffs. As I trespassed into physical anthropology, I learned about the physical damage to bones and muscles and bodies caused by hard labor in tobacco, rice, cane and cotton fields. The dazzling collections of the Museum of African Art exposed me to the creative heritage that enslaved people brought with them in their hearts and minds that remains the source of the vibrant American expressive cultures Betty Wood and I studied for our coauthored book *Come Shouting to Zion: African American Protestant Christianity in the American South and the British Caribbean to 1830*.[7]

Through it all, and from opposite ends of the historiographical spectrum, I received support from Peter Wood and Eugene Genovese, both highly influential in setting the agenda for the historiography of slavery. Genovese, who self-identified as a reader for Princeton University Press, noted that although he disagreed with parts of my argument—which was closer to Wood's—he insisted that the press should publish the manuscript. Wood wrote copious notes on my manuscript and pushed me harder to listen for the slightest whisper coming through the documents.

To say that men helped me advance my career is not to say that I didn't experience discrimination of the sort that was and is systemic in academia. Because salaries were considered to be "private," I was unaware that mine was significantly lower than those of my male colleagues of the same rank until I was elected to the departmental executive committee, which was charged with responsibility for allocating cost-of-living and merit raises. When I protested, my genial and decent chair reminded me that my male colleagues had "families to support" and that several had entered the department at a time when base starting salaries were higher; he argued that it would therefore require patience on my part until my salary could "catch up," an argument I was unwilling to concede, and the department consequently made an appropriate adjustment.

Although I had been granted tenure without issue, there was at the time no concurrent advancement in rank, which was governed by separate terms. Considering that I met the criteria for promotion, the department recommended my promotion to the rank of associate professor. The University Tenure and Promotion Committee, chaired by a woman dean, denied my promotion without explanation. Given that I had equally attractive credentials as my male colleague, whom the committee passed without issue, gender discrimination seemed a likely explanation. I would like to say that my march to the newly established Equal Employment Opportunity Office on campus was motivated by a feminist ideology. But as Sara Evans, the historian and civil rights activist, said of the early women's movement, I and we did not have a gendered vocabulary to help us understand, much less challenge, discrimination. My understanding of equality was developed from and was still limited to race. For me, the promotion decision was about fundamental fairness. Whether he saw it as unfair or discriminatory or simply wished to avoid adverse publicity, the provost apparently found reasonable cause to question the decision. In the fall he reconvened the Tenure and Promotion Committee with instructions to review the case. They reversed the decision unanimously. However modest my intentions, in retrospect it served as a wake-up call that gender mattered.

My personal awareness of the need to take gender as seriously as other forms of discrimination developed in tandem with the women's movement. Although women appeared in *The British Solider in America*, it was only in peripheral roles, more in the wings than at center stage.[8] In 1980, as a struggling assistant professor at what was then Sophie Newcomb College, the oldest coordinate college in the country, I won a Woodrow Wilson National Fellowship Foundation award to attend a summer institute on women in U.S. history at Princeton University. The institute faculty represented the first time in my career that I would have female mentors. And what a group of mentors it was! Carol Berkin, Linda Kerber, Lois Banner, and Sara Evans. The institute would have been provocative in any context, but given the fact that it was on the leading edge of the emerging women's studies movement, the subject was all the more challenging. The publication of Kerber's *Women of the Republic* and Mary Beth Norton's *Liberty's Daughters* the same year gave impetus to the emerging field, which faced enormous resistance both inside and outside the academy.[9]

I acquired from each institute faculty member resources and methods that would stand me in good stead. Carol Berkin sent us to the archives, where Marion Morton and I discovered many of the documents that formed the collection we coedited and published in 1986 as *New World, New Roles: A Documentary History of Women in Pre-Industrial America.*[10] Back at Tulane, I introduced the first course on women in U.S. history. In my teaching, I followed the logical progression of women's historiography. In 1993, as Andrew W. Mellon Professor, I built my graduate seminar with gender as the analytical framework. The participation in the seminar of two of the most distinguished members of what would become the Delta Women Writers group greatly enriched it and my own intellectual life. Emily Clark in her first year as a graduate student brought intellectual maturity and acuity far beyond most of her peers. As a guest lecturer, Elizabeth Payne, whom I had met earlier at Cambridge, where we were both doing research, introduced me and my students to the rich cache of photographs, and the haunting face of Myrtle Lawrence, she had discovered through her research on tenant farmers.

In *Water from the Rock*, women were closer to the center of action but not yet an integral part of my work. At the time Betty Wood and I were researching and coauthoring *Come Shouting to Zion*, women were still largely absent from the political mainstream of American history. As we explored church archives on both sides of the Atlantic, we discovered, not to our surprise, that women were frequently at the forefront of the process of religious transformation from traditional African religions to Protestant Christianity. Unseen, unrecognized by later generations of historians, women are very much a visible presence in Baptist disciplinary records, in the Methodist fondness for counting and recordings statistics, in Anglican missionary reports, occasionally as preachers but more often as leaders in the conversion experience. How should their story be told? In many summer walks along the banks of the Cam River, we decided that instead of carving out distinctive social roles for women, or including them in a separate chapter or chapters as though their lives were experienced apart from their fathers, brothers, and husbands, we would integrate them into the text, where they could rightfully be seen both as actors in their own right and in interaction with the world around them.

Working collaboratively with Betty Wood was a new experience for me, intellectually stimulating and mind-expanding. Aside from editing a documents collection with Marion Morton, I had always worked alone, as do most historians. Our need to work through the documents to reach agreement on potentially controversial interpretative readings brought me to Cambridge on a regular basis and introduced me to a different intellectual community of scholars from throughout the United Kingdom. My appointment as Visiting Mellon Scholar in the spring of 1993, and an invitation to serve as Pitt Professor of American History in 1997–98, followed by my election as Honorary Fellow of Newnham College, were highlights of my academic career. My experiences at Cambridge reinforced my natural tendencies as a colonialist, and a student of Anglo-American history, to view the world through an Atlantic lens.

History is, for the most part, a solitary profession. But it also is or can be a collective experience. My collaboration with Betty Wood led eventually to a collaborative project between the faculties of history of Tulane and Cambridge. Over a six-year period, a group of senior scholars convened by Tony Badger, Paul Mellon Professor at Cambridge, and Betty Wood and myself, with considerable help from then graduate student Emily Clark, met alternately in New Orleans and Cambridge to examine the differential effects of two broad structural changes—the establishment of slavery and the coming of emancipation—on race, class, and gender in societies of the Atlantic world. The inaugural conference brought together scholars of empires that built the Atlantic world system of slavery—notably Britain and Portugal—and the

Caribbean and North American slave societies that emerged. The series culminated in 2001 with a focus on social justice and anticolonial movements in the Atlantic world. A forty-year retrospective on the Freedom Rides, the conference featured a discussion by five of the original Freedom Riders, including Diane Nash, and incorporated a professional development component for K-12 teachers from throughout the southeastern United States.

Open to the public, the conference drew a large and diverse audience and generated a highly animated discussion. Why, local civil rights leaders demanded to know, are our faces and voices absent in this conference on civil rights? Why are we invisible, our stories untold? Their insistence on their right to be heard recalled to mind two questions raised by Marc Bloch seventy years ago: What is the use of history? What is its value?[11] I said earlier that history chose me; it also changed me. On a personal level, research and writing about the history of race and racism, class and gender, helped me to know myself and to define the personal values that shape my understanding of the world and my place in it. But the opportunity to engage with the public in events like Tulane-Cambridge opened my eyes to the possibility of using history as a route to bring about social change. I do not intend to engage in the academic history/public history divide here. Nor do I mean to make a case for any one particular approach. Suffice it to say that I was becoming more interested in alternative ways of doing history. As a member of the Board of Advisors of the television series *Africans in America, America's Journey through Slavery,* and also *Liberty,* the PBS television documentary on the American Revolution, I had the opportunity to communicate what research had taught me through a medium that translated words into images.

A call in 1998 from the distinguished Caribbean scholar Hilary Beckles, inviting Tulane to host the first meeting of UNESCO's Transatlantic Slave Trade Education Project (TST) in the continental United States, turned me onto the path of social activism. Part of a global effort to "break the silence" about the international slave trade and the unhealed wounds of slavery, including modern forms of racism and slavery, the project forged triangular links between more than one hundred schools affiliated with ASPNet (UNESCO Associated Schools Project Network) in twenty countries in a massive effort to breach racial, ethnic, cultural, national, and international boundaries. The invitation presented a rare opportunity for Tulane's newly established Deep

South Regional Humanities Center—of which I was reluctant founding director—to join this global effort to improve teaching through enrichment of content knowledge and intercultural dialogue.

My nine years of service as national coordinator and member of the TST's International Task Force lay at the nexus of academic and public history. The TST International broke down the barriers between what Marc Bloch famously called "the watertight compartments" of disciplines by inviting university faculties, museum curators, archivists, and scholars from research centers to share the stage with classroom teachers, whose stories formed the core of every conference agenda. What I originally thought was to be a teaching experience turned out to be a learning experience for me and for most of the participants in the project. Our first TST meeting at Tulane in 2000 was open to the public, and like the earlier Tulane-Cambridge conference, it attracted a diverse audience of humanists, preservationists from local plantations, teachers and local activists, many of them descendants of enslaved people. Local activists from the African American community lauded the TST mission and its inspiring human rights discourse but noted the lack of cultural inclusion that deprived them of an opportunity of representing their own narrative on the public stage. At a later meeting in Charleston, South Carolina, an angry African American woman voiced a different complaint: "You come," she said of the TST, "and bring us hope, and then you leave, and nothing changes."

Although improvements in the daily lives of marginalized people were probably not significantly changed, the TST did help to create and spread a creative pedagogy based on shared international teaching materials and the infusion of new research on the tangible and intangible heritage of the slave trade. The international project continues today, but the TST/USA initiative held its last meeting in 2008, a victim of the recession that began that year. My experience with the program had suggested to me new ways to make the past "live in our world," as Bloch put it, by linking ideas to action. But it made me at least vaguely aware of its limits. My life as a historian had been dedicated to finding the voices of the voiceless, all of whom were dead and whose voices were largely lost to memory. But the plaintive appeal of the Charleston woman and the insistence of the living on their right to speak for themselves was a reminder that the living have speech, but we render them voiceless when we exclude them from discourse about their own history.

The Tulane-Cambridge Atlantic World Studies Group, UNESCO's Transatlantic Slave Trade Education Project, residency at the Smithsonian Museum and the John Carter Brown Library were fundamental to my development as a historian. But all of it also prepared me in unanticipated ways for another way of being a historian. In 2004, after a lifetime of research and writing, I was ready to shed my identity as an academic historian. I boxed my entire library and offered it to graduate students; what was left I donated to the university library. I shredded all of my notes, the accumulation of decades spent in happy isolation in archives and libraries. But my retirement did not quite put a bracket to end my career as an academic historian. I continued to publish articles and was well along in research on a new book project dealing with the Haitian Diaspora, a subject to which I continually circled back. But the Haitian Diaspora was of a different sort than the forced migration of African slaves. Although it was involuntary, it was multiracial, including enslaved people and free people of color fleeing the violence of the revolution. Many of the émigrés, like my subject, the Pierre Lambert family, belonged to a community of thriving French-Haitian coffee planters. Their story lies at the intersection of several powerful developments in Atlantic history: the Haitian Revolution; the dispersal of thousands of French-Haitians and their settlement in family clusters in Santiago, Cuba, and elsewhere; their establishment of coffee cultivation in eastern Cuba; the cultural wars between France and Spain precipitated by the Napoleonic invasion in 1809 that drove ten thousand of them—the Lambert family among them—to the French-speaking port of New Orleans.

A five-month tenure as Senior Mellon Research Fellow at the John Carter Brown Library (JCB) on the Brown University campus gave me access to the incomparable collections on the colonial history of the Americas, and also the opportunity to engage with pre- and postdoctoral fellows and independent scholars who made up a unique interdisciplinary community of researchers from Europe and North and South America. A deeply enriching experience that nourished me intellectually, it pointed me professionally in two directions: to Santiago and the Spanish archives to complete my research; and to a world outside the archives with a different, more actively engaged intellectual life. My lack of the portfolio of skills of the public historian, and my daily encounters with predoctoral fellows at the JCB—many of them highly trained in theory and new methodologies—told me that it just might be time to surrender the field to the rising generation.

Then came Katrina. In retrospect, I believe that I was always conscious at some level of my ancestral history of displacement. I do not mean to compare my seven-week evacuation experience with the dislocations suffered by tens of thousands of my New Orleans neighbors. At best victims of discrimination, at worst of racism, many of them have become part of a permanent internal dislocated population, in a sense a new diaspora. But Katrina and the first-hand experience of rupture from home and place changed the city and me in fundamental ways. In the face of the profound physical and emotional disaster, a flag and the *fleur de lys* became the ubiquitous symbol for a wide range of meanings and interpretations. For some the Bourbon *fleur de lys* connected the past with a new sense of survival, of togetherness, of unity, of community. For others, it was a troubling reminder of the shame of history associated with the city's European roots and the deep and persistent fragmentation of society that was and is a legacy of slavery.

As the city's lights came on and the discarded, fruit-fly infested refrigerators disappeared from the sidewalks, the multiplicity of meanings incorporated in the flag slowly became unified in a single acronym, NOLA. New Orleans has always defined itself in terms of a vocabulary of food and music. Nola is a location, a destination, a place. Recovered from the floodwaters, Nola translates as defiance, survival, resilience, home, sweet home. It expressed itself in a tentative optimism, a sense of community rooted in a place—Nola. A wave of civic activism, much of it "wearing lipstick and carrying a purse," as Pam Tyler memorably described it, drove recovery efforts and produced a mixed bag of results.[12] Although optimism faded and activism waxed and waned, an undercurrent persisted, kept alive by many of the neighborhood leaders of civic organizations raised by the storm.

Like many people across the social and political spectrum, I too felt a need to engage on issues of serious social concern. I signed petitions, made contributions, and attended public meetings called by One Greater New Orleans, one of the most successful female-led reform organizations, in a personal search for community. After forty years away from religion, I began attending a United Methodist Church whose brilliant female pastor preached a gospel of unity and tolerance. "All means all," she said, a three-word definition of my own understanding of community. Small steps leading to no place in particular. My improbable second career was launched by an invitation from three female friends, all formerly associated with Newcomb College, who wanted to create a woman-centered project to celebrate the three-hundred-year anniversary of the city's birth.

Little realizing what I was committing to, I casually signed on to what I imagined would be an avocation. Instead it became my late-life vocation. Like many academics in retirement, I was drawn into the nonprofit world by the desire to see the fruits of my academic labor make a tangible difference in people's lives. I had spent decades studying and writing about race and gender-based inequalities, but always at one step removed from day-to-day life. Katrina provided me with the incentive; Nola4Women offered me the opportunity to make the past meaningful in today's world through direct engagement with the community. Like most academic historians, I had no experience in social activism. In working with Nola4Women, I have essentially undergone a civics crash course, learning about and learning from the tireless work of civic and grassroots organizations from the ground up.

The name we chose for our nonprofit, Nola4Women, embodies our mission to call attention to the needs of the most vulnerable sectors of New Orleans society—low-income, underemployed, and working poor women and their children—through community-based and community-driven initiatives. To implement our vision, Nola4Women has developed a consensus-building model that breaks down the institutional silos that divide the philanthropic and research worlds. In contrast to most nonprofit community organizations, our role is to convene cultural and civic organizations with a dual purpose in mind: rewrite the narrative of New Orleans history that showcases the contributions of all women; and produce and advocate for a policy agenda based on community consensus that radically addresses the needs of underserved women and children. Time-consuming and labor-intensive, the process of bringing people together in informal venues where collective knowledge is shared and ideas are cross-fertilized appeals to my experience as an educator at the same time that it satisfies my desire to act as an education activist. It does more than that. It erases the sharp line drawn between academic and public history. It recognizes that the living have voices and that change, if it is to endure, must be led by the community itself, which in practice means the right to speak for themselves.

As Nola4Women has matured as an organization, our goals have become both narrower and more ambitious. Our immediate target is the racial- and gender-based discrimination that exists in exaggerated form in our community and in our region. But the problems faced by women are universal, recognized by the United Nations as the most urgent human rights issue of our time. Our ultimate goal is to develop a collaboratively defined action agenda, one that draws from and is inspired by conversations with key community stakeholders, from both the nonprofit world and academic research centers, with their global counterparts from developed and developing countries around the world.

Our society separates academic history from public history, but the division is more imagined than real. Both are in the business of trying to understand the world and to make it a better place. Never before, perhaps, has there been such a public need for history as there is today. In a recent article titled "Professors, We Need You," the noted *New York Times* journalist Nicholas Kristof called on professors to stop marginalizing themselves like "medieval monks" and use their knowledge to provide the historical context for some of the most controversial issues of our time.[13]

The response to Kristof's call was fierce. Blogs and online media are "FULL" of academics, Claire Potter pointed out.[14] Potter was speaking for many academic historians whose contributions to public knowledge go largely unnoticed and unreported. The "medieval monks" Kristof was speaking to from his privileged perch on the editorial pages of the *Times* are mostly tenured professors at some of the country's most elite institutions who eschew the role of public intellectual. Potter's forthright rebuke of Kristol, and by implication the "medieval monks," was an attempt to call attention to scholars like my friends and colleagues of the Delta Women Writers group who are successfully addressing larger audiences not only through classroom teaching and their contributions to the historical record but through the quiet dialogue they carry on with the public through active engagement with social media and community public history projects that create a link to the past and a connection between the public and the academy.

I have been a member of this remarkable organization since its founding. A diverse group from public and private institutions, the membership cuts across racial, class, and generational lines. As individuals and as a group, the Deltas have redefined collegial culture. The discourse at biannual meetings is a model for organizational cultures of all types—more inclusive, more democratic, more collaborative, more supportive, a place where ideas are freely discussed, and vibrant, even controversial, ways of thinking are encouraged. As a member of the Delta Women Writers group and a cofounder of Nola-4Women, I inhabit two parallel but connected communities where my twin roles of educator and social activist converge, a space where crossing and recrossing boundaries between the academy and the general public is both approved and practiced.

As I look toward the end of my professional life, I reflect back to the question I asked myself in the opening paragraph of this essay: What makes us who we are? My answer to myself is heritage and experience, a combination of geography, ethnicity, education, and luck. Genetics and family heritage made me sensitive to displacement, if only at an unconscious level, which formed the core of my research. As a young girl growing up in a small southern town, my life was of a piece with those of my friends and other girls of my generation. In other ways it was singular. My college experience, sheltered and limiting though it was in many ways, formed my beliefs and values, changed me as a person, and translated into my professional life. Support from senior colleagues opened doors for me that are otherwise largely closed to southern women of my social and educational background. In many ways, my professional journey has been a response to life-shaping events, most notably the stultifying conformity of the 1950s and the exhilarating 1960s demand for an end to discrimination in all its forms. Women were present in every event, though often pushed to the wings. Today my work as cofounder of Nola4Women is a small part of a general female-powered movement that stands as a thoroughgoing rejection of resurgent racism and sexism. It is an appropriate bracket to the ending of my professional life.

NOTES

1. Susan Faludi, *In the Darkroom* (New York: Picador, 2016).

2. Kathryn S. Olmstead, *Red Spy Queen: A Biography of Elizabeth Bentley* (Chapel Hill: University of North Carolina Press, 2003).

3. Ibid.

4. Jesse Lemisch, "Jack Tar in the Streets: Merchant Seamen in the Politics of Revolutionary America," *William and Mary Quarterly* (July 1968): 371–407.

5. Benjamin Quarles, *The Negro in the American Revolution* (Chapel Hill: University of North Carolina Press, 1961).

6. Sylvia Frey, *Water from the Rock: Black Resistance in a Revolutionary Age* (Princeton: Princeton University Press, 1991).

7. Sylvia Frey and Betty Wood, *Come Shouting to Zion: African American Protestant Christianity in the American South and the British Caribbean to 1830* (Chapel Hill: University of North Carolina Press, 1977).

8. Sylvia Frey, *The British Soldier in America: A Social History of Military Life in the Revolutionary Period* (Austin: University of Texas Press, 1981).

9. Linda Kerber, *Women of the Republic: Intellect and Ideology in Revolutionary America* (Chapel Hill: University of North Carolina Press, 1980); Mary Beth Norton, *Liberty's Daughters: The Revolutionary Experience of American Women, 1750–1800* (Boston: Little, Brown, 1980).

10. Sylvia Frey and Marion Morton, eds., *New World, New Roles: A Documentary History of Women in Pre-Industrial America* (Westport, CT: Greenwood, 1986).

11. Mark Bloch, *The Historian's Craft* (Manchester, UK: Manchester University Press, 1992).

12. Pam Tyler, "The Post-Katrina, Semi-Separate World of Gender Politics," *Journal of American History* (December 2007): 780–88.

13. Nicholas Kristof, "Professors, We Need You," *New York Times*, February 15, 2014.

14. Claire Potter, "Dear Mr. Kristof: A Letter from a Public Intellectual," *New York Times*, February 18, 2014.

THE PAST SHOULD BE FOREVER

ELIZABETH ANNE PAYNE

I was born six days before Christmas in 1943, in a house standing on land near the Tombigbee River, land claimed by my great-great grandfather after the Chickasaws left the area in the 1830s. When Mama, my maternal grandmother, learned that Mother was pregnant with her first grandchild, she insisted that Mother return home from Connecticut to give birth to me in the same bed where she had delivered Mother, and by the same country doctor. After all, Mama explained, doctors in the North did not know how to take care of mothers and babies. Mother honored Mama's request and traveled back to northeast Mississippi on a train loaded with soldiers.

My father soon followed. When Mother went into labor, Mama's friends assembled to assist in the delivery. Most Mississippi babies were born at home in the 1940s. It was not until I read Laurel Thatcher Ulrich's *A Midwife's Tale: The Life of Martha Ballard*, published in 1990, that I began to understand the important role that women friends and neighbors played in delivering babies in the rural South prior to the 1950s.[1]

No doubt, I was a welcomed baby. Mother told me that immediately after my birth, my father entered the birth room, knelt by the bed, and kissed my hand. My fourteen-year-old uncle Billy found a perfectly shaped holly tree full of berries and brought it into Mother's bedroom. I later found a letter my uncle had written to my grandfather, who worked in Corinth as a telegrapher for the Gulf, Mobile, and Ohio Railroad, telling him, "We have a baby, and her name is Elizabeth Anne."

I grew up in a close-knit family with my maternal grandparents and bachelor uncle living next door. Another uncle, his wife, and their little son lived on the other side. I loved tagging along with my grandparents when they visited relatives. My grandmother often warned her friends and relatives, saying: "She's a peculiar child. She will ask you a thousand questions." Fortunately, relatives generously welcomed my questions and often invited me to share a slice of chocolate cake as well. What I most enjoyed, however, were their stories about the past. I was an intense listener.

Eudora Welty's recollections in describing family outings on Sunday afternoons bring back memories of my childhood. She explained in *One Writer's Beginnings* that no seat in the car should be empty, and her mother often invited a neighbor to accompany the family on the outings. Small Eudora liked to sit between her mother and the neighbor. Once situated, Eudora looked up at them and said, "Now *talk.*" And the neighbor did—in a dialogue of "I said, '. . .' He said, '. . .' And I am told that she plainly said, '. . .'"[2] I loved listening to older people talk about the past. In fact, I preferred the companionship of elderly adults to that of children.

My grandmother loved quilting and often invited her friends over for an afternoon of easy conversation as they created beautiful quilts of scraps from dresses she had made for herself and her daughters. Mama's quilting frame was attached to the ceiling of the living room. I watched with anticipation as she lowered the frame. After the ladies sat down and began their needlework, I crawled under the frame and sat quietly for up to two hours. I was mesmerized by the rhythm of the needles pointing down from above and then disappearing beyond my sight but pulling thread behind them. I sat quietly looking back and forth at the moving needles and then at the four pairs of laced-up "granny" shoes. But what especially interested me were their stories—should I say their gossip?—about their youth and young adulthood.

Family cemeteries especially interested me. My father often took me for a Sunday-afternoon visit to his family burial ground, a Methodist cemetery named "New Chapel" that dated back to the Civil War. He obviously went for two reasons: he had a highly developed sense of responsibility and wanted to check the tombstones and fences; he also wanted to share memories with me of his dead kin. It was a time of sadness but also of sharing and intimacy. I was his oldest child, and I think he wanted me to know who among the dead had been generous and who had been scandalous. He told me of his half brother who died of swine flu fever in a North Carolina boot camp in 1918 and also of his grandfather's opening a box of apples for his store and pricking his thumb on a rusty nail. Tetanus raged in that area of the South, and his grandfather died two weeks later. The stories continued to build upon each other. Later on, I would learn from William Faulkner that "The past is never dead. It's not even past."[3]

In the 1850s, the Conwill and Hawkins families arrived in Monroe County, Mississippi, in covered wagons from Monroe County, Alabama, the site of Harper Lee's novel *To Kill a Mockingbird*.[4] My maternal grandfather's family cemetery continues to fascinate me. The cemetery sits atop the mile-long hill above the Tombigbee River. Until "straightened" by the Tenn-Tom Waterway in the 1970s, the Tombigbee meandered and curved, creating rich bottomland among hills of red clay. Even now when I walk into the cemetery, I feel that I have entered a different time, even a different world.

Southern rural families in the nineteenth century often created cemeteries on their own land. The Conwill cemetery is a short walk from the spot where the Conwill home stood. At the time Daniel Goodwin Conwill arrived, Indian mounds peppered the landscape of northeast Mississippi. A small mound stood on the Conwill property. Whether the mound was a ceremonial site or burial ground is unknown as the mound was never excavated. What is certain, however, is that Daniel Conwill, born in South Carolina in 1790, looked upon the Indian mound as a sacred site during a time when many settlers were turning mounds into rows of cotton and corn. He asked that he be buried on the mound; he died on July 31, 1863, just after Confederate troops fell to the Union army in the doomed Battles of Vicksburg and Gettysburg.

My maternal grandfather, Pa, died in 1978. He was the intellectual in my family. He taught Latin when he was in his twenties, and he celebrated my mother's birth by buying her a set of the eleventh edition of *The Encyclopaedia Britannica*, a gift which was handed down to me and will be given to my grandson at my death.[5] Two years before he died, I had asked Pa to go with me to the Conwill cemetery to record the names of all the dead and their relationships to him. I had four nephews at that time. I wanted them to know something of the suffering, but also the joy, of generations before them. At that time Pa was the only living person who knew where each person was buried. Importing marble and other metamorphic rocks had rarely been possible due to the difficulty of transporting heavy rock to a remote area. And also, marble was costly. Thick planks of wood were used instead, but they, of course, decayed. Memories had to substitute for marble.

The visit with my grandfather awakened memories that I had almost forgotten. Pa spoke of the enslaved elderly man, Dock, who chose to remain on the Conwill farm, even after being given his freedom. Dock, as Pa was told, asked to be buried on the edge of the mound. Dock's request was honored. I asked about another grave near Dock's. Pa hesitated, then looked away from me and said, "Shay [the name my family likes to call me], I hate to tell you this. She was my first cousin. She had a baby out of wedlock." I wondered how Pa could tell me about a family slave in a matter-of-fact manner but could not face me about an unwed mother in the family.

My family lived on the outskirts of my hometown, Nettleton. A black family, the Burts, lived across the road. I loved the mother of the family, whose name was Daisy. I played with her children. When she called them to dinner (the noon meal), I tagged along. I was so small that Daisy turned the chair around so I could stand and lean across the back of the chair to eat. I was warmly embraced in her home.

Daisy ironed for my grandmother. Although barely three, I remember clearly my grandmother's calling out to me, "It's dinnertime." I waited for Daisy to come with me to our dining table. I was stunned when she finished the garment and started ironing another. I said more loudly, "Daisy, it's dinnertime." She finished another garment, and to my frustration, she began another. I became angry and stomped my foot saying, "Daisy, it's dinnertime!" I pitched a minor temper tantrum. She would not look at me, and she badly hurt my feelings, something she had never done before. At that point, my grandmother came to the door and said, "Daisy will want to eat later." I instantly knew something was dreadfully wrong. I looked back and forth between Mama and Daisy, two people I deeply loved. At that moment, my sphincter muscle tightened, something that happened only once again that I remember—when I received a "U" on a second-grade spelling test! Psychologist Erik Erickson associated this phenomenon with feeling shame about oneself or another.[6]

Mississippi had the largest percentage of African Americans of any state in the country. I, however, do not remember experiencing a difference between "colored"—the term used to avoid the "n" word—and white people until my shock at Mama's not inviting Daisy to dinner. Nevertheless, by the time I entered school at age five, I was aware that my friend Emma Dee, Daisy's daughter, went to another school and rode on a different bus.

When I was eight years old, I learned about a controversy that had emerged in Nettleton. I attended a small Methodist church named "Shiloh." My paternal great-grandfather had been one of the twelve men who organized the church, where many of his descendants still attended. In fact, most of the members were kin to each other. A member-couple in their early forties had adopted Jimmy, a beautiful, one-year-old boy whose later picture is still in my scrapbook. As Jimmy approached the sixth grade, Miss Betty Lou, a sixth-grade teacher from a wealthy local family, demanded that he be tested to ensure he was white. She did not realize that blood did not prove one's color.

After church, it was the tradition that either Mama or another female relative prepared the meal. After eating, the men retreated to a separate room from the women and children and closed the door to discuss "serious" and political issues. I pulled a chair close to the door and pressed my ear to the wall. That particular afternoon I learned that Nazis had turned the skins of Jews into lampshades. I also learned that Miss Betty Lou had made her complaint official. The men tossed the issue back and forth. When my father had something important to say, he always cleared his throat as though to signal his decision. The chatter subsided, and he said: "This is what I think. He's Gilbert and Ludie's son. He's been a member of our church since he was a baby. No, men, there should be no test." Suddenly, there was consensus. And amazingly, there was indeed no test.

One day after school started, I was running late to my class because the school bus had mechanical problems. I turned a corner and heard moaning in the distance. As I got closer, I saw a huge teacher dressed in black lying on the stairs and obviously in pain. She was so heavy that she could not get up. I recognized her immediately as Miss Betty Lou (who always dressed in black) but felt no inclination to get help for her. I walked by slowly and said to myself: "That's what she gets for trying to kick Jimmy out of school. God punishes people who do things like that." I seated myself in my classroom and did not mention the scene outside.

After about fifteen minutes, however, I felt as though God had probably punished her enough. I raised my hand and told my teacher that Miss Betty Lou was lying on the steps when I came by. She ran for help. To this day, I have never felt any guilt about walking by fallen Miss Betty Lou and leaving her there on the steps to suffer. On the other hand, I was delighted that Jimmy became a terrific dancer, was popular with the girls, and was a member of the football team that won the state championship his senior year.

My father decided on Easter Sunday in 1956—the first Easter after the murder of Emmett Till—not to go to church but instead to visit the Shiloh National Military Park. It surprised us because Mother had made beautiful pink-and-white striped dresses for the three of us and had bought white straw hats with navy-blue binding. He drove us around the park, and we ended up facing cannons across the Tennessee River. My father explained how Union boats appeared around a bend in the river and surprised Confederate troops, resulting in the South's losing the battle.

My sister became agitated and asked, "Do you mean that if the Yankee boats had not come around the bend at just that time, we would have won the battle?" My father looked across the river with his eyes cast beyond the cannons. I could tell that he was about to say something important as he swallowed, and his Adam's apple seemed particularly prominent: "Well, the South might have won the battle, but it would not have won the war. It should not have won the war. Slavery was wrong, girls, very wrong!" I looked up at him in awe and with delight and thought, "My daddy knows something my teachers don't know."

On Monday morning two weeks later, Mother waked me at five o'clock, saying: "Your daddy is ill. You need to stay with him. I'm going to get Pa." I walked into the den and spoke to my father. I suddenly realized that his eyes were empty and that he did not know me. My grandfather and mother entered at that point. Pa took one look and said, "It's a stroke." I had no idea what a stroke was, but I knew my father was in a grave condition. At that time no ambulance was available in rural areas. Mother and Pa got Daddy into the car; Mother drove; I sat in the back seat with Daddy. Within three hours, the hospital's visiting room was filled with our relatives. Daddy was thirty-five; I was twelve. My world turned upside down that morning.

On Friday, Daddy spoke a single word and expressed a semblance of consciousness. It was obvious, however, that the stroke had taken a severe toll.

He had no feeling on his right side; in fact, he was paralyzed on that side of his body. Even as a businessman returning to his work, he had to sign his name with an X. Furthermore, he had two serious heart attacks in the next few months.

Daddy's stroke was not the only thing that devastated my family and me that year. On June 14, my four-year-old cousin Roger, who lived next door to us, walked with Mama across the road to the mailbox. After collecting the mail, he turned and ran in front of a car. He was instantly killed. To my sisters and me, Roger was more like a little brother than a cousin. My father was ordered by his physician not to attend the funeral. Even though I was only twelve, I felt the irony in my sisters and me wearing to Roger's funeral the pink-and-white striped dresses that Mother had made for us to wear on Easter Sunday. To this day, I wonder who Roger would have become as an adult. He was a beautiful child; he would have been a handsome man. There is still a space in my heart left empty because of his death.

After a near fatal stroke and two heart attacks, my father decided to move us to Houston the next year to be near Dr. Michael DeBakey, the prominent heart surgeon at Methodist Hospital who had been a key contributor to the development of the heart-lung machine. We moved in August. DeBakey immediately gave Daddy his prognosis: with no surgery, he would die within two years; with surgery, he had a fifty-fifty chance of surviving. My father asked, "When is your next opening?" DeBakey answered, "Friday." That was three days away; Daddy said, "I'll take it." Mother recalled to me that she focused on Dr. DeBakey's hands, thinking, "His hands could save my husband's life." One of DeBakey's residents was the son of the dean of Liberal Arts at the University of Mississippi. He showed Daddy the operating room and explained how the heart-lung machine worked. In addition, Dr. Lewis slept in the empty chair the night before the surgery. The surgery was successful; Daddy lived ten more years. My sisters and I grew up having a father.

Except for Methodist Hospital, Rice University, and the nearby park with huge live oaks, I hated Houston. It seemed soulless. The school I attended was huge, and I remember having only one friend, a girl named Marie, who was Hispanic. We sat together in class and genuinely liked each other. In retrospect, I think we probably recognized each other as outsiders. I did not like the teachers. My science teacher ridiculed me for asking about the working of mitosis, the process of cell division. I also did not feel comfortable with my money-hungry Payne relatives who lived in Houston. I insisted on going back home; Mother finally relented, and I returned to Nettleton to live with my grandparents.

My parents and two sisters moved back to Nettleton the next year. My father became a successful contractor. I admired both of my parents. I do not recall having experienced a stage of teenage rebellion. My mother made it clear that I, as the oldest of the children, should be a model of good behavior. My father had feminist instincts. Once he told my sisters and me, "I am working this hard so that you can tell any man who does not treat you right to hit the road." And once when we were discussing cheerleading, he commented, "I don't want one of my daughters making a fool of herself over some boy catching a ball." During my junior year in high school, I entered a beauty pageant and won. My father's response the next morning was, "I guess once is okay, but I hope you don't let it happen again." I didn't.

By high school I had discovered the Methodist church, with its camps, conferences, and meetings. At Mississippi camps, I met young people from all over the state. I became president of the state board of the Methodist Youth Fellowship (MYF). The summer after my eleventh grade, I attended an assembly at Lake Junaluska in North Carolina. We saw *Unto These Hills,* an outdoor play about the Cherokees.[7] I met a young African American man from Atlanta, the son of a Morehouse professor, and quickly learned that he knew a lot more than I. The Methodist church became the window from which I began to view the world. I loved the diversity, the interests, and the concerns that I began to experience. I took note that although the State of Mississippi prohibited integration, the Methodist church always had at least one person of color at camps. I remember particularly Christians from Japan and India. On one occasion, I complimented an Indian woman on the beauty of her sari, and I asked her how she wrapped the garment. She invited me to wear one and carefully wrapped me with an especially beautiful sari. I still have the photograph in my album of us side by side, showing off the beautiful saris.

During high school I became interested in women characters in novels. I was fortunate to have the mother of my best friend as my teacher. She gave our class a long list of books from which to choose, and she suggested which books I might like. In our junior year we read American literature, from poetry to novels. I especially liked Ellen Glasgow's *Barren Ground* and *Vein of Iron*. Until a friend wrote his dissertation on Glasgow, however, I had no idea her books were a social history of Virginia. I was deeply moved by Helen Hunt Jackson's *Ramona*, which portrayed the character of a mixed-race Scottish and Native American woman in the midst of a developing Southwest and California. In our senior year we read the literature of other countries. I chose Richard Llewellyn's *How Green Was My Valley*, set in a Welsh mining community. The lovely Bronwyn appealed to me as a character due to both her gentleness and her strength. I thought if I ever had a daughter, I would name her Bronwyn.[8]

In some ways I was a rebel. I read a number of college catalogues and noticed that applicants needed at least three years of math. At my high school, the junior class was divided into homerooms. During the first period, boys took geometry; girls took shorthand. Determined to take geometry, I explained to my English teacher that I needed the course for college. She reported my request to the superintendent, who responded, "What will Elizabeth do when the county nurse comes?" My teacher convinced him that arrangements could be made for me to hear the nurse's discussion of intimate female issues. The superintendent relented. I sat on the front seat, loved geometry, and did well. Gender-divided homerooms ended after that year.

When I finished high school, I decided to attend the "W," the Mississippi State College for Women, the first state-supported college for women in the United States. I had three reasons in mind: the tuition was modest (I did not want to burden my parents financially), my best teachers were graduates of the "W," and it was the closest four-year college to my home. If my father became ill, I could be home in one hour. By the end of my first college year (1962), however, I had decided that I needed to leave Mississippi. My attitudes, especially about race, were becoming more pronounced. I took summer courses in order to shorten my time at the "W."

The following semester was traumatic. On September 30, James Meredith, an African American Mississippi native and air force veteran, was escorted to a dormitory room on the University of Mississippi campus by United States Marshals. Meredith's admission had been ordered earlier by a three-judge panel from the U.S. Fifth Circuit Court of Appeals, the circuit covering the

Deep South. United States Supreme Court Justice Hugo Black, an Alabamian who had jurisdiction over interlocutory orders from the Fifth Circuit, upheld the judges' decision.

I had gone home that weekend, mainly to talk with my parents about the emerging Meredith situation. Many of my male friends belonged to the National Guard. Since Mississippi governor Ross Barnett had not honored his agreement with President Kennedy regarding Meredith's admission, the state's National Guard was nationalized one minute after midnight on September 30, 1962. Unrest began to grow when students and agitators learned of Meredith's ordered admission to the university. By evening a crowd had begun to assemble, mainly in response to the rhetoric and incitement of the segregationist governor, whom Judge Minor Wisdom of the Fifth Circuit called a "weasel of the worst kind."[9]

As I headed back to the "W," I saw trucks full of friends and relatives in Nettleton lined up waiting for their orders. They were terrified; so was I, for their sake. Already United States Marshals were trapped inside the Lyceum, the oldest and most important building on campus, with tear gas as their only protection. The Oxford unit of the National Guard was ordered to free the Marshals but was also trapped. Many were wounded. More units arrived only to be trapped as well.[10]

By 10:00 p.m., few students remained. The angry crowd, however, continued to throw metal pipes, rocks, bricks, and bottles. One Union County resident drove his bulldozer onto the steps of the Lyceum, seeking to smash into the building. Fortunately, he ran out of gas. A reporter had been murdered. The National Guard unit from my hometown arrived at the Oxford Armory exactly at the time President Kennedy gave the order to issue ammunition. Although they were tank crews untrained in riot control, the Nettleton unit was ordered to reach the entrapped Marshals and National Guard units and to use their loaded M1 rifles if necessary. My future brother-in-law was ordered to lead the trucks back to the Oxford Armory and to use force if necessary. His windshield was broken and his tarp was on fire, but he created a path which others followed. As he exited the campus, he faced a blockade of Mississippi Highway Patrolmen. He gunned his truck; the patrolmen and their vehicles scattered. Years later, I asked him why he had not stopped. He answered: "I was a soldier with a loaded M1 rifle. I did not stop because I was afraid I'd have to kill somebody." I was amazed at the discipline of the U.S. Marshals, the military, and the National Guardsmen.

The Meredith events and the following week took a severe toll on me. The "W" had a large dining hall; we dined together. I tired of the students rising and singing "Dixie." I hated the discussion of how much they detested President Kennedy and the federal government. My roommate went home on Friday night. I was alone. In the middle of the night, I awakened to a scream different from any I had ever heard. It was long and deep and terrifying. It took me several seconds to recognize I was the screamer. My throat throbbed with pain. Lights went on in the dormitory. Girls ran to the bathroom to see who had committed suicide in the shower. The next morning at breakfast the talk was of "the scream." I never told anyone that I was the person who screamed in the middle of the night. But I concluded one thing: I would never let myself be dominated by people who hated, especially those who valued only their own ethnicity. Somehow in that scream, I found a voice of freedom, and I promised myself that I would never let it go. I never had to scream again.

The following summer, I was elected to represent the Methodist Youth Fellowship at the national meeting at Evansville College (now the University of Evansville) in Evansville, Indiana. I became a member of the national council and was appointed the student representative to the General Board of Christian Social Concerns, which met that summer the week before the March on Washington. Dr. Martin Luther King spoke to the three thousand of us who assembled in downtown Chicago. As he exited the room, I positioned myself in order to shake his hand. I said, "I am from Mississippi, and I thank you." His answer was, "You're welcome." Somehow, that simple handshake was deeply satisfying.

The board to which I was elected included a diverse group. One was a young Japanese man whose family was robbed of its orange grove during World War II. He planned to become a minister and expressed a sense of grace and peace. Another was a young woman from Montana who planned to study religion; she became a professor at Harvard Divinity School. Another was a young African American man from Dallas who wanted to attend law school. Another was a young man from upstate New York who wanted to be a minister.

At the end of the meeting, we new members stood together to be photographed for a picture to be published in the *Christian Advocate*, the national Methodist publication. I stood next to Eddy, the young man from Dallas. Two months later the photograph appeared. I came home to learn that one of our church members had taken the paper to every merchant in my hometown saying, "Look what Dauley Payne's daughter is doing." When my father heard this, he said to me, "Put on your [red] blazer, and let's go downtown to have coffee." I realized while we were sitting together in Nettleton's only restaurant that Daddy was saying he was proud of me and that he did not give a flip what anybody said about me.

At the 1963 annual meeting of the National Council of the MYF at Christmas, I was chosen to be a lobbyist in Washington, D.C., for the following summer. The responsibility involved keeping abreast of legislation, informing state councils of upcoming proposals, and writing congressmen. It was a terrific experience. I had an office in the Board of Christian Social Concerns with a window that looked out on the Supreme Court Building. The job, however, involved long hours and extensive research. I tracked changes in proposed legislation as committees battled over minute differences. I focused on the Civil Rights Act and the War on Poverty. Even though I returned to Washington the next summer to lobby for the 1965 Voting Rights Act, I had realized by the end of the summer of 1964 that I did not want to be a bureaucrat or a politician. What I enjoyed most about the job was the research. Although I was deeply concerned about social justice, I also felt a yearning for spiritual needs that had lately been unmet.

I began to think about going to seminary. I wanted to learn more than I did at the "W." I did have encouragement from two professors, one who taught a course in Western civilization. His grandmother lived on the Cherokee Reservation in Oklahoma, and he occasionally referred to her. One day, he stepped away from his notes and discussed with excitement how the Spanish learned to make lace. I felt liberated from dates and monarchs. He made me glad that I had chosen history as my major. When another professor, a philosopher, handed back a paper I had written, he leaned over and quietly said, "Miss Payne, you should go to graduate school"—whatever that was!

Thinking about going to seminary made me remember a special event when I was sixteen, sitting on the front steps of my home in Bermuda shorts.

A large butterfly alit on my right knee. That beautiful creature began to spread its wings and gracefully move them back and forth. I became mesmerized by the beauty of its color and movement. I began to have thoughts I had never considered before: "Is that butterfly real; am I real? Or am I an idea in the mind of God?" Finally, *the* question: "Why is there something rather than nothing?" That experience lived on in me with questions like, "Why *should* there be something rather than nothing?" and "How do I know I am real?" In a philosophy course five years later, I learned that Gottfried Leibniz, a German philosopher who had lived more than three hundred years earlier, had explored *the* question I had asked. I later learned that the question, "Why is there something rather than nothing" is the fundamental question of metaphysics. At age sixteen, I had never heard the word "metaphysics," but I remember that a butterfly connected me with everything and everyone who existed.[11]

After lobbying for the Civil Rights Act and the War on Poverty over the summer, I entered Perkins School of Theology at Southern Methodist University. The fall 1964 entering class had ninety-two members, including three women seeking a bachelor of divinity (changed later to master of theology) degree. Our first gathering became memorable when Professor John Deschner held up his arm, pointed his finger skyward, and said: "When we Methodists say there is one way, we are not saying that there is *only* one way. We mean that our beliefs are salvific." He went on to say that there were many ways to have a salvific understanding of life. For me, his words were liberating.

Unlike many of my classmates who had previously studied theology and church history, I struggled at first. Frankly, I did not like the first half of the required church history sequence called "Patristics"—what woman would? One of my favorite courses, however, was the history of the liturgy, a course which began with the Nicene Creed and continued to the present. Some days I ended the class leaning over, eager to learn what the church would do next. I had taken history classes but none like this one. I saw the church literally creating itself.

Halfway through my three years in divinity school, I had gained confidence in my intellectual ability. The seminary curriculum required that all students in their second year take two semesters of systematic theology. More than one hundred of us attended the riveting lectures of our two leading theologians. We shared a common reading and wrote a paper. Each week one of the professors asked the student deemed to have written the best paper to read it to the class and then discuss it. I was shocked to hear my name called. In retrospect, I think that was an epiphany in my academic life—I could do it!

The "W" had not truly challenged or excited me academically. Professors teaching speech, for example, advised students on the first day of class that during our debate sessions, we could choose any topic we wanted except race, which could not be discussed. Perkins was as stimulating to me as the "W" was boring. Visiting professors from other institutions taught courses. I especially remember Viktor Frankl, the author of *Man's Search for Meaning*, a meditation on his three years in a Nazi concentration camp during World War II. His perspective on life encouraged us to ponder and explore the meaning of transcendent experience and to embrace the reality of human moral freedom.[12]

Late in my first year I fell in love with a classmate from Arkansas who, I thought, embodied everything I wanted in a partner. He had been a National Merit Scholar and an Eagle Scout. He was preparing to be ordained. *Plus* he was a southerner. We married in January 1966 with both sets of parents blessing our union. For the next few years, I followed him from Dallas to Durham, North Carolina, and to Chicago, where he enrolled in the University of Chicago PhD program in religion and psychology.

While at Perkins, I became interested in ordination and got nothing but encouragement from my husband, professors, and classmates. When I inquired about ministry in my husband's conference (the Methodist church divides into state conferences and regional jurisdictions), however, the district superintendent said: "Yes, we will ordain you. And we'll assign your husband to Podunk and make you his assistant." I had become close to the Reverend James Thomas, who worked as a staff member at the Methodists' Board of Education in Nashville. He became the youngest bishop in the Methodist church in 1964 and the only African American to serve in the North Central Jurisdiction of the church. I shared with him my experience of the Arkansas superintendent, and he said: "Come to Iowa. We'll ordain you." I would have loved serving under Bishop Thomas, but I shuddered at the idea of winters in Iowa.

The first year in Chicago, I taught fourth grade in an all-black community on the South Side of Chicago. I was heartbroken that only eight of the thirty-two children could read at grade level. I still think of Stephen Boyd, my favorite student. He was smart, kind, and gentle. He won the award for the best science exhibit in the district. I hope adulthood did not rob him of his gentleness.

I loved Chicago with its ethnic enclaves and its wonderful, inexpensive restaurants. I took the "El" and spent Saturday downtown exploring the wonderful architecture designed by Louis Sullivan and Frank Lloyd Wright. Before I lived in Chicago, I hated cities. I found Washington, D.C., interesting for two summers, but it never appealed to me beyond that. I hated Houston and Dallas. I was enthralled by Chicago's difference. I felt liberated.

Illinois offered free tuition to public school teachers who wanted to return to graduate school at public institutions. I enthusiastically enrolled in the history MA program at the University of Illinois at Chicago, which employed a stunning list of faculty members. Mayor Richard Daley had for years wanted his own university. At the time, he had the money to raid Ivy League institutions, as well as the University of Chicago. I took advantage of auditing professors like Stanley Mellon, a French historian who had been recruited from Yale's faculty. I remember vividly how he ended an undergraduate class on World War I: "And so, my dear students, this country gave Europe exactly what it did not need—a set of winners and a set of losers." I was stunned. I could not leave my seat. My mind went directly to the New Chapel and Conwill cemeteries. That one sentence has remained with me. Each time I taught a course which included the end of World War I, I concluded the course quoting Mellon's exact words, giving him credit with delight.

I entered graduate school thinking I would become a high school history teacher. Three women professors and one male led me to change my mind. One night I attended Anne Firor Scott's presentation on her book *The Southern Lady: From Pedestal to Politics, 1830–1930*. I had seen her on campus while a counselor at Duke Women's College during the academic year 1967–68, but I had never spoken with her. She impressed Duke students with her bobbed hair, flat shoes, no makeup, and fast walk. This was the first time I heard her speak. I have never forgotten her light-blue linen dress and black pumps. Her book riveted me, in part because she so eloquently captured the lives of southern, white, middle- and upper-middle-class women.[13]

The fruitful intersection of the publication in 1970 of Scott's book with the rising women's movement led historians to respond with a keen interest in both the approach and message of the book. Using women's diaries, letters, and other personal documents, Scott brilliantly demonstrated that the familiar dichotomy of personal versus public and private versus civic that had dominated traditional scholarship about men could not be made to fit women's lives. In doing so, she helped to open up vast terrains of women's neglected experiences for historical study. The book has never gone out of press. That night, I knew I wanted to be a historian, in fact, a woman historian like Anne Scott.

At the conclusion of course work for my MA, I faced the challenge of comprehensive exams, and I was terrified. One day I walked into the history office, and Professor Joan Scott—yes, *the* Joan Scott—asked when I planned to take the exams. I responded that I was planning to take another semester to study. She whirled around from the copy machine, put her hands on her hips, and said: "Elizabeth Payne, don't you realize that every morning when I am brushing my teeth, I say to myself, 'Joan Scott, today is the day somebody will find out that you are a fraud!' Now take the exams." I did and was invited to continue into the PhD program. I took my PhD comprehensive exams in 1976 and did well.

Chicago had been a labor center since the early 1880s. In 1886, violence broke out at Haymarket Square, where labor leaders and anarchists fought the police. Three years later, Jane Addams moved into a dilapidated mansion on South Halstead Street where she welcomed all—whom she called "neighbors." Hull House stood at the corner of the Illinois, Chicago campus. I often found myself wandering through the Hull House museum, gradually learning about the Chicago women who regarded the social settlement as an oasis of social reform. I especially appreciated Addams's dining room, as she metaphorically described democracy as a banquet to which all were welcome.

While taking a research seminar, I discovered the National Women's Trade Union League (NWTUL), established in 1903. I became especially interested in the League because it was an organization of working women and "allies," upper-middle-class women who were typically women of faith. The NWTUL had three major local associations: Chicago, New York, and Boston. Chicago and New York were the strongest, and they were led by two of the Dreier sisters: Margaret in Chicago and Mary in New York. They were activists of the most energetic kind. Mary Dreier, who was president of the New York WTUL, was arrested while marching with garment strikers in New York City in 1909. The next day her picture appeared on the front page of the *New York Times*, giving the public a vision of the conditions of women workers in the Garment District. The New York strike sparked one in Chicago in early 1910. Allies in both cities supported the strikes. Chicago allies marched in the picket lines with factory women opposing Hart, Schaffner, and Marx. A number of strikers were arrested and held in the city jail. One ally, Bertha Honore Palmer, showed up that night to offer bail. The officer said bail would be impossible because of the amount of money needed. Mrs. Palmer responded, "Would the deed to the land on which the *Chicago Tribune* stands be adequate?"

As I learned more about the NWTUL, I decided to focus on Margaret Dreier Robins, a Brooklyn-born woman and daughter of wealthy German immigrants, who became president of the League in 1907 and served in that position for fifteen years. On the paper which I submitted to fulfill my research requirement for the MA, my advisor, Professor Burton Bledstein, wrote, "Nice!" He then added that perhaps I might like to pursue the topic. I did.

My first book, *Reform, Labor, and Feminism: Margaret Dreier Robins and the Women's Trade Union League*, was the third book published in the University of Illinois Press's Women in American History series. Anne Scott, Jacquelyn Hall, and Mari Jo Buhle, editors of the series, made preparing the book for publication a joy.

In the meantime, my husband and I had moved to Macomb, Illinois, where he taught for four years at Western Illinois University. Then we came back to Hyde Park, where he taught at Chicago Theological Seminary for the rest of his career. Frankly, I had missed Chicago. I also awaited a baby who never arrived, but I was surrounded with the Regenstein Library and Newberry Library. My home had a third-floor study which looked out at John Dewey's Laboratory School and the Midway, the site of the World's Columbian Exhibition held in 1893. I was happy with my study, with its microfilm reader and with what I was learning.

After teaching at Roosevelt University and a number of other Chicago institutions, I was offered a position as a visiting assistant professor at the University of Illinois, Urbana-Champaign, during the academic year 1982–83.

At the annual meeting of the Southern Historical Association that year, I attended a stunning panel on lynching. Elizabeth Jacoway and Virginia Durr asked probing questions from the audience. I was especially impressed with Jacoway, who introduced herself simply as "Elizabeth Jacoway from Newport, Arkansas."

I was then offered a position of visiting assistant professor at Northwestern University for three years. Everything seemed to be moving along smoothly, except for my husband's asking for a divorce. I was especially appreciative of the support and generosity of the history faculty. Robert Wiebe agreed to read my manuscript and offered suggestions. Karen Halttunen and I went antique shopping together. Karen advised me of an open position in my field at the University of Arkansas at Fayetteville. I applied and accepted the position.

I loved the university, Fayetteville, and the Ozark Mountains. And I got to know Elizabeth Jacoway. Best of all, I adopted a beautiful three-day-old baby girl whom I named Conwill. I was asked to direct the honors program at Arkansas, where I became acquainted with faculty throughout the university. A group of us submitted a proposal to the National Endowment for the Humanities to revamp the core requirements in the honors program. It worked; we received a grant of $240,000. Those courses are still being taught, and I am delighted that Lynda Coon, my dear friend, is now dean of the honors college. I was awarded the university's Fulbright Fellowship at the Lucy Cavendish College at Cambridge University in 1992–93.

Anne Scott and Sylvia Frey spoke at the Cambridge History Department's monthly seminars. The following year, Sylvia invited me to Tulane to speak about Myrtle Lawrence, an illiterate white woman who joined the Southern Tenant Farmers' Union (STFU) in Arkansas. At the Tulane seminar, I met Emily Clark, who is both brilliant and beautiful!

My interest in Myrtle Lawrence and the STFU has spanned decades. When I arrived in Fayetteville in 1985, I remembered a comment made in a graduate seminar by Gilbert Osofsky, author of *Harlem: The Making of a Ghetto, Negro New York, 1890–1930*. I was the only southerner in the class, and Osofsky asked me several things about my experiences in the South. He ended the conversation with saying that he had always thought Arkansas governor Oval Faubus would end right where he had begun: at Commonwealth College and the Southern Tenant Farmers' Union. He, of course, did not speak literally but figuratively. I did not tell Professor Osofsky that I had never heard of the STFU.[14]

I decided to explore the STFU. I began reading the papers of the union, which were interesting enough, but I wanted to do a bottom-up book. I finally called H. L. Mitchell, cofounder of the STFU. He put me in touch with Priscilla Robertson, who, with her Vassar classmate Louise Boyle, a photographer, had gone to Arkansas in 1937. I hit the motherlode: the two women had spent two weeks in September with STFU organizer Myrtle Terry Lawrence documenting the STFU through photographs. Lawrence had been until two months earlier illiterate. Robertson had met Lawrence at the Southern Summer School for Women Industrial Workers in Arden, North Carolina. The school had just shown *King Cotton's Slaves* in *The March of Time* film series, and Myrtle had instantly sensed the power of the documentary.[15] Lawrence invited Robertson and her photographer friend to come to Arkansas and "take all the pictures you want."

When I called Robertson, she listened to me describe my research for thirty minutes. Then she asked me what I thought of Mitchell. I responded that I thought he was a misogynist, and she said, "I can forgive his peccadilloes but not his misogyny." She followed up with inviting me to come to Lexington and read her papers. If I were still interested, I could have copies of her papers because, she said, "I am too old to learn computers, and I am too arthritic to type." I, of course, flew to Lexington that summer of 1989.

Priscilla Robertson thought that when Myrtle Lawrence first got involved in the STFU, she was probably thinking of feeding her family but then discovered she had an extraordinary gift. Lawrence's rise in the STFU was meteoric; she quickly earned a reputation for being an extraordinarily effective organizer. By the spring of 1937 she had come to be regarded as the union's best organizer of African Americans. Myrtle at times apparently taunted male organizers by volunteering for difficult tasks and dangerous activities that men found too formidable. Even H. L. Mitchell remembered her as the best white woman organizer in the STFU.

In opening her home to Priscilla Robertson and Louise Boyle, Myrtle set the stage for documenting the story of the STFU from her perspective. By inviting Boyle to use her own life as a human document, Myrtle manifested confidence that her audience would not only find her struggle interesting, but that they would respond with empathy. Entirely missing from the photographs that Louise Boyle took is "*The* look—mournful, plaintive, nakedly near tears," the look pursued by Margaret Bourke-White and many Farm Security Administration (FSA) photographers.[16] While learning to read and write, therefore, Lawrence encountered an art form with an audience that bypassed local social hierarchies. In asking for the camera to be turned on her, she inverted the documentary.

Thus, Myrtle Lawrence herself invited a photographic project that would tell her own story to a country she had reason to hope would give a sympathetic ear to the injustices of farm laborers in the Arkansas Delta. Seeing *The March of Time*, organizing for the STFU, and studying at the summer school in North Carolina taught Myrtle Lawrence that a public, however distant, was interested in what she had to say. And in 1937, forty-six-year-old Lawrence stood ready for her audience. The intersection of Lawrence, Robertson, and Boyle remains historically compelling although unacknowledged.

Lawrence determined the places Robertson and Boyle went and the people whom they met. Robertson and Boyle worked as a team: Robertson collected notes and handled the flash; Boyle took the pictures over a ten-day period. These three women—Robertson, Boyle, and Lawrence—cooperated with each other to present a different and more hopeful image of the southern poor, one in sharp contrast to that of the hapless victim worn down by oppressive landlords and brutal weather. Their work together forged an active partnership: conceived by Lawrence, designed by Boyle, and executed by Robertson. Their collaboration left graphic evidence of southern sharecroppers and their world, for Boyle's photographs illustrate their daily home lives, their social gatherings, and their community rituals as well as their union activities.

Although I loved Fayetteville and the University of Arkansas, three things brought me to the University of Mississippi at Oxford. I had met Ken Rutherford at Camp Lake Stephens, a Methodist church camp just outside Oxford, during the summer of 1963. Our two-hour conversation in the dining hall began a lifelong friendship. For thirty-two years we had an entirely platonic relationship. In 1995, however, we both realized that our friendship had taken a romantic turn. We married the next spring.

In 1997 Jim and Sally Barksdale gave an endowment to establish an honors college at their alma mater in Oxford. They announced that they wanted to stop the brain drain out of Mississippi. I was offered and accepted the directorship of the honors college. At the same time, it had become apparent that Mother's health was declining. I wanted to live nearer her and my two sisters.

In the meantime, I was introduced to a tall, elegant, fabulously dressed woman who spoke with a wonderful southern accent—Martha Swain—at a Southern Historical Association annual meeting. As we chatted, it became obvious that we had similar interests, especially Mississippi and women. In 1997, Martha Swain; Joanne (Jan) Hawks, the director of the Sarah Isom Center for Women and Gender Studies; and I gathered on a spring day. We sat at an outdoor café on State Street in Jackson across the street from Millsaps College to discuss a project centering on the history of Mississippi women. Jan had surveyed sources from all of the eighty-two counties in the state. Within two hours, we had outlined essays for not one, but two volumes.

We were timid about taking to a publisher our proposal for two volumes—the first of biographies and the second of themes. Happily, however, Nicole Mitchell, the director of the University of Georgia Press, and Nancy Grayson, its editor in chief, made it easy. At the 1998 SHA meeting, Martha and I sat with Susan Ditto, who assisted with the editing, with our work spread out on a table. Nancy eyed our table full of papers and came over to ask us how our work was coming. She quickly looked at our work and said, "Come down to meet Nicole this afternoon." Nicole said immediately that she would like to publish our work and gave us everything we wanted: two volumes, paperback, and seventeen articles in each volume. We named our work the Mississippi Women's History Project.

Our template was followed by historians in Alabama, Arkansas, Georgia, Kentucky, Louisiana, North Carolina, South Carolina, Tennessee, Texas, and Virginia. Nineteen volumes in the Southern History Series have been published, and another is one the way. Martha and I enjoyed seeing our project expand. Janet Allured, my first PhD student, coedited *Louisiana Women*, volume 1.[17] Unfortunately, Jan Hawks did not see the fruit of her work. She unexpectedly died of a heart attack in the summer of 1998.

The University of Mississippi honors college was a success as soon as the doors opened. We had a Rhodes Scholar the second year, and by the fourth year we had four Truman Scholarships. The Barksdales enlarged their endowment in the fourth year, and we hired more staff. In the summer of 2000, Anne Firor Scott taught a remarkable course to my students entitled "Parallel Lives: Black Women; White Women," which one of my students later remembered as a life-changing experience. In spite of the honors college's success, my superior called me into her office and told me that she would not renew my contract at the end of the fifth year because, she said, "You are exhausted from giving birth to the honors college."

To my disappointment, my history chairman arranged for the position to go to a male associate professor who had no academic administrative responsibilities and had never taught any courses in the honors college. When I realized the role my history chair and my successor had played, I went to the professor and told him that I felt raped. His response was, "Babe, [nobody in academia had ever called me that], maybe in a year or two, we can have coffee." I stood up and said, "Don't count on it." I slammed the door. Although the position was advertised as a national search, in fact the provost, my chair, and the internal candidate had an agreement from the beginning. The provost changed the name of the head of the honors college from director to dean and raised the salary. Heretofore with my academic and professional work, I had always been treated fairly. I learned a lot from this experience, including that women do not necessarily look fondly on the success of another woman.

When I left the honors college, my honors students presented me with a photograph of William Faulkner's desk and typewriter. It hangs in my living room. I became a full-time history professor, became more involved with the Southern Association for Women Historians, and began publishing again. I enjoyed organizing the 2008 Porter Fortune Symposium and bringing leading women historians to our campus. I was given total freedom in choosing the historians, and I enjoyed editing *Writing Women's History: A Tribute to Anne Firor Scott.*[18] I was awarded a fellowship at the National Humanities Center during the academic year of 2008–9. I was the center's first Fellow from the University of Mississippi.

Writing Women's History resulted not only from the Porter Fortune Symposium but also the Delta Women's Writing Symposium. Betsy Jacoway said to me afterward: "You and I have been talking about creating a group of women historians from this area. So, let's do it!" We contacted women in the area who had attended the symposium. We met in late May in Oxford. We discussed some other women who might be interested. Ten years later, we still share our writing and our lives.

As I look back on my career, I vividly remember the Southern Historical Association's (SHA) meeting at Lexington, Kentucky, November 8–11, 1989. I presented in one panel and showed several of Louise Boyle's photographs. Priscilla Robertson and Anne Firor Scott, president of the SHA that year, were in the audience. One of the photographs showed Myrtle Lawrence in the office of Arkansas governor Carl Bailey with her hand on her hip, obviously advising him on an issue important to her. Anne Scott said during the question-and-answer session: "I want to know how a sharecropper woman could be in the office of the governor. That would never happen in North Carolina." I fumbled for an answer. I realized that I was in the presence of two remarkable historians. I took Priscilla to dinner the next evening, and just before we left the restaurant she said: "I am so happy that you are writing about these photographs. I feel as though a little piece of me has not been wasted." Her obituary appeared in the *New York Times* two weeks later.[19]

In my small study at home, I have two posters which remind me why I became a historian. One of them is titled "Eudora Welty's Symposium, Mississippi University for Women—October 10–12, 1991," which I attended. A dated Royal typewriter with a page half-typed sits in front of a group of rural Mississippians—one in overalls lighting a cigarette, standing next to a middle-aged woman with sagging breasts, a man whose face is not painted, but who is obviously next to his wife, and finally a curious young boy trying to make sense of what he is seeing. The other poster, advertising Arkansas Archaeology Society's "Archaeology Week/April 1–6, 1991," pictures an Indian mound with trees growing above. I see the words that drew me into the poster: "THE PAST SHOULD BE FOREVER."

NOTES

1. Laurel Thatcher Ulrich, *A Midwife's Tale: The Life of Martha Ballard, Based on Her Diary, 1785–1812* (New York: Knopf, 1990).

2. Eudora Welty, *One Writer's Beginnings* (Cambridge: Harvard University Press, 1983), 14.

3. William Faulkner, *Requiem for a Nun* (New York: Random House, 1950), 73.

4. Harper Lee, *To Kill a Mockingbird* (New York: Lippincott, 1960).

5. *The Encyclopaedia Britannica: A Dictionary of Arts, Sciences, Literature and General Information*, 11th ed., 29 vols. (New York: Encyclopaedia Britannica Company, 1910–11).

6. Erik Erikson, *Identity and the Life Cycle* (New York: Norton, 1959).

7. A revised version of *Unto These Hills* by Kermit Hunter, performed outside at Cherokee Mountainside Theatre, Cherokee, North Carolina.

8. Ellen Glasgow, *Barren Ground* (New York: Doubleday, Page, 1925); Glasgow, *Vein of Iron* (New York: Harcourt, Brace, 1935); Helen Hunt Jackson, *Ramona* (New York: Little, Brown, 1884); Richard Llewellyn, *How Green Was My Valley* (London: Michael Joseph, 1939).

9. http://repository.wustl.edu/concern/videos/dj52w630r, filmed with Judge John Minor Wisdom, conducted for *Eyes on the Prize*.

10. For details about Meredith's suit and the university's response, see Charles W. Eagles, *"The Price of Defiance": James Meredith and the Integration of Ole Miss* (Chapel Hill: University of North Carolina Press, 2009).

11. Maria Rose Antognazza, *Leibniz: An Intellectual Biography* (Cambridge: Cambridge University Press, 2009).

12. Victor E. Frankl, *Man's Search for Meaning: An Introduction to Logotherapy* (Boston: Beacon, 2006). Originally published in German in 1946; and in English in 1959 as *From Death-Camp to Existentialism.*

13. Anne Firor Scott, *The Southern Lady: From Pedestal to Politics, 1830–1930* (Chicago: University of Chicago Press, 1970).

14. Gilbert Osofsky, *Harlem: The Making of a Ghetto: Negro New York, 1890–1930* (New York: Harper and Row, 1968).

15. *King Cotton's Slaves*, in *The March of Time* series, vol. 2, no. 8, 1936, by Editors of *Time, the Newsmagazine* (RK Radio Pictures, Distributor Copyright 1936, Time, Inc.).

16. William Stott, *Documentary Expression and Thirties America* (New York: Oxford University Press, 1973), 60.

17. Jane Allured and Judith F. Gentry, eds., *Louisiana Women: Their Lives and Times* (Athens: University of Georgia Press, 2009).

18. Elizabeth Anne Payne, *Writing Women's History: A Tribute to Anne Firor Scott* (Jackson: University of Mississippi Press, 2011).

19. "Priscilla Robertson, 79, Historian and Teacher," *New York Times*, November 29, 1989.

AFTERWORD

STEPHANIE ROLPH

The extraordinary women whose memoirs comprise *No Straight Path* have contributed a jewel in these pages. Within their stories, and their beautiful diversity, resides an intricate network of lineage that led to the birth of the Delta Women Writers. I, unlike the women who narrate their personal paths with the dexterity and wisdom of whole lives, fully explored, joined this collection of scholars in 2010, at the very beginning of my career. Only a year and some months out of graduate school, I was returning from a one-year position that turned into a tenure-track search that resulted in an offer to "the other candidate," when Martha Swain called me and invited me to join a group of women historians who met twice a year at my alma mater, Millsaps College. Millsaps also happened to be the institution where I was about to begin a one-year position that turned into two one-year renewals, and, in my third year, a tenure-track search that resulted in an offer to "the inside candidate," who, this time, was me. In 2015, when the *Journal of Southern History* accepted my submission for publication, the first people with whom I shared my success were members of this group. The next spring, when the dean of Millsaps College offered me tenure, these women were the first to know.

I have heard stories at our Delta gatherings. When the "hard-nosed" critiques end, and we retreat to cocktail hour and a long dinner, the past moves around our table like a wraith. Many times it surfaces, as one might expect among a group of historians. But as the distance between that dinner table and the daily routine of our "real lives" expands, the stories of "former lives" appear as answers to questions. When I reflect on my own winding path within the profession, the snippets of memory and experience that these women have offered me feel like pieces of a much larger fortune carefully passed down to me, like an inheritance. When I share my stories with them, I hear the assenting murmurs of recognition. I feel their generosity in our shared celebrations of completed projects and professional accolades. And through these ongoing exchanges, experienced in different places and in different lifetimes, we feel the bonds of shared kinship. It is the kind of belonging that we study and write about in our own scholarship when we strive to locate our subjects within the geographies of family, place, and time to make better sense of their lives. After reading their stories, these women who have been so critical to my own formation within the discipline have become more than my mentors; they have become my sisters.

In these pages resides a landscape of women who reach far and wide over space and time. In some cases, they are found on the dusty shelves of an archive, recaptured in the monographs and essays that stitch together a scholar's lifetime. They are at times elusive, like Janann Sherman's Phoebe Omlie, and at other times they are faithful custodians of future generations, like Pamela Tyler's women managers of the Poydras Home. At other moments in these essays, women appear in flesh and blood, like Anne Firor Scott, with gentle coercion to quietly guide an adolescent career into the next stage in its maturity. Friendships surface across the pages, crystallizing in the moments following a compelling conference panel or an office meeting. In every description of these encounters, self-doubt, awe, and fascination pervade, whether our authors are witnessing a historical marvel in their subjects or they are admiring the strength and accomplishments of a fellow traveler who, over time, becomes a dear friend.

My first encounter with the Delta Women Writers encapsulated all of these responses. At first I felt nearly invisible next to these venerable women, sure that in my first submission to the group, a severely underdeveloped draft of what would become a chapter in my first book, they could have detected a dramatic misjudgment in welcoming me into their sophisticated ranks. But over eight years, these women have encircled me, personally and professionally. In the stories they have so generously shared in *No Straight Path*, I suddenly realize that I am a scion of an abundant inheritance that I am charged with bequeathing to other scholars.

But this collection is not a "how to make it in the academy" guidebook for women scholars. It does not rely on nostalgia or retrospective wisdom as its driving thesis. Instead, what the reader will discover, what I have discovered in these women whom I believed I knew so well, is the humility we should embrace in our observations of each other in the present and in our reflections on the past. For, at its core, *No Straight Path* presents historians as self-reflecting subjects. Professional accomplishments are redefined not only as completed projects, sitting on a bookshelf, but as moments in high school classrooms, administrative offices, community planning meetings, and on factory floors. Personal milestones are not always located in the formal unions written into family Bibles. Sometimes they linger around the final dissolution of a long-labored relationship, or in the discovery that the expectation of a tidy life has actually been an obstacle hiding in plain sight.

I sympathize with Beverly Bond when she explains the difficulty in writing about one's own life. As good historians we should all wonder what they chose to leave out, what and whom they have chosen to keep for themselves. In these pages, the beginning of future investigations sits, waiting for a wide-eyed scholar curious about these women to ask her own questions about where to go next to find crumbs of insight into these rich and complex lives. I have the privilege of looking toward the next time we sit around our table and ask the same questions of men and women long departed, residing in libraries and newspapers, diaries and living memory. But the next time we gather, I will watch with a scholar's eye these dear friends of mine who have navigated lives and careers in both traditional and unorthodox ways. I will see them not only as precious mentors and friends, but as branches of my family tree.

COLLECTIVE BIBLIOGRAPHY

BEVERLY GREENE BOND

"'Educating the Common Man': Developing the Public School Systems in Memphis and Shelby County, 1820–1944." In *The Dynamics of School Consolidation: Race, Economics, and the Politics of Educational Change*, edited by John M. Amis and Paul M. Wright, 21–56. Knoxville: University of Tennessee Press, 2018.

"Taylor-Made: Envisioning Black Memphis at Mid-Century." In *An Unseen Light: Black Struggles for Freedom in Memphis, Tennessee*, edited by Aram Goudsouzian and Charles McKinney, 107–29. Lexington: University of Kentucky Press, 2018.

"'Ma . . . Did Not Make a Good Slave': African American Women and Slavery in Tennessee." In *Tennessee Women: Their Lives and Times*, vol. 2, edited by Bond and Sarah Wilkerson Freeman, 7–35. Athens: University of Georgia Press, 2015.

——— and Sarah Wilkerson Freeman, eds. *Tennessee Women, Their Lives and Times*. Vol. 2. Athens: University of Georgia Press, 2015.

——— and Janann Sherman. *University of Memphis: A Pictorial History*. Charleston, SC: Arcadia, 2012.

——— and Janann Sherman. *Dreamers, Thinkers, Doers: A Centennial History of the University of Memphis*. Virginia Beach, VA: Donning, 2011.

"Millie Swan Price." In *Tennessee Women: Their Lives and Times*, vol. 1, edited by Sarah Wilkerson Freeman and Bond, 44–67. Athens: University of Georgia Press, 2009.

——— and Sarah Wilkerson Freeman. *Tennessee Women: Their Lives and Times*. Vol. 1. Athens: University of Georgia Press, 2009.

——— and Betty Huehls. "Sue Shelton White." In *Tennessee Women: Their Lives and Times*, vol. 1, edited by Sarah Wilkerson Freeman and Bond, 140–64. Athens: University of Georgia Press, 2009.

——— and Janann Sherman. *Images of America: Beale Street.* Charleston, SC: Arcadia, 2006.

"Roberta Church (1914–1996): Race and the Republican Party in the 1950s." In *The Human Tradition in African American History: Portraits of African American Life since 1865*, edited by Nina Mjagkji, 181–97. Wilmington, DE: Scholarly Resources, 2003.

——— and Janann Sherman. *Memphis in Black and White.* Charleston, SC: Arcadia, 2003.

"'Every Duty Incumbent upon Them': African American Women in Nineteenth-Century Memphis." *Tennessee Historical Quarterly* 59, no. 4 (Winter 2000): 254–73. Reprinted in *Trial and Triumph: Readings in Tennessee's African American Past,* edited by Carroll Van West, 203–26. Knoxville: University of Tennessee Press, 2002; and in *Tennessee Women in the Civil War: The Best of the Tennessee Historical Quarterly,* vol. 8, edited by Antoinette G. van Zelm, 140–62. Nashville: Tennessee Historical Society, 2014.

"'The Extent of the Law': Free Women of Color in Antebellum Memphis, Tennessee." In *Negotiating the Boundaries of Southern Womanhood: Dealing with the Powers That Be,* edited by Janet Coryell, Thomas Appleton Jr., Anastatia Sims, and Sandra Gioia Treadway, 7–26. Columbia: University of Missouri Press, 2000.

EMILY CLARK

"Slave Testimonies: The Long View." In *Slave Narratives in French and British North America, 1700–1848,* edited by Trevor Burnard and Sophie White. London: Routledge, 2019.

———, Ibrahima Thioub, and Cécile Vidal, eds. *New Orleans, Louisiana, and Saint-Louis, Senegal: Mirror Cities in the Atlantic World, 1659–2000s.* Baton Rouge: Louisiana State University Press, 2019.

"Genre et conversion religieuse des esclaves: La Nouvelle-Orléans 1729–1800." In *Les Laïcs dans la mission, Europe et Amériques, xvie–xviiiem siècles,* edited by Aliocha Maldavsky, 183–94. Tours: Presses Universitaires François Rabelais, 2017.

"Missionary Orders in French Colonial New Orleans." In *New Orleans: The Founding Era,* edited by Erin Greenwald. New Orleans: Historic New Orleans Collection, 2017.

"The Ursuline Nuns and the Roots of New Orleans Catholicism." In *New Orleans and the World: 1718–2018 Tricentennial Anthology,* edited by Nancy Dixon. New Orleans: Louisiana Endowment for the Humanities, 2017.

"The Tragic Mulatto and Passing." In *The Palgrave Handbook of Southern Gothic,* edited by Susan Castillo Street and Charles Crow, 259–70. London: Palgrave Macmillan, 2016.

"The Women across from Congo Square." In *Louisiana Women: Their Lives and Times,* vol. 2, edited by Mary Farmer Kaiser and Shannon Frystak, 11–24. Athens: University of Georgia Press, 2016.

——— and Greg Lambousy. "Archivist Meets Historian: A Conversation." In "Atlantic World Archives of Louisiana," special issue, *Collections: A Journal for Museum and Archive Professionals* 11, no. 3 (August 2015): 259–67.

——— and Greg Lamousy, eds. "Atlantic World Archives of Louisiana." Special issue, *Collections: A Journal for Museum and Archive Professionals* 11, no. 3 (August 2015).

——— and Greg Lambousy. "A Note from the Guest Editors." In "Atlantic World Archives of Louisiana," special issue, *Collections: A Journal for Museum and Archive Professionals* 11, no. 3 (August 2015): 163–66.

"Atlantic Alliances: Marriage among People of African Descent in New Orleans." In *Louisiana: Crossroads of the Atlantic World,* edited by Cécile Vidal, 165–83. Philadelphia: University of Pennsylvania Press, 2014.

The Strange History of the American Quadroon: Free Women of Color in the Revolutionary Atlantic World. Chapel Hill: University of North Carolina Press, 2013.

"When Is a Cloister Not a Cloister? Comparing Women and Religion in the Colonies of France and Spain." In *Women and Religion in the Atlantic Age, 1550–1900,* edited by Clark and Mary Laven, 67–87. London: Ashgate, 2013.

——— and Mary Laven, eds. *Women and Religion in the Atlantic Age, 1550–1900.* London: Ashgate, 2013.

——— and Cécile Vidal. "Les familles d'esclaves à La Nouvelle-Orléans et sur les plantations environnantes sous le Régime français (1699–1769)." *Annales de Démographie Historique* 122 (2011–12): 99–126.

"Refracted Reformations and the Making of Republicans." In *Empires of the Imagination: Transatlantic Histories of the Louisiana Purchase,* edited by Peter J. Kastor and François Weil, 180–203. Charlottesville: University of Virginia Press, 2009.

"How American Is New Orleans? What the Founding Era Has to Tell Us." In *Place, Identity, and Urban Culture: Odesa and New Orleans,* Kennen Institute Occasional Paper no. 31, edited by Samuel C. Ramer and Blair Ruble, 27–34. Washington, DC: Woodrow Wilson International Center for Scholars, 2008.

"Elite Designs and Popular Uprisings: Building and Rebuilding New Orleans, 1721, 1788, 2005." *Historical Reflections/Réflexions Historiques* 33, no. 2 (Summer 2007): 1–22.

"Hail Mary down by the Riverside: Black and White Catholic Women in Early America," In *The Religious History of American Women: Reimagining the Past,* edited by Catherine A. Brekus, 91–107. Chapel Hill: University of North Carolina Press, 2007.

Masterless Mistresses: The New Orleans Ursulines and the Development of a New World Society: 1727–1834. Chapel Hill: University of North Carolina Press for the Omohundro Institute of Early American History and Culture, 2007.

Ed. and trans. *Voices from an Early American Convent: Marie Madeleine Hachard and the New Orleans Ursulines, 1727–1760*. Baton Rouge: Louisiana State University Press, 2007.

"Patrimony without Pater: The New Orleans Ursulines and the Creation of a Material Legacy." In *French Colonial Louisiana and the Atlantic World*, edited by Bradley G. Bond, 95–110. Baton Rouge: Louisiana State University Press, 2005.

"Felicite Girodeau: Racial and Religious Identity in Antebellum Natchez." In *Mississippi Women: Their Histories, Their Lives*, vol. 1, edited by Elizabeth Payne, Marjorie Spruill, and Martha Swain, 4–20. Athens: University of Georgia Press, 2003.

"Peculiar Professionals: The Financial Strategies of the New Orleans Ursulines, 1777–1825." In *Neither Lady nor Slave: Working Women of the Old South*, edited by Michele Gillespie and Susana Delfino, 198–220. Chapel Hill: University of North Carolina Press, 2002.

——— and Virginia M. Gould. "The Feminine Face of Afro-Catholicism in New Orleans, 1727–1852." *William and Mary Quarterly*, 3d ser., 59, no. 2 (April 2002): 409–48.

"'By All the Conduct of Their Lives': A Laywomen's Confraternity in New Orleans, 1730–1744." *William and Mary Quarterly*, 3d ser., 54, no. 4 (October 1997): 769–94.

SYLVIA FREY

"La Nouvelle-Orléans: Mélangeur culturel du monde atlantique, 1718–1803." In *La Louisiane au carrefour des cultures*, edited by Nathalie Dessens and Jean-Pierre Le Glaunec, 15–36. Quebec City: Université Laval, 2016.

"Beyond Borders, Revising Atlantic History." In *Louisiana: Crossroads of the Atlantic World*, edited by Cécile Vidal, 184–204. Philadelphia: University of Pennsylvania Press, 2013.

"Acculturation and Gendered Conversion: African-American Catholic Women in New Orleans, 1726–1884." In *Beyond Conversion and Syncretism: Indigenous Encounters with Missionary Christianity, 1800–2000*, edited by David Lindenfeld and Miles Richardson, 213–41. Oxford, UK: Berghahn, 2011.

"Remembered Pasts: African Atlantic Religions." In *The Routledge History of Atlantic Slavery*, edited by Gad Heuman and Trevor Burnard, 153–69. London: Routledge, 2010.

"Resistance and Revolts in North American Slave Societies." In *Slavery, Abolition and Social Justice, 1490–2007*. Digital Slavery Program. London: Adam Matthew Digital, 2010.

"The American Revolution and the Creation of a Global African World." In *From Toussaint to Tupac: The Black International since the Age of Revolution*, edited by Michael O. West, William G. Martin, and Fanon Che Wilkins, 47–71. Chapel Hill: University of North Carolina Press, 2009.

"The Visible Church: Historiography of African American Religion since Raboteau." *Slavery and Abolition: A Journal of Comparative Studies* 29 (March 2008): 83–110.

"Cultural Migrations: A Time and Space Outline of Black Evangelical Protestantism." In *Diasporas: Consciousness and Imagination*, edited by Genevieve Fabre and Benedicte Alliote, 83–99. Amsterdam: Rodopi, 2004.

"Causes of the American Revolutions." In *Blackwell Companion to Colonial American History*, edited by Daniel Vickers, 508–29. Oxford, UK: Blackwell, 2003.

"Inequality in the Here and the Hereafter: Religion and the Construction of Race and Gender in the Postrevolutionary South." In *Inequality in Early America*, edited by Carla G. Pestana and Sharon V. Salinger, 87–108. Hanover, NH: University Press of New England, 1999.

——— and Betty Wood, eds. *From Slavery to Emancipation in the Atlantic World*. London: Frank Cass, 1999. Published simultaneously as a special issue of *Slavery and Abolition: A Journal of Comparative Studies* 20 (April 1999).

——— and Betty Wood. *Come Shouting to Zion: African American Protestant Christianity in the American South and the British Caribbean to 1830*. Chapel Hill: University of North Carolina Press, 1997.

"Rethinking the American Revolution." *William and Mary Quarterly* 53, no. 2 (April 1996): 367–72.

"'The Year of Jubilee Is Come': Afro-American Christianity in the Plantation South in Post-Revolutionary America." In *Religion in a Revolutionary Age*, edited by Ronald Hoffman and Peter Albert, 87–124. United States Capitol Historical Society Symposia Publication Series. Charlottesville: University Press of Virginia, 1994.

"'Shaking the Dry Bones': The Dialectic of Conversion." In *Black and White Cultural Interaction in the Antebellum South*, edited by Ted Ownby, 23–54. Jackson: University Press of Mississippi, 1993.

"Republicanism: Sources, Meanings, and Usages in American History." *Historical Journal* 35 (1992): 471–85.

"Slavery and Antislavery." In *The Blackwell Encyclopedia of the American Revolution*, edited by Jack P. Greene and J. R. Pole, 379–91. Cambridge, MA: Basil Blackwell, 1991.

Water from the Rock: Black Resistance in a Revolutionary Age. Princeton: Princeton University Press, 1991.

"Josephine Louise Newcomb." In *Encyclopedia of Southern Culture*. Chapel Hill: University of North Carolina Press, 1989.

"The British Armed Forces and the American Victory." In *The World Turned Upside Down*, edited by John Ferling, 165–83. Westport, CT: Greenwood, 1988.

"Between Two Wars: The Rise and Fall of Chattel Slavery in Georgia." *Slavery and Abolition: A Journal of Comparative Studies* 8 (1987): 216–25.

"Liberty, Equality and Slavery: The Paradox of the American Revolution." In *The American Revolution: Its Character and Limits*, edited by Jack P. Greene, 230–52. New York: New York University Press, 1987.

——— and Marian J. Morton, eds. *New World, New Roles: A Documentary History of Women in Pre-Industrial America*. Westport, CT: Greenwood, 1986.

"Between Slavery and Freedom: Virginia Blacks during the American Revolution." *Journal of Southern History* 49 (August 1983): 375–98.

The British Soldier in America: A Social History of Military Life in the Revolutionary Period. Austin: University of Texas Press, 1981.

"Courts and Cats: British Military Justice in the Eighteenth Century." *Military Affairs* 43 (February 1979): 5–11.

"The British and the Black: A New Perspective." *Historian* 38 (February 1976): 225–38.

"The Common British Soldier in the Late Eighteenth Century: A Profile." *Societas: A Review of Social History* 5 (Spring 1975): 117–31.

ELIZABETH JACOWAY

"Daisy Lee Gatson Bates (1913?–1999): The Quest for Justice." In *Arkansas Women: Their Lives and Times*, edited by Cherisse Jones-Branch and Gary Edwards, 197–222. Athens: University Press of Georgia, 2018.

——— and Tim Watson. *Images of America: Newport and Jackson County*. Mount Pleasant, SC: Arcadia, 2016.

Turn Away Thy Son: Little Rock, the Crisis That Shocked the Nation. New York: Free Press, 2007.

"Richard C. Butler and the Little Rock School Board: The Quest to Maintain 'Educational Quality.'" *Arkansas Historical Quarterly* (Spring 2006): 24–38.

"Not Anger but Sorrow: Minnijean Brown Trickey Remembers the Little Rock Crisis." *Arkansas Historical Quarterly* (Spring 2005): 1–26.

"*Brown* and the 'Road to Reunion.'" *Journal of Southern History* (May 2004): 303–8.

"Daisy Bates." In *Notable American Women*, vol. 5, edited by Susan Ware and Stacy Braukman, 44–46. Cambridge: Harvard University Press, 2004.

"Vivion Brewer of Arkansas: A Ladylike Assault on the 'Southern Way of Life.'" In *"Lives Full of Struggle and Triumph": Southern Women, Their Institutions, and Their Communities,* edited by Bruce L. Clayton and John A. Salmond, 264–82. Gainesville: University Press of Florida, 2003.

"Jim Johnson of Arkansas, Segregationist Prototype." In *The Role of Ideas in the Civil Rights South,* edited by Ted Ownby, 137–56. Jackson: University Press of Mississippi, 2002.

"Down from the Pedestal: Gender and Regional Culture in a Ladylike Assault on the Southern Way of Life." *Arkansas Historical Quarterly* (Autumn 1997): 345–52.

"Understanding the Past: The Challenge of Little Rock." In *Understanding the Little Rock Crisis: An Exercise in Remembrance and Reconciliation,* edited by Jacoway and C. Fred Williams, 1–22. Fayetteville: University of Arkansas Press, 1997.

——— and C. Fred Williams, eds. *Understanding the Little Rock Crisis: An Exercise in Remembrance and Reconciliation.* Fayetteville: University of Arkansas Press, 1997.

"The South's Palladium: The Southern Woman and the Cash Construct." In *W. J. Cash and the Minds of the South,* edited by Paul Escott, 112–33. Baton Rouge: Louisiana State University Press, 1992.

———, Dan T. Carter, Lester Lamon, and Robert C. McMath, eds. *The Adaptable South: Essays in Honor of George Brown Tindall.* Baton Rouge: Louisiana State University Press, 1991.

"Little Rock," "Orval Faubus," and "Civil Rights and Business." In *Encyclopedia of Southern Culture.* Chapel Hill: University of North Carolina Press, 1989.

Ed. *"Behold, Our Works Were Good": A Handbook of Arkansas Women's History.* Little Rock: Rose, 1986.

"Civil Rights and the Changing South." In *Southern Businessmen and Desegregation,* edited by Jacoway and David Colburn, 1–11. Baton Rouge: Louisiana State University Press, 1981.

"Taken by Surprise: Little Rock Businessmen." In *Southern Businessmen and Desegregation,* edited by Jacoway and David Colburn, 12–41. Baton Rouge: Louisiana State University Press, 1981.

——— and David Colburn, eds. *Southern Businessmen and Desegregation.* Baton Rouge: Louisiana State University Press, 1981.

Yankee Missionaries in the South: The Penn School Experiment. Baton Rouge: Louisiana State University Press, 1980.

"Education for Life: The Penn School Experience." In *South Atlantic Urban Studies,* vol. 2, edited by Jack R. Censer and N. Steven Steinert, 89–103. Columbia: University of South Carolina Press, 1978.

GAIL SCHMUNK MURRAY

"Taming the War on Poverty: Memphis as a Case Study." *Journal of Urban History* 43, no. 1 (January 2015): 70–90.

"African American Female Civil Rights Activists." In *Women and Social Movements in America*, edited by Thomas Dublin and Kathryn Kish Sklar. Binghamton, NY: Alexander Street Press, 2010.

"Jocelyn Dan Wurzburg: Race Woman." In *Tennessee Women: Challenging Boundaries, Claiming Identities*, edited by Sarah Wilkerson Freeman and Beverly Bond, 381–402. Athens: University of Georgia Press, 2009.

"Children in Antebellum America." In *Social Perspectives in the Jacksonian Era*, edited by Mark R. Cheathem, 35–54. Santa Barbara: ABC-CLIO, 2008.

Ed. *Throwing off the Cloak of Privilege: White Southern Women Activists in the Civil Rights Era*. Gainesville: University Press of Florida, 2004.

"White Privilege, Racial Justice: Women Activists in Memphis." In *Throwing off the Cloak of Privilege: White Southern Women Activists in the Civil Rights Era*, edited by Murray, 204–9. Gainesville: University Press of Florida, 2004.

American Children's Literature and the Construction of Childhood. History of Childhood in America Series, edited by N. Ray Hiner and Joseph M. Hawes. New York: Twayne, 1998.

"Charity within the Bounds of Race and Class: Female Benevolence in the Old South." *South Carolina Historical Magazine* 96, no. 1 (January 1995): 54–70.

"Rational Thought and Republican Virtue: Children's Literature from 1789–1820." *Journal of the Early Republic* 8, no. 2 (Summer 1988): 159–77.

ELIZABETH ANNE PAYNE

Ed. *Writing Women's History: A Tribute to Anne Firor Scott.* Jackson: University Press of Mississippi, 2011.

———, Hattye Raspberry-Hall, Michael de L. Landon, and Jennifer Nardone. "The Forgotten Grandmother: African-American Memory and Lives of Service in Northern Mississippi." In *Mississippi Women, Their History; Their Lives*, vol. 2, edited by Payne and Martha Swain. Athens: University of Georgia Press, 2010.

——— and Martha Swain, eds. *Mississippi Women: Their Histories; Their Lives.* Vol. 2. Athens: University of Georgia Press, 2010.

"Myrtle Terry Lawrence." In *Notable American Women: The Modern Period*, vol. 5, edited by Susan Ware and Stacy Braukman, 372–73. Cambridge: Harvard University Press, 2004.

———, Martha Swain, and Marjorie Julian Spruill, eds. *Mississippi Women: Their Histories; Their Lives*. Vol. 1. Athens: University of Georgia Press, 2003.

"Margaret Dreier Robins." In *Women Building Chicago, 1790–1900: A Biographical Dictionary*, edited by Rina Lunin Schultz and Adele Hart, 758–60. Bloomington: Indiana University Press, 2001.

"Women's Trade Union League." In *The Oxford Companion to United State History*, edited by Paul Boyer, 837. New York: Oxford University Press, 2001.

"'The Lady Was a Sharecropper': Myrtle Lawrence and the Southern Tenant Farmers' Union." *Journal of Southern Cultures* 4, no. 2 (1998): 5–27. *Southern Cultures* has twice released this article online (in 2017 and 2018) during Women's Month.

"Evelyn Smith Munro." In *Encyclopedia of the American Left*, 495–96, edited by Mari Jo Buhle, Paul Buhle, and Dan Georgaskas. Urbana: University of Illinois Press, 1992.

"'What Ain't I Been Doing': Historical Reflections on Women's Lives in the Arkansas Delta, 128-149." In *Arkansas Delta*, edited by Jeannie Whayne and Willard Gatewood. Fayetteville: University of Arkansas Press, 1992.

"Culture of Caring: Delta Women." In *The Arkansas Delta: A Landscape of Change*, edited by Tom Baskett Jr., 118–33. Helena, AR: Delta Cultural Center, 1990.

Reform, Labor, and Feminism: Margaret Dreier Robins and the Women's Trade Union League. Women in American History Series. Urbana: University of Illinois Press, 1988.

"Friendship and Ritual in the Women's Trade Union League." In *Women in the American Theatre*, edited by Helen Drich Chinoy and Linda Walsh Jenkins, 25–28. New York: Crown, 1981.

"Mary Elizabeth Dreier." In *Notable American Women, The Modern Period*, edited by Barbara Sicherman, 204–6. Cambridge: Harvard University Press, 1980.

JANANN SHERMAN

"Carol Lynn Gillmer Yellin: Conscience of the Mid-South." In *Tennessee Women of Vision and Courage*, edited by Charlotte Crawford and Ruth Johnson Smiley, 157–64. North Charleston, SC: Create Space Independent Publishing, 2013.

——— and Beverly G. Bond. *University of Memphis: A Pictorial History*. Charleston, SC: Arcadia, 2012.

Walking on Air: The Aerial Adventures of Phoebe Omlie. Jackson: University Press of Mississippi, 2011.

——— and Beverly G. Bond. *Dreamers, Thinkers, Doers: A Centennial History of the University of Memphis*. Virginia Beach: Donning, 2011.

"Phoebe Fairgrave Omlie: Wing Walker, Parachute Jumper, Air Racer." In *Tennessee Women: Their Lives and Times*, vol. 1, edited by Sarah Wilkerson Freeman and Beverly Greene Bond, 114–39. Athens: University of Georgia Press, 2009.

——— and Beverly G. Bond. *Beale Street*. Charleston, SC: Arcadia, 2006.

——— and Beverly G. Bond. *Memphis in Black and White*. Charleston, SC: Arcadia, 2003.

Conversations with Betty Friedan. Jackson: University Press of Mississippi, 2002.

"Margaret Chase Smith: Wartime Congresswoman." In *The Human Tradition in the World War II Era*, edited by Malcolm Muir Jr., 121–38. Wilmington, DE: Scholarly Resources, 2001.

"'Senator-at-Large for America's Women': Margaret Chase Smith and the Paradox of Gender Affinity." In *The Impact of Women in Public Office*, edited by Susan J. Carroll, 89–116. Bloomington: Indiana University Press, 2001.

No Place for a Woman: A Life of Senator Margaret Chase Smith. New Brunswick: Rutgers University Press, 2000.

——— and Carol Lynn Yellin. *The Perfect 36: Tennessee Delivers Woman Suffrage*, Knoxville: Iris, 1998.

"'The Vice Admiral': Margaret Chase Smith and the Investigation of Congested Areas in Wartime." In *The Home-Front War: World War II and American Society*, edited by Kenneth Paul O'Brien and Lynn Hudson Parsons, 119–38. Westport, CT: Greenwood, 1995.

"'They Either Need These Women or They Do Not': Margaret Chase Smith and the Fight for Regular Status for Women in the Military." *Journal of Military History* (January 1990): 47–78.

SHEILA SKEMP

Afterword to *Women in the Era of the American Revolution*, edited by Barbara Oberg. Charlottesville: University of Virginia Press, forthcoming.

The Making of a Patriot: Benjamin Franklin at the Cockpit. New York: Oxford University Press, 2012.

"America's Mary Wollstonecraft: Judith Sargent Murray's Case for the Equal Rights of Women." In *Revolutionary Founders*, edited by Alfred Young and Gary Nash, 289–304. Boston: Beacon, 2011.

"Judith Sargent Murray and American Religion." In *Biographical History of Women Biblical Interpreters*, 379–81. New York: Baker Academic, 2011.

The Making of a Patriot, 1757–1776." In *A Companion to Benjamin Franklin*, edited by David Waldstreicher, 46–64. Cambridge, UK: Blackwell, 2011.

First Lady of Letters: Judith Sargent Murray and the Struggle for Female Independence. Philadelphia: University of Pennsylvania Press, 2009.

"William Franklin." *Time*, July 7, 2003.

"Deborah Franklin: Goodwife." In *Benjamin Franklin and Women*, edited by Larry Tise, 19–36. Philadelphia: Franklin Institute, 2000.

"Judith Sargent Murray: The American Revolution and the Rights of Women." In *The Human Tradition in the American Revolution*, edited by Nancy L. Rhoden and Ian K. Steele, 285–306. Wilmington: Scholarly Resources, 2000.

——— and Bruce C. Daniels, eds. *The Colonial Metamorphoses in Rhode Island: A Study of Institutions in Change*, by Sydney V. James. Hanover, NH: University Press of New England, 2000.

"William Franklin: The Most Intimate Enemy." *Pennsylvania Magazine* 65 (Winter 1998): 35–45.

Judith Sargent Murray: A Brief Biography with Documents. Boston: Bedford, 1994.

Benjamin and William Franklin: Patriot and Loyalist, Father and Son. Boston: Bedford, 1990.

William Franklin: Son of a Patriot, Servant of a King. New York: Oxford University Press, 1990.

"Newport's Stamp Act Rioters: Another Look." *Rhode Island History* 63 (1989): 41–59.

——— and Winthrop D. Jordan, eds. *Race and Family in the Colonial South.* Jackson: University Press of Mississippi, 1988.

"A World Uncertain and Strongly Checker'd." In *Adapting to Conditions: War and Society in the Eighteenth Century*, edited by Martaan Ultee, 84–103. Tuscaloosa: University of Alabama Press, 1986.

"Freedom of Religion in Rhode Island: Acquidneck's Reluctant Revolutionaries." *Rhode Island History* 44 (1985): 3–18.

"William Franklin: His Father's Son." *Pennsylvania Magazine of History and Biography* 59 (1985): 145–78.

——— and Joanne Hawks, eds. *Sex, Race and the Role of Women in the South.* Jackson: University Press of Mississippi, 1983.

"George Berkeley's Newport Experience: An End to Reform." *Rhode Island History* 37 (1978): 58–73.

MARTHA SWAIN

———, Elizabeth Anne Payne, and Marjorie Julian Spruill, eds. *Mississippi Women: Their Histories, Their Lives.* Vol. 2. Athens: University of Georgia Press, 2010.

——— and Dorothy S. Shawhan. *Lucy Somerville Howorth: New Deal Lawyer, Politician, and Feminist from the South.* Baton Rouge: Louisiana State University Press, 2006.

"Prelude to the New Deal: Lou Henry Hoover and Women's Relief Work." In *Uncommon Americans: The Lives and Legacies of Herbert and Lou Henry Hoover,* edited by Timothy Walsh, 151–66. Westport, CT: Greenwood, 2003.

———, Elizabeth Anne Payne, and Marjorie Julian Spruill, eds. *Mississippi Women: Their Histories, Their Lives.* Vol. 1. Athens: University of Georgia Press, 2003.

———, Janet Coryell, Elizabeth Hayes Turner, and Sandra Treadway, eds. *Southern Women: Beyond Image and Convention.* Columbia: University of Missouri Press 1998.

"A New Deal for Southern Women: Gender and Race in Women's Work Relief." In *Women of the American South: A Multicultural Reader,* edited by Christie Farnham, 241–57. New York: New York University Press, 1997.

Ellen S. Woodward: New Deal Advocate for Women. Jackson: University Press of Mississippi, 1995.

"Loula Dunn: Alabama Pioneer in Public Administration." In *Stepping out of the Shadows: Women in Alabama, 1819–1990,* edited by Mary Martha Thomas, 132–53. Tuscaloosa: University of Alabama Press, 1995.

"Keith Frazier Somerville: In War and in Peace, 1888–1978." In "*'Dear Boys': World War II Letters from a Woman Back Home, 1943–1945,* edited by Judy Litoff and David Smith, 23–40. Jackson: University Press of Mississippi, 1991.

"Ellen Woodward and Eleanor Roosevelt: A Partnership for Women's Relief and Security." In *Without Precedent: The Life and Career of Eleanor Roosevelt,* edited by Joan Hoff-Wilson, 135–52. Bloomington: Indiana University Press, 1984.

"The Public Role of Southern Women, 1930–1980." In *Sex, Race, and the Role of Women in the South,* Sheila Skemp and Joanne Hawks, 37–58. Jackson: University Press of Mississippi, 1983.

Pat Harrison: The New Deal Years. Jackson: University Press of Mississippi, 1978.

PAMELA TYLER

"'Oh Lord, How Long': New Orleans Was a Battleground for the Woman Suffrage Movement." In *New Orleans and the World: 1718–2018 Tricentennial Anthology,* edited by Nancy Dixon, 74–78. New Orleans: Louisiana Endowment for the Humanities, 2017.

New Orleans Women and the Poydras Home: More Durable Than Marble. Baton Rouge: Louisiana State University Press, 2016.

"Corinne Claiborne 'Lindy' Boggs." In *American National Biography Online,* edited by Susan Ware. Oxford University Press. www.anb.org, 2015.

"Martha, Hilda and Natalie: Newcomb's Furies." In *Newcomb College 1886–2006: Higher Education for Women in New Orleans*, edited by Susan Tucker and Beth Willinger, 303–20. Baton Rouge: Louisiana State University Press, 2013.
"A Tale from Sophie Newcomb College, the Class of 1909." *Louisiana History* 52 (Summer 2011): 300–323.
"Woman Suffrage in Louisiana," "Lindy Boggs," "Margaret 'Polky' McIlhenny," "Hilda Phelps Hammond," "Ella Brennan." In *knowLouisiana.org, Encyclopedia of Louisiana*, edited by David Johnson. Louisiana Endowment for the Humanities, 2010–. http://www.knowlouisiana.org.
"Louisiana Women and Hurricane Katrina: Some Reflections." In *Louisiana Women: Their Lives and Times*, vol. 1, edited by Janet Allured and Judith Gentry, 324–43. Athens: University of Georgia Press, 2009.
"The Post-Katrina, Semi-Separate World of Gender Politics." *Journal of American History* 94 (December 2007): 780–88.
"May Craig," and "Clare Booth Luce." In *Women and War: A Historical Encyclopedia from Antiquity to the Present*, edited by Bernard Cook. Santa Barbara: ABC-CLIO, 2006.
"'Blood on Your Hands': Conservative White Southern Responses to Eleanor Roosevelt." In *Before "Brown": Civil Rights and White Backlash in the Modern South*, edited by Glenn Feldman, 96–115. Tuscaloosa: University of Alabama Press, 2004.
"Warm Personal Friend, or Worse Than Hitler? Southern Women's Views of Eleanor Roosevelt." In *Lives Full of Struggle and Triumph: Southern Women, Their Lives, Their Communities*, edited by Bruce Clayton and John A. Salmond, 181–200. Gainesville: University of Florida Press, 2003.
"The Impact of the New Deal and World War II on the South." In *The Blackwell Companion to the American South*, edited by John Boles, 444–60. Malden, MA: Blackwell, 2002.
Silk Stockings and Ballot Boxes: Women and Politics in New Orleans 1920–1965. Athens: University of Georgia Press, 1996.
"'Women of Brains and Standing': The New Orleans League of Women Voters, 1934–1950." *Gulf Coast Historical Review* (Spring 1994): 6–28.
"The Ideal Southern Woman: As Seen by the *Progressive Farmer* in the 1930s." *Southern Studies* 2 (Fall 1981): 276–94. Reprinted in *Southern Studies* (1991): 315–33; and also in *History of Women in the United States: Historical Articles on Women's Lives and Activities*, edited and with an introduction by Nancy F. Cott. Berlin: De Gruyter, 1993 and 2012.

CONTRIBUTORS

BEVERLY GREENE BOND is an associate professor of history at the University of Memphis. She is the coeditor of the two-volume *Tennessee Women: Their Lives and Times;* coauthor of *Memphis in Black and White* and *Beale Street;* and co-author of two books on the history of the University of Memphis—*Dreamers, Thinkers, Doers: A Centennial History of the University of Memphis* and *University of Memphis: A Pictorial History*. She was codirector of the "Memphis Massacre Project" and is currently editing, with Susan O'Donovan, a collection of the essays on the 1866 Memphis Massacre. She is a wife, mother, mother-in-law, and grandmother. She teaches at the University of Memphis.

EMILY CLARK is Clement Chambers Benenson Professor of American Colonial History at Tulane University. Before taking a PhD in history in 1998, she received a BA in classics and worked as an archaeologist in Greece, a social worker in New Orleans, and an administrator at Tulane. Post PhD, she taught in Cambridge, England; Mississippi; and Oregon before joining the faculty at Tulane. Clark is the author of four books, including *Masterless Mistresses: The New Orleans Ursulines and the Development of a New World Society: 1727–1834* (2007) and *The Strange History of the American Quadroon: Free Women of Color in the Revolutionary Atlantic World* (2013).

SYLVIA FREY is a professor of history emerita at Tulane University in New Orleans. She is the author/editor of five monographs and more than twenty-five scholarly articles. Her scholarly honors and awards include Senior Mellon

Research Fellow at the John Carter Brown Library; Pitt Professor of American History at the University of Cambridge; NEH Distinguished Professor at the University of Richmond; Andrew Mellon Professor at Tulane University; Honorary Lifetime Fellow, Newnham College, University of Cambridge; and Smithsonian Institution Senior Postdoctoral Fellow. She has served on a number of advisory and editorial boards, including the Amistad Research Center, Executive Council of the Southern Historical Association, ABC-Clio *Encyclopedia of the American Revolutionary War*, Board of Editors of the *William & Mary Quarterly*, *Journal of American History*, and the *Journal of Military History*.

GLENDA GILMORE is the Peter V. and C. Vann Woodward Professor of History, African American Studies, and American Studies at Yale University. She earned her PhD at the University of North Carolina at Chapel Hill. She is the author of *Defying Dixie: The Radical Roots of Civil Rights, 1919–1950*, which was one of the American Library Association's Notable Books of 2008, and the *Washington Post*'s Best Books of 2008. Her first book, *Gender and Jim Crow: Women and the Politics of White Supremacy in North Carolina, 1896–1920*, published in 1996, won the Frederick Jackson Turner Award and the Julia Cherry Spruill Prize, among others.

ELIZABETH JACOWAY earned her BA from the University of Arkansas in 1966, and her PhD from the University of North Carolina in 1974. She has taught at the University of Florida, the University of Arkansas at Little Rock, and Lyon College. Since 1974 she has been an independent scholar and has lived for forty years in a small town in rural Arkansas. She has remained visible in the profession through her service, especially to the Southern Historical Association and the Southern Association for Women Historians, and her writing. She is the author or editor of nine books and a dozen articles, including *Turn Away Thy Son: Little Rock, the Crisis That Shocked the Nation* (2007).

GAIL SCHMUNK MURRAY earned a BA from the University of Michigan in 1966 and a MSEd at the University of Central Arkansas in 1968. For the next twenty years she followed her husband's career and reared three children while doing some adjunct lecturing. She completed a PhD at the University of

Memphis at age forty-seven and joined the history department of Rhodes College that same year. She retired after twenty-four years, including four years as the department's first female chair. She is the author of several articles, the edited collection *Throwing off the Cloak of Privilege: White Southern Women Activists in the Civil Rights Era*, and one book, *American Children's Literature and the Construction of Childhood.*

ELIZABETH ANNE PAYNE earned a BA from Mississippi State College for Women, an MDiv from Southern Methodist University, and MA and PhD degrees in history from the University of Illinois at Chicago. After directing the honors college at the University of Arkansas, she moved to the University of Mississippi in 1997 to become the founding director of its honors college. She is the author of *Reform, Labor, and Feminism: Margaret Drier Robbins and the Women's Trade Union League*; and she coedited *Mississippi Women: Their Histories, Their Lives*, volumes 1 and 2. She edited *Writing Women's History: A Tribute to Anne Firor Scott.*

STEPHANIE ROLPH is an associate professor in the History Department at Millsaps College, and academic director for the Shepherd Higher Education Consortium on Poverty. Her work has appeared in *The Right Side of the Sixties: Reexamining Conservatism's Decade of Transformation* (2012) and in the *Journal of Southern History.* Her book *Resisting Equality: The Citizens' Council, 1954–1989* (2018) looks at the long history of organized white resistance to civil rights and its impact on national conservatism.

JANANN SHERMAN first attended college at a small Community College in Arkansas, at age thirty-five. She earned her PhD at Rutgers University at age forty-nine and moved into her first academic job as assistant professor of history at the University of Memphis at fifty. She taught at Memphis for nineteen years, the last nine of which she served as the first woman chair of the History Department. Sherman has published eight books, including biographies of Senator Margaret Chase Smith and aviation pioneer Phoebe Fairgrave Omlie, and four volumes of Memphis history, coauthored with colleague Beverly Bond. She retired in 2013.

SHEILA SKEMP is Clare Leslie Marquette Professor Emerita of American History at the University of Mississippi. She received a BA in history at the University of Montana in 1967 and her PhD in history at the University of Iowa in 1974. She was a visiting assistant professor in a number of colleges and universities before joining the faculty at the University of Mississippi in 1980. She is the author of four books, including *William Franklin: Son of a Patriot, Servant of a King* (1990) and *First Lady of Letters: Judith Sargent Murray and the Struggle for Female Independence* (2009).

MARTHA SWAIN received her BA from Mississippi State College and her MA and PhD from Vanderbilt University, working under Dewey Grantham. She taught for twenty-one years at Texas Woman's University, then returned to teach at Mississippi State University in her hometown of Starkville. She is the author of *Pat Harrison: The New Deal Years; Ellen Woodward: New Deal Advocate for Women;* and, with Dorothy Shawhan, *Lucy Somerville Howorth: New Deal Lawyer, Politician, and Feminist from the South;* and coeditor of *Mississippi Women: Their Histories, Their Lives,* volumes 1 and 2.

PAMELA TYLER worked as a high school history teacher after graduating from Georgia Southwestern College. Belatedly realizing that she could not deal with sixteen-year-olds forever, she enrolled in graduate school at Tulane University and earned a PhD in 1989. She taught at North Carolina State University for sixteen years, but the shock of Hurricane Katrina moved her to find a position closer to her beloved New Orleans. She retired from the University of Southern Mississippi as professor of history in 2017. She is the author of two books, *Silk Stockings and Ballot Boxes* and *New Orleans Women and the Poydras Home.*